NOBODY
CARES
WHO
YOU
ARE

NOBODY CARES WHO YOU ARE

THE LIFE & TIMES OF ACEMAN, A WIDESPREAD PANIC ROADIE
BOOK I: THE SEARCH FOR HIS MUSE

LARRY ACQUAVIVA

Deeds Publishing | Athens

Copyright © 2016 — Larry Acquaviva

ALL RIGHTS RESERVED—No part of this book may be reproduced in any form or by any electronic or mechanical means, including information storage and retrieval systems, without permission in writing from the authors, except by a reviewer who may quote brief passages in a review.

Published by Deeds Publishing in Athens, GA
www.deedspublishing.com

Printed in The United States of America

Cover design and text layout by Mark Babcock

Library of Congress Cataloging-in-Publications data is available upon request.

ISBN 978-1-944193-67-6
EISBN 978-1-944193-68-3

Books are available in quantity for promotional or premium use. For information, email info@deedspublishing.com.

First Edition, 2017

10 9 8 7 6 5 4 3 2 1

This book is dedicated to my parents, two people who gave me all the strength, talent, and tools I've ever needed to live my life according to my own dreams.

ACKNOWLEDGMENTS

THERE ARE A NUMBER OF PEOPLE I WANT TO MENTION FOR VARIOUS reasons in regards to this book. Every one of these people have inspired me tremendously throughout this process. The first is my sister Katherine, "The Trusty Soldier," who supplied most of the pictures for this volume and has always been a great friend. George Davidson, for his wisdom and insight, and a man who has constantly carried me to newer heights through his friendship. Leara Rhodes, for being the definition of a teacher and a woman who has allowed for me to see things just a little bit clearer in ways only a good teacher can. Dan Stoneburner, an astral traveler who one day decided to make Planet Earth a stop on his journey and has enriched my life ever since. And finally, Mark Brill, a true friend and confidant who has helped to make this dream a reality. To all these people, and many, many more, I owe a huge debt of thanks.

—Larry Acquaviva, May 2016

INTRODUCTION

FROM THE TIME I CAN REMEMBER, I'VE BEEN SEARCHING FOR SOMEthing deeper in life. Something magical, something strange, something on the edge and something that has always, *always* been alive. I've never cared about where this search would take me, and I certainly have no idea where it's going, but one thing is for sure, it has been a lot of fun getting there and one hell of an adventure along the way. I was born into a world teetering on the edge and I'm going to leave it with a bang, no matter when or where that happens. One thing life has taught me is that, in the end, no one on this planet has any of the answers to anything in this world but I've also got a feeling that collectively, we are going to discover some age-old insights to some very confusing questions in the years to come.

My life has been a lot of fun, laced with some very deep and profound pain, just like everyone else on the planet. I don't consider this story to be anything other than the tale of one life, one quest, as a single man attempts to navigate his way through the wild and explosive journey called living. Being a student of history, I've always been fascinated by the lives of the Everyday Joes, those individuals who've made up the fabric of the world and created a foundation of strength upon which the rest of us can now stand. I believe that history is important, very important in fact, and that without it we would all be lost within a sea of confusion with absolutely no way of guiding ourselves into the future. That's what this tale is, a history of one man and the times he lived through as he searched for what he needed out of life: his own voice, his own dream, and the determination to forge his own way in the world.

In the fall of 1987, I met the boys in Widespread Panic. From the moment I laid eyes on them, I knew on a very basic and instinctual level that I needed to spend some quality time exploring their world. What I found was myself. This is a journey through the streets of Detroit, Michigan, my hometown, which I had the misfortune of watching disappear right before my eyes as my family life swirled within a cyclone of confusion and uncertainty, and a journey to find the music I needed to live a meaningful life. From those earliest days in Detroit, I knew that on some level, music was a guiding force and eventually embraced a lifestyle that would lead me straight to her, through a turbulent childhood, an explosive adolescence, a confused early-adulthood, and to the streets of Athens, Georgia in the late 1980s, where I met the boys who would change my life.

The journey to get to Athens was incredible, as I was forced to fight my way through a debilitating cloud of turbulence and recklessness that had me on a direct collision course with self-destruction. Along the way I made a few discoveries, not only about the world but myself, and met some very interesting, wise, and colorful characters who made the odyssey a tolerable, if not completely wonderful, experience to behold. And when all is said and done, that is all any of us could possibly ask for out of life.

This tale is a journey of the mind, body, and soul, one that was forged in the foundry of Detroit, Michigan, and one that I took across North America as I pursued my dreams. No matter where I was or what I was forced to endure, music was always there, leading the way and pointing me in the direction I was meant to go. I came to see that music, in all her wonder, in all her glory, and in all her selflessness, was something that would allow me to become my own man and live my life according to my own wishes and desires. Music, man, *music*, without her I cringe at the prospect of what this world would be. But I can tell you this much: I hope I never have to find out…and pray that I never will…

This is a true story. Most names and some incidents have been changed to ensure that nobody gets stepped on.

—Larry Acquaviva, May 2016.

PART I: THE BEGINNINGS OF LIFE

1. THE BEGINNINGS OF LIFE

I WAS BORN LAWRENCE LEONARD ACQUAVIVA ON GOOD FRIDAY, APRIL 16, 1965. I was the second youngest of seven children and the youngest of five boys. I have, clearly preserved in my mind, two distinct early memories—what could be considered my initial impressions of life.

The first, without a doubt, is music. The specifics are anyone's guess, but there is a strong possibility that it was either The Beatles or Motown. You see, I was born on the east side of Detroit, Michigan, smackdab in the middle of the city that produced Diana Ross and The Supremes, Smokey Robinson and The Miracles, Little Stevie Wonder, The Temptations, Aretha Franklin, The Queen of Soul, and so many others. The music of Motown was a constant in the life of anyone who lived in the city, and no matter where you went, you could not escape that sound; it permeated the air and rang clearly throughout the factories, machine shops, immigrant neighborhoods, and cramped streets of Detroit twenty-four hours a day.

The second memory I have is one of a different nature, and one which immediately established what my life would be throughout my infancy, childhood, and formative years: that of a wild, volatile, broken home. Being rocked awake by a disturbing sound saturating our working class home one night, my six siblings and I gathered around the doorway of the house's lone bathroom to investigate. There on the floor was my mother, crying and fading in and out of consciousness. Sitting on the commode was my father. He had gathered us together to watch my mother fight for her life.

"Your mother has tried it again, kids. Same old story, same old bullshit."

My mother, defeated and broken, simply continued to weep as she lay on the floor and my siblings and I attempted to digest what was going on.

In her misery, in her confusion, my mother had tried to kill herself by swallowing a bottle of aspirin. She was tired of the charade, she was tired of living a lie, and she was tired of being trapped in a marriage that brought nothing but heartache. She wanted out…and this was the way she chose to do it.

My father, still sitting on the commode, then stuck his fingers down my mother's throat until she vomited, ultimately saving her life. I don't ever want to entertain the thought of what my life would have been like if she had succeeded in her attempt to end her own. It's amazing how one incident can change things.

Such was the beginning of my life.

Now, I'm forty-eight-years-old as I write this—relatively intelligent, and a man who not only appreciates logic, but craves it as well. Without logic, I believe, one does not have a foundation on which to stand and observe life properly. One of the aspects of life in the city of Detroit, which I grew to respect immediately, was the fact that you could not escape logic. Life in the city dictated as much. If you screwed up or crossed a line, you paid the price instantly. Growing up in the environment that I did, there were no gray areas to cloud perspective. In my experience, there was only black and white; what you saw was what you got.

As I look back over my childhood now, I view a mad romp through confusion and recklessness, and have to search deep and wide to find happy moments with my family. The ones I do have are fleeting and far-between. I see no benefit in sugarcoating the facts: in a nutshell, everyone in my family was filled with rage, frustration, jealousy, and insecurity, including myself. I wish it were different...but again, logic paints a striking picture not obscured by sunshine and rainbows. I learned early on that if I wanted to survive the experience, both physically and emotionally, I had to forge my own life as far away from my family as I could get. I removed myself from the reality of family life early on, through music and a never-ending imagination bestowed upon me by the situation I was in. If I hadn't, I would not have emerged in one piece.

Now, just to make this clear, I loved my family dearly, and still do to this day. My mother, whom I love more than I can express, was a great provider who struggled mightily to keep the family together. I will never forget the sacrifices she made, and I am extremely proud, not only of who she is, but how stoically she endured the hardships of raising seven children on her own. My mother is one of the strongest people I have ever known and my respect for her is endless. To put it sharply, my mother had balls—and so did every one of her children. This is what life on the east side of Detroit had established in us, and when all is said and done, this tale is not meant to throw anyone under the bus. It is merely the story of my life, and nothing more.

In light of this, my formative years were laced with violence, anger, and misguided intention, just like everyone else in the family. In fact, my childhood was no different from anyone else's in the neighborhood—but clearly, I don't remember much nurturing, coddling, or guidance of any kind, other than one, simple rule: if I didn't do as I was told, I would pay the price immediately, no questions asked. Deal with it, or suffer the consequences.

Now, just to make *this* point clear, I do not now, nor have I ever, blamed anyone for the situation I grew up in, including my parents and siblings. They were a product of their times and were subjected to the same reality that I was. And just like anyone else in their position, they acted accordingly in order to survive life in the city. To try and place blame is pointless and non-productive, and certainly not logical. As a matter of fact, in my early twenties, I even came up with a slogan which sums up my feelings on the subject to a T: "Blame The Big Bang."

Where do you begin to place blame for anything in this world? At whom do you point the finger to release the pain of a world steeped in the horrors of endless warfare, continuous genocide, rampant hunger, devastating disease, and mindless destruction? In logic, do we blame God, the Devil, or Creation itself? Do we blame, as religion dictates, the Supreme Being who instigated this mess? Do we blame Him, Her, or It for putting us in this situation in the first place? Do we blame The Big Bang? Or do we simply accept our fate, and make the best of a no-win situation—so that our own hearts, our own minds, and our own souls can be at peace and move forward in a world lost and frightened by its own shadow?

To defy that which has been established, and fight with all our might to rise above it all, and do the right thing; is this not the definition of what it means to be a good man, a good woman, a good human being? Is this not the definition of what it means to be a rebel, a revolutionary like Jesus or Gandhi, in a world dominated by greed, avarice, and personal self-gain? I do not blame anyone for what I've experienced, and never will; logic forbids it. The whole point of life is to accept responsibility, and attempt to rectify a situation that is obviously wrong. And in truth, I've always appreciated my upbringing simply because it prepared me for the realities of life.

Just to set the record straight, I do not consider my life to be any different from anyone else's. Humility is a big thing and was pounded into my head from the time I can remember. In fact, I know many, many people who have struggled more than I have, and in a lot of ways, I believe that most people I've met have lived lives infinitely more extraordinary than mine.

Take a man off the streets of Baltimore, or a woman from the hills of Kentucky, and I guarantee you that they will blow your mind with endless tales that are extraordinary, fascinating, and true. Being abandoned as a child and having to fend for themselves in a lonely, decrepit shack somewhere. Incest, rape, and general debauchery, and tales of longing and acceptance on an amazing scale, from describing the beauty of a rose they picked at age ten, to watching their father being gunned down over a simple card game when they were four.

Everyone has a story to tell and every life must come to an end. The key is to preserve these tales, like a historian, a keeper of time, or a builder of promise, who swims in the oceans of eternal space. This is why we live and this is why we die, alone in our minds with the puzzle of life: that infinity, that beauty, that confirmation of existence, there before us every second of every day. This place is alive, man, it's *alive*, and if there's one thing I've learned it is that there ain't nothing for free, never has been and never will be. As Madman Morrison said all those years ago, "No one here gets out alive." I'm proud of my upbringing... but it took me years to get there.

Years ago I learned about intention: the reasons behind those things we say and do every day, and the end result we wish to come from such actions. It's a question I ask myself daily: *Are your intentions good or are they bad?* I always attempt to make my intentions proper, based on what is good for me, the people I love and the world in general. Down to my core, I believe that I am a decent human being with proper intention. With this in mind, I understand that this tale I share with you now is based in proper intention. I'm merely telling a story, the story of my life. And to the best of my knowledge, I believe that my parents shared a similar view throughout their lives, and have never based their beliefs in hate or misguided deeds. Again, I say this to the best of my knowledge. What was in their hearts and minds is simply for them to discern.

What I write now are my memories, and mine alone.

★

Both my parents were born in the mid-1930s, at the height of The Great Depression. Their formative years could not have been more different. My mother, Adrianna Juliet Righetti, was, for the most part, born into privilege and opportunity, with proper guidance as the foundation for a life of promise. By my mother's own account, her parents loved her, and each other; they created a life for my mother and her three younger siblings steeped in love, strong religious beliefs, and eternal support.

What the true fabric of daily life was like for her is anyone's guess, and the one thing I've learned is that every family—and I mean *every* family—has its dark secrets and hidden skeletons. Throughout my life, my mother has shared with me those aspects of her family that were good and positive; if she has chosen to focus on those things, that's her choice. I've heard rumors and tales that are not so flattering—but again, these are based in hearsay and innuendo; who knows the actual truth? Certainly not me. Despite this, my mother's childhood and teen years appear to have been happy and carefree, with the only discontent coming from petty sibling rivalries and youthful jealousies. My mother, for all intents and purposes, lived a charmed life.

In stark contrast, my father—Angelo Leonardo Acquaviva—was a product of Italian immigrant parents who settled in Detroit in the

1930s. My father grew up on the streets near downtown, succumbing to the vices of sex, drinking, gambling, and fighting at an early age. My pops had a tough childhood. Some of the stories I've heard about my old man's early years are brutal and tough to digest. He was abused, neglected, and forced to grow up at a young age. Knowing no better, and living life according to the rules of the street and the machismo of Italian heritage, he grew into a man governed by his times.

To me, my father is the definition of the average, blue-collar man. In short, he grew into the man he felt he was destined to become, for better or for worse, and lived the life he felt he was meant to pursue, dictated by what was handed down to him by past generations of his own family. My father was a tough, streetwise man who dealt with his situation the best way he knew how. He despised his mother (with good reason) and spent as much time away from her as he possibly could. He had no curfew, ran wild on the streets, and was exposed to things I could only imagine. He returned home at night only because his friends had to.

My parents' upbringings could not have been more different, so how they came together is beyond my comprehension. But one thing I do understand is that they were young, real young, when they met. Because of this, and this alone, I've come to see that carnal explorations based in youthful desires were at the source. They were hot for each other from the moment they met.

Almost immediately, both my mother and father fell into the roles expected of them in the early 1950s—roles they didn't have the understanding to break away from. Being a student of history, it always blows my mind when I hear people romanticize the past, as if the history of mankind is shrouded in all things good and loving. As a matter of fact, the further you go back in time, the more brutal, ignorant, and unforgiving the reality of daily life becomes. In truth, the early 1950s in America was a time when the roles of men and women were solidified as concretely as Ken and Barbie at a beach party, and to buck the system was never an option. For the most part, men ruled the roost and women maintained the nest, plain and simple.

My parents were no different than the norm, and fulfilled their roles as dutifully as was expected. Entering a bond of marriage only entrenched their lives even further into the destiny for which they were groomed. To live their lives in any other way would have gone against everything they knew to be true. Again, being a student of history, I can't imagine what my parent's comprehension of life must have been. One thing I do know is that what they saw and understood in their youths was far different from what I saw in mine. It's amazing what a 30-year separation in time can do to perception. The world my parents grew up in was far different from the one I experienced.

I do believe, on some level, that my parents truly did love one another. In fact, they probably loved each other a bit too much, and allowed those feelings to dominate their logical selves. I believe that both wanted to change the other into what they felt was the perfect mate — a fallacy unobtainable under the definition of true love. This phenomenon still exists today, and continually disturbs me when I see it. Love does not control, and love does not want us to change simply to appease another. Love is free and forgiving. Love grows together, as one. This is what my parents lacked in spades, and they lacked it to the point of self-destruction from the moment they said, "I do."

By the time I was born in April of '65, I believe that my mother had had enough of dirty diapers, screaming babies, and a life dictated by an unhappy marriage; she'd been pregnant nine times in eleven years, losing two of the children prematurely, one early in the marriage and one later on. To her credit, she stayed the course, despite a life of broken promises and unfulfilled dreams. How she maintained a shred of sanity is beyond me — an aspect of my mother's personality I have respected to this day.

In fact, I love her dearly for what she had to endure, and because of this, consider her a great woman with a strong moral character most human beings could only dream of possessing. Many of my traits — my personality, disposition, strength, and artistic abilities — come straight from my mother. This much cannot be disputed. But to fool myself into believing that I was a welcome addition to a loving, caring family is something I can never acknowledge, simply because it's not true. The fact of the matter is, by the time I arrived, my family was already seriously fractured, and would only become more damaged as time went on. From my earliest memories, this was as plain as the nose on my face; it became even clearer with every day I grew older.

The memory of my mother lying on that bathroom floor with my father leaning over her is not only emblazoned on my mind for all time, but it also instigated one unsettling and whacked-out event after the other from that point forward. By the time this episode unfolded, when I was three or four years old, my parents were on their last legs as a married couple. This event may very well have been the death knell of their union. No more than four years later they were divorced, and my father had already moved out of the house.

Divorce is a terrible thing. It destroys families. And in our case, that is exactly what happened. Because of it, I never got to know my father or his family, a regret I still have. My father virtually disappeared once the divorce was finalized, coming around on Sundays and some holidays. During those final four years of their marriage, I have, unfortunately, less than a handful of memories of my father being around, and felt he was absent long before the final divorce proceedings were executed. I have fleeting memories of playing hide-and-seek with my father, and sitting on his lap playing with his hair, but not much else.

There were no afternoon baseball games, no trips to the park, no rounds of catch, nor evening chats on the front porch alone with my father. He was long gone, emotionally and physically, years before I became aware—and sadly, he wasn't much of a factor in my life at any time during my childhood or formative years. He was never the kind to offer advice or guide me in any way. In recent years, I've learned that my father never wanted a divorce in the first place, and that he was forced by my mother to stay out of my life. Apparently, my mother didn't want him influencing me. My mother once told me that my father wanted two or three children, that was it; the rest, he simply wanted nothing to do with. Over the years, my father has told me a different story, which contradicts this, and somewhere in between lies the truth. What that truth is, I have yet to decipher.

Yet my father did give me several gifts for which I have been eternally grateful. First, the man gave me logic. My father was, and still is, a simple man who understood the rules of the world in a very direct, to-the-point fashion; what you saw was what you got. Detroit was a no-bullshit city, and it produced no-bullshit men like my father—a man who lived his life based in logic. By birth alone I was given this understanding; I know down to my core that my affinity for logical thought comes straight from my old man, and this was perhaps his greatest gift to me.

Not only was my pops a man of logic, but he was also an incredibly funny guy. Blessed with a biting, streetwise sense of humor, his observations of life were absolutely hysterical. One of the memories I have of my old man was when one of my sisters would become emotional over some trivial issue. Standing before my pops, my sisters would plead their case; Dad, in silence, would mimic pulling a violin from its case, place it to his chin, tune his instrument to perfection, then unleash a torrent of sorrow from his grieving, sympathetic hands. This would inevitably send my sisters over the edge, causing them to burst into tears of frustration as they ran screaming from the room. Pops' antics always had us boys rolling on the floor like little lunatics. My pops was a funny guy, and handed his sense of humor down to us kids.

Those years leading up to my parents' divorce (when I was eight years old) were filled with anger, mistrust, and a demented approach to entertainment embraced by siblings and me. When my parents were together, they fought constantly. All other times were spent either dealing with the wrath of my siblings or spending as much time alone as I possibly could. The Detroit of my youth was a perfect palette for a child with a ravenous, creative mind. Our neighborhood, like most in the city at that time, was self-contained. We lived on Goulburn Avenue and alongside East McNichols Road, also known as 6 Mile Road, on the east side.

6 Mile contained everything we needed to survive. We lived next to a bakery, a sausage factory, and a plumbing supply store. On the opposite side of 6 Mile was an ice cream factory (Alinosi's) and a pharmacy (Waltham Drugs). Down from there was a candle shop, a cobbler, a hardware store, and several other shops. Our neighborhood offered numerous nightclubs, mom-and-pop grocery stores, filling stations, a bowling alley, restaurants, an adult movie theater, and various party stores. It even offered a music theater: The Ramona Theater, where the likes of Iggy and The Stooges, Deep Purple, and many other great bands were rumored to have played live.

Our neighborhood was populated by immigrant factory workers of every nationality, living in small, post-World War II box houses. Most were Catholic, had large families, and were as angry and frustrated as we were. There was nonstop activity in our neighborhood, twenty-four hours a day. Having four older brothers also made for interesting times. There were initiation rites, contests of will and strength, games of chance, and an endless excursion into mayhem.

Initiation rites consisted of climbing buildings (and then jumping off of them), shoplifting, and throwing mud balls filled with rocks at passing cars in the summertime and snowballs laced with stones in the winter. This was all done in hopes of being chased through the labyrinth of streets and alleyways by infuriated drivers intent on revenge. Several times, I escaped by the skin of my teeth; a few other times, I was caught and had to endure their wrath. What these episodes taught me was to never get caught again. I became very proficient at escaping, developing into a gold medal climber of trees, garages, fences, houses, and other buildings to ensure I would live to see another day.

Burning things was another favorite pastime my brothers and I shared. In order to get the matches needed to initiate this rite, we devised a clever (and ultimately ill-fated) scheme. Whether our overseer was my mother or a babysitter (commonplace in such a large household), our plan of action was the same: two of us boys would stage a fight on the front lawn of our house while another alerted our mother (or the young, female babysitter) to the melee taking place out front. When they would appear, yet another brother and our youngest sister Katherine would steal away to the back door and into the kitchen. Once inside, Katherine would be hoisted up to the cupboard where the matches were stored and snag a pack or two. Upon her return, the two battling brothers were supposed to end the staged fight so we could execute the final phase of the plan. (Though it was fairly rare to actually complete the mission; more often, the "fake" fight would erupt into a very real brawl, which would have to be extinguished by not only my mother or the babysitter, but the other brothers as well.)

Once in possession of the matches, everything was fair game, and it is a minor miracle that our house and garage (both constructed mainly of wood) survived the recklessness of children with fire. Several times things nearly got out of control, and we learned early on to always have a water source nearby.

Now, to say that there were not happy times in my childhood would be a misstatement of vast proportions, because there were many ways to bring joy to life in the city. For hours, in our youngest years, my siblings and I would play "house," "diner" and "truck stop." There were neighborhood baseball games at the local ball field, where dozens of kids would play for hours on end in the summertime. There were street hockey matches, basketball games, and bike riding excursions, which lasted into the wee hours of evening. There was a crazy game called "Spider," where my siblings and I would stretch string all around the basement in a wild pattern. The object of the game was to move about the basement with someone acting as the spider. If you touched the string, you were "stuck" and the spider could then "get you." This was a terrifying game, which engendered many a nightmare in my mind, and brought those nightmares to life when I lay down to sleep, tormenting me in ways I can only imagine now.

Other experiments simply got out of hand. I remember one incident where my brothers tinkered with a chemistry set they had gotten for Christmas and nearly blew up the house. There was an explosion, which rocked the walls and a feeling that we had just crossed the line. I remember my mother coming home as we attempted to hide the evidence, including a thick, rank sulfur cloud, which permeated every inch of the house. No one escaped my mother's wrath that day.

On the milder side, there were also games of hide and seek, scavenger hunts, and another diversion my brother Stephen invented called "Spy." Stephen would assemble his siblings before him and give us each a "spy kit": a tin band-aid box filled with string, paper, a small pencil, and a paperclip or two. He would then send us off, armed with our makeshift espionage gear and walkie-talkies, to climb trees, houses, and local buildings as we attempted to outsmart the other teams and locate our opponents before we were discovered. Katherine was my constant companion, and we made for a formidable team. "Spy" was a great game.

The alleyways that ran behind the rows of box houses offered even more entertainment. It was within these alleyways where my mind erupted into creativity. For hours a day, I would play army, or cowboys and Indians. I'd catch butterflies and explore the neighborhood. I created new worlds, envisioned alternate realities, and searched for lost treasure. Whenever plausible, I joined my siblings in these excursions, but soon found that it was better to be by myself, simply out of self-preservation. Inevitably, time spent with my siblings would erupt into violence—which solidified my belief that it was best to be left alone.

Shortly after becoming conscious and witnessing my mother on that bathroom floor fighting for her life, something strange began happening to me. To this day, I'm not certain what this phenomenon was...but I am certain it was an experience not of this world.

As I'd sit on a chair in our living room, my entire being would suddenly become seized by some outside force. I would then begin to feel a sensation akin to moving through a tunnel. This feeling would start slow and steady, but quickly escalated in intensity. Within seconds, momentum would build, energy would increase, and the sensation of moving through the tunnel would amplify until I felt I was being shot through at mindboggling speeds. During this phenomenon, I was aware of my surroundings; I could see our living room, and hear the familiar sounds of voices and everyday routines as this experience ravaged me.

I'd grip the arms of the chair as my insides shook, rattled, and careened down the tunnel. My peripheral vision would become blurred, as I could see only a pinpoint of light while traveling at an incredible rate, reaching the point of barely hanging on. As the experience reached a crescendo—as it felt I was about to be ripped apart by the intensity, as I began to enter an entirely new realm of understanding—the experience would suddenly, and inexplicably, come to a jarring halt. Instantly, everything would be back to normal, leaving me trying to decipher what had just taken place. And as any child would do in that situation, I resumed my normal routine.

What this event was is anyone's guess, but in later years I would hear similar stories about people in their early years reliving the experience of traveling through the birth canal. I could have been experiencing this, but have my own theories as well. Even when this was happening I felt as if I were traveling through a portal of some kind, like a doorway to another dimension or alternate reality. Or maybe it was a way in which I could escape my own unstable family life. Who knows? Certainly not me. I've always felt that it had more to do with inner space than outer space, but also that it was definitely a combination of the two. This experience occurred numerous times in those early years, and would always leave me asking, *What the hell was that?*

I can clearly remember the feelings I had when it *was* over, for it would take several moments to gather my senses while pondering its meaning. The first time it happened I was certainly unnerved. But every time following, I became more comfortable with the experience, eventually accepting it with no questions asked. When I would feel it coming on, I'd simply grip the arms of the chair, holding tightly but enjoying every second. It was an experience unlike any other, and proved to me that there is much more going on in this world than any of us are aware of.

At some point, this phenomenon simply stopped; it has not occurred since. To this day, I am thankful that it happened, and have accepted it for what it was: a mystery of life never to be deciphered.

It was shortly after the "Tunnel of Light" experiences that I was exposed to two more ethereal phenomena, each of which has left an indelible impression upon me. The first was simple enough, but brought an understanding that there is definitely more going on in this world than I could possible fathom: the world of puddles.

Puddles of rain on a windswept day would, to put it mildly, blow my mind. For hours at a time, I would sit before a puddle and manipulate the surface; I could see clearly within them other worlds. The reflection of the neighborhood and the sky above became, to a child with a rabid imagination, a window into the other side of the universe. I felt as if I could enter these puddles and slip through a portal that would send me to another dimension; in my mind I would enter these alternate realities at will. It was here where I learned to groom my imagination and allowed it to stretch to the farthest reaches of exploration.

These meditations solidified my understanding of inner space as well as outer space, and gave me the tools I needed to explore each. It also allowed me to enter the spirit world and has given me the tools I needed to always pursue those realms.

The other experience I had early on only solidified this new understanding.

I was raised Catholic, and although I never accepted the teachings, I did have an episode which altered my thinking. One Sunday night following Mass, I was relaxing on my bed; I must have been four or five years old. As I contemplated the words of the priest earlier in the day, I could feel myself changing. The priest had spoken of eternity, and the infinite possibilities of that concept. As I lay on the bed, I could feel my head split open and expand, as if my mind, body, and soul were entering the vast, endless universe. I could feel my mind rushing out into the stratosphere as my body followed suit. It was a relaxing feeling, and one that showed me the true scope of the human mind while opening up an entirely new understanding of life. I realized right then and there that life never truly begins or ends, but rather simply passes from one reality to the next. It was an event I never forgot, and one that has forever fueled me. If our minds could only comprehend the reality of this world, it would simply explode. The truth is that powerful.

These were just a few examples of the experiences I had that hinted of a world beyond immediate comprehension. It seemed my childhood was filled with such experiences.

From the time I was three years old, my mother told me that I was drawing pictures depicting little blue men fighting little silver men and calling it "The Silver War." From that point forward, and until I was nearly in high school, my mother said that she thought I was a former Civil War soldier, either from Louisiana or Mississippi, who had fought and died at the Battle of Gettysburg.

From the time I can remember, I was not only fascinated with the Civil War but also dreamed about it, recreated it, wrote short stories about it, drew pictures, read books, and watched films depicting this most horrific period in American history—all as if I had firsthand knowledge on the subject. I could feel something stirring in my heart, in my soul, which brought forth memories of the past, as if I were reliving the experiences all over again. It was a surreal perception, one which lasted throughout my entire childhood, and one that once again proved to me that we know very little about the inner workings of this world. Nor will we ever fully understand what we see on a daily basis.

When I was older and doing research for a school paper on the subject of the Civil War, I came across some documentation that may have proven my mother's theory. I learned that at Gettysburg, several regiments from Mississippi and Louisiana had fought in that brutal battle, and many, many men died there while serving proudly for those two Southern states. To this day, I have a connection to the Civil War, which, on an intellectual and logical level, makes absolutely no sense. There is no way I can describe what I feel about this phenomenon because the one thing I've learned is that, when all is said and done in this crazy world, most aspects of life are never meant to be understood, on any level, for as long as we live. And so my life continued with these new understandings, and onward I grew...as life all around me erupted into chaos.

As I said, violence and mayhem were a daily reality we all had to face. If the neighborhood wasn't bad enough, my four older brothers assured that I understood what anger was. Unfortunately, I passed some of this down to my youngest sister Katherine, whom I loved more than any of my other siblings. Later in life, Katherine assured me that my torment towards her wasn't extreme, and was more on the lenient side—a tidbit of information that has done little to alleviate my guilt, because I know better. I brought Katherine some serious pain and am not proud of the abuse I unleashed on her. If I could take it back, I would, in a heartbeat. Some of the things that my brothers did to me, I did to Katherine. Unfortunately, shit runs downhill.

Again, because of environment and circumstance, we all knew no better. Through this, my brother Michael became *my* nemesis. Michael was an excitable kid, and a kid I grew to admire and respect. Michael had numerous good qualities and taught me a great deal in my youth, and I loved Michael more than any of my other brothers. Michael was a great kid. But Michael was, without a doubt, a fighter. Attempting to pinpoint the first time I felt his wrath is impossible. It probably first came to fruition when I was still in the crib. But the things I do remember are powerful enough, and at the same time, downright humorous to boot. Although Michael and I went at it like rabid dogs, all my brothers made me understand who was in charge.

Some of their favorite pastimes were pinning me to the floor with my head between their legs. Unable to move, they would perform what was known as Chinese Water Torture: a continuous pecking of the forehead with a raw knuckle designed to drive one insane. I do believe that my brothers achieved their ultimate goal. This ritual was a constant throughout my childhood and one that, again, I passed down to Katherine. Living in our house was *The Lord of the Flies* brought to life, a reality that prepared us all for the realities of the world.

My brothers would turn on me at the drop of a hat, unleashing their rage when I least expected it. One day while walking just paces behind one of them in our backyard, my brother suddenly turned and whipped a rock at me. The swiftness of the experience and the forcefulness in which he threw that rock were astonishing. Even before I understood what was happening, I could feel in my mouth not only the rock, but a part of my right front tooth as well. To this day, that tooth is chipped. And, as if nothing had happened, my brother and I carried on and prepared to enter an entirely new phase of exploration.

One summer day, while on the front porch, one of my brothers was having his way with me: slapping, punching, and cursing like a drunken sailor. On one of the rare occasions my mother was around, she burst out of the front door, grabbed my brother by the throat and pinned him against the wall. Wanting me to defend myself and turn the tables, my mother directed me to even the score.

"Hit him, Larry!!!" my mother cried. "Goddamn it, Larry, hit him!!!"

I remember looking at the two of them in confusion and declining the offer.

"I can't," I replied in defeat, "he's my brother."

My mother then did what I was unable to do. It would take several more years before I had had enough of my brothers' aggression and learned to defend myself, despite what I felt for them. But when I did finally learn to retaliate, the abuse from my brothers came to a swift and immediate end. Unfortunately for me though, that time was still years away.

Violence and anger came from everyone in the family—excluding my father, who wasn't around. I have not a single memory of my father ever raising a hand to me. Truth be told, I'm thankful as can be for such a reprieve, because my father had a reputation as a vicious fighter who embodied pain. Despite this, I received my full complement of pain from everyone else, including my mother, who most of the time didn't even know who she was angry with.

One of my mother's favorite threats was, "Don't make me come up there or I'll knock you into next week!" Inevitably, my siblings and I would laugh hysterically upon hearing those words. We couldn't help but wonder just how cool it would be to travel through time. Our reaction would then prompt my mother to attempt carrying out her threat. We must have driven that woman crazy: seven screaming rug-rats running wild day and night. We were a handful.

Our house had a basement, a dark, damp, and frightening place occupied by spiders, centipedes, crickets, and whatever else thrived in the climate. It housed the laundry room, a pantry, and other areas where we kept our toys and games. The basement also boasted a "teen room," an area my mother sectioned off with hanging sheets and blankets where the record player, dozens of L. P. s, and a couple of couches resided to entertain my older siblings. The basement was a tolerable place when it was daytime and well lit, but was also a source of terror when dark and unoccupied.

One day, a few of my brothers thought it would be a gas to tie me to a support beam in the basement, turn out the lights, and put a Walt Disney record entitled "Sounds of Horror and Dementia" on repeat mode. I was six years old. For several hours I sat tied to that pole in the dark with who-knows-what crawling over me, and the sound of vampires, werewolves, monsters, and blood-curdling screams wafting through the darkness. Where my mind traveled to during that experience is unknown even to myself, but I guarantee you that a psychiatrist would have a field day deciphering what this episode did to me.

When my mother did finally come home, she eventually came

downstairs to do a load of laundry. Upon entering, she heard me whimpering in the dark, realized what was happening, and untied me while cursing my brothers. Once I was untied, my mother simply walked away while still cursing—and I attempted to maintain a hold on my sanity. It's no wonder I turned out to be the man I am today. One thing this experience did teach me, however, was a lesson I feel fortunate to have learned at such a young age: a sense of humor is essential to survival, something I have never forgotten.

Now, I'm going to say something here that might upset some people and it may very well be politically incorrect, but as I said before, I don't have the time or temperament to sugarcoat the facts. Not only do I feel fortunate to have grown up in the situation I did, but am very thankful for being put in my place time and again by my mother and siblings. Again, the one thing life in Detroit taught me was that this is a cold, nasty, and unforgiving world we live in—and if you act the fool, you will immediately suffer the consequences. I grew up in a time and place where if you fucked up while down the street, by the time you got home, your mother knew what you had done and you paid the price for your indiscretions.

One of the things I've noticed as I've gotten older is that every successive generation following mine has continually become softer, less responsible for their actions. It has gotten to the point that if parents discipline their children in any way, they face the possibility of jail time or intervention from Child Services, making proper discipline from grown-ups a thing of the past. And do not fool yourself into believing that the children of today don't understand this and use it to their advantage every chance they get. If a parent looks cross-eyed at their kids today, these winey, spoiled, undisciplined brats call the cops and drop dime for having their day upset.

As a matter of fact, just recently, a friend of mine found herself in the back of a police cruiser after her teenage son called the cops on her. This kid was drinking, doing drugs, and stealing from neighbors. When my friend—who was raising the child on her own—became angry with the boy and demanded that he stop, he called the police and reported physical abuse. I love my friend, but she did it to herself. She never disciplined the boy...and now she's suffering the consequences. Unfortunately, this is happening all across the country.

Again, I am thankful for the experiences I have had, simply because it taught me that if you fuck up, you pay the price. Today, parents have no control over their kids, a reality implemented by the government and ultra-liberal meatheads who want to control everything we do—while essentially accomplishing nothing but nurturing generations of people who have no understanding of consequence or responsibility. The belief of "let the children do as they please" is one of the main reasons we live in the world we do today, and is one of the biggest fallacies I've ever been privy to. What would do the world a load of good is to implement stern discipline upon these kids to prove who is in charge. We allow children to believe that *they* are in charge, and then paradoxically wonder why we can't control them. This policy is going nowhere and is doing no one any good, especially "the children." It's a weak game that needs to come to an end. If it doesn't, this country is going to become even more mired in selfishness, laziness, and irresponsibility. And the reality of the situation is that children want to be disciplined. They crave it, need it, and pine for it. Another fact based in truth.

By the time I was four or five years old, my personality—as predicted by Freud—was already well formed. My imagination, love of music, and need for creativity crystallized around this age, setting me down the path I follow to this day. Although this understanding was hard earned, I would have it no other way. Discipline, through an iron hand, had everything to do with this. Not only was life rigid and regimented at home, the same held true at Catholic school. You see, I was alive at the tail end of an era where strict discipline in Catholic schools still thrived. It was not uncommon for teachers, nuns, and priests to use force to control the kids. Again, whether or not this is right isn't the point. The point is that it worked, and worked extremely well. We grew to fear our teachers, and rightfully so.

Life at home also became a daily grind of waking, doing chores, and going to school. Coming home simply meant more chores and seemingly endless amounts of homework. Finally, hard-earned free time was offered before bed. The discipline learned during this time has never left me, and has been the foundation upon which I still live. Without a certain understanding of discipline, one cannot live a life of promise or productivity. Again, another reality succeeding generations appear to lack.

I can clearly remember the day our parents informed us of their disunion. We were all upstairs in an area known as the playroom, a small space of floor that led to the two bedrooms my brothers and I shared and a door leading to the attic. Huddled together, we all cried as the news was revealed, ending an aspect of my life I never felt a part of in the first place: my parents' marriage. While surrounded by my family, I remember thinking how odd it was that we were here discussing divorce when I never felt the security of a healthy family unit in the first place. I simply accepted the news for what it was: the end of the family.

As unsettled as I felt leading up to the divorce, I had no idea what awaited me. If I did, I would have most assuredly slung a gunnysack over my shoulder and hit the rails along with the hobos. But unfortunately for me, and everyone else in the family, the worst was yet to come.

My mother may have turned over a new leaf and entered a phase free of her marriage, but not us children. We were now headed towards an entirely new realm of the experiment—and not a single one of us would be able to escape the harshness of my mother attempting to raise seven children on her own, struggling to maintain a healthy home amidst chaos. The worst was yet to come, and I, an eight-year-old boy, was about to learn just what it meant to hide from reality and forge a life of creativity out of desperation, fear and loneliness. And these were the experiences that would come to shape my life, for better or for worse, as I grew into manhood. My life was about to begin...and my journey through this world without my family as a guiding force had just been unleashed.

2. GODZILLA

FOR TWO YEARS IN A ROW—WHEN I WAS NINE AND TEN YEARS OLD—I had the same dream, each time on the night before Easter Sunday. The dream, which was actually an incredibly disturbing nightmare, was one of the most vivid night visions I have ever had. In the dream, I was in the back alley behind our house and the sun was just beginning to crack the new dawn. The sky, a gruesome deep purple in color, was swept wide with thin, spacious clouds clinging to the atmosphere high above. Our neighborhood, usually stirring with people heading to work in the early morning hours, was eerily silent and still. As I gathered in my surroundings, I could feel the heavy moisture saturating the early spring air. There was an overpowering feeling of danger hanging above the entire neighborhood.

Suddenly, from behind me and down the alley, I heard a disturbing sound. Slowly turning, I was horrified to see Godzilla—the monstrous, towering icon of Japanese film—bearing down on me. He was seething, horrific, the very definition of terrifying...and he had me in his hungry sights. Turning to run for my life, my feet suddenly became mired in the heavy soil of the alley floor. It felt as if I were somehow running through quicksand; my feet were lifeless and unable to break free of the thick muck beneath me.

As I looked over my shoulder, I could see Godzilla, spitting fire and baring his teeth, as he quickly closed in on me. With every step he took, the ground shook with the force of an earthquake. With every step I took, the more bogged down I became. Within seconds, I was unable to move any further as I struggled with all my might to escape certain death. Closer Godzilla came. Closer Godzilla surged. Closer Godzilla lumbered to where I fought to free myself from this journey through madness. I remember screaming, I remember crying out from the depths of my being. I remember thrashing about wildly and clawing at the ground in an effort to release myself from the wrath of this monster swooping down on me.

As Godzilla drew closer, I remember distinctly crossing over to the realm of insanity once it became clear that I could not escape. My cries became maddening, my fears all encompassing, and my entire being fought in desperation to remove myself from a situation that was now inescapable.

Godzilla was suddenly upon me, screeching and gnashing as he reached for me with razor-sharp claws. In those final moments, I moved beyond insanity and entered a place of acceptance, giving in to my fate like a condemned man. I sealed my eyes shut and covered my ears to extinguish the horror crashing down on me. My life was over, my time had come, and my mind went blank as I removed myself from the world. I could feel Godzilla's scorching breath on my skin; I could feel the weight of his body pressing down on mine and could feel my life slipping away to the eternal emptiness of endless space. I no longer wanted to live. In a flash, I had entered the land of the lost.

It was then and only then that I would wake from this nightmare, alone and terrified, while attempting to cling to a single measure of sanity. In the pre-morning darkness, I tried to hold on to who I was and who I wanted to become. Alone, I fought to hold onto my life.

My parents finally divorced in 1973, succumbing to the inevitable following eighteen years of disagreements, mistrust, and misguided intention. The final blow for my mother was that now-infamous birth announcement she received in the mail from one of the women my father had impregnated during their marriage. That was the last straw. Despite her stern Catholic beliefs of marriage at all costs, my mother bucked the system and demanded an end to the institution that had brought her so much grief, pain, and uncertainty. Suddenly, their marriage was no more.

My mother once told me that prior to her union with my father she had received numerous marriage proposals from several men. Following their divorce, my mother once again fielded several more proposals from men who worshipped her. Even in her mid-40s, my mother was a gorgeous woman, and men were coming out of the woodwork to ask for her hand. Being understandably gun-shy, my mother resisted these as she elected to spend time playing the field, an honor she rightfully deserved. I remember several men drifting in and out of our lives in the months following the divorce.

One was a chess champion from India who taught my siblings and me the ancient game of kings and queens. He was a cool guy who sincerely took a liking to me. Another was a guy who exposed the family to the world of vegetarian cuisine. At the time, this new realm of soy products and tofu dishes was tough to digest, but would eventually become more appealing as I grew older. (I've always been appreciative for having been exposed to this world at such a young age. Back then, the vegetarian lifestyle was definitely not the norm, and to see it existing on the blue-collar streets of Detroit was as exotic as harems and geisha girls.)

There was another man, a tall, athletic cat who took us to his softball games where I would spend my time playing catch with him in between innings. He was a really sweet man who loved my mother dearly and was one of many who proposed. To his dismay, my mother declined.

And then there was a man named Kip. Kip, an Episcopal priest, was a thin, smarmy guy with dark-rimmed glasses; he had an air about him that was sleazy and untrustworthy. I never felt comfortable around the guy and actually have no memories of spending time alone with him. Despite this, Kip proposed and my mother accepted, becoming the man who was to be my new stepfather. But with wedding preparations in full swing, my mother unfortunately discovered some disturbing news about her future husband.

She had received a phone call from a mystery woman who claimed to be engaged to Kip herself. The woman, Kip's secretary, said that she, too, was about to become Kip's bride, and that she had only recently found out about my mother (and Kip's intentions towards her). Both women were now hell-bent on revenge. Employing the services of my brothers Mark, Paul, and Steven, and my sister Maria, my mother loaded into the old family truckster and headed to Kip's apartment.

There, my mother and siblings took delight in ripping apart Kip's apartment: clothing, bedding, kitchenware, plates, glasses, photos, toiletries — anything they could get her hands on. They ravaged that apartment from top to bottom, destroying everything in sight, even spray painting the walls and pictures thoroughly. The pride I felt for my mother was only surpassed by my disappointment at not being invited along for the mission. Apparently, I was too young to experience such mayhem...but was filled with pride, nonetheless, for my mother's actions.

Around this time, my mother was working at a bar down the street from our house, one of three jobs she juggled simultaneously to support her large family. My mother worked as a waitress, slinging drinks to factory workers, blue collar Johnnies, local drunks, and general down-and-outers. The bar was dark and sleazy (like Kip), and seemed a desperate choice of employment for a woman as beautiful as my mother. Inevitably, my mother had to endure an endless barrage of catcalls, drunken proposals, and slimy offers of carnal indiscretions on a nightly basis.

Somehow, our phone number made its way to the bathroom wall of the bar. I remember several late-night calls, which I personally received. Answering the phone, I would hear the voice of some seedy man describing to me what he would like to do to my mother, all in stark and graphic detail. Now, having five older siblings, I learned at an early age what sex was, but to hear the full scope of possibilities described in such detail was an eye-opener, especially when relating to my own mother. Knowing no better, I would listen intently as these lowlifes unleashed their sexual fantasies while intimating just how much my mother would enjoy them. I can clearly remember answering their twisted questions and hearing the descriptions of their darkest desires. Man, what a sick fucking world we live in.

Looking back on these episodes, I'm amazed that my mother wanted to deal with the male of the species at all. Why she didn't become a nun or consider a life of celibacy is beyond me, for her experiences had certainly been harsh enough to warrant such a move. But my mother did continue to see men, and jumped right back on that horse following the debacle with Kip. The next man to come around was a man who was a priest in the Catholic Church, and a man I would eventually come to know as Godzilla: another low-life philanderer who would use his position and status in the Church to bamboozle not only my mother, but my entire family. This man, who embodied my worst and most frightening Godzilla nightmares, was named Chris Mercer. Chris entered my life like a tempest, bringing even more uncertainty to a reality already swirling with the ferocity of a cyclone.

Chris Mercer was approximately the same age as my mother and was, as I said, a priest in the Catholic Church. My mother and Chris had actually dated when both were in school at the University of Detroit, before my mother married my father. Chris had even proposed to my mother but she declined; by that time, my mother was already in love with my father. During my parents' marriage, Chris visited us on numerous occasions, staying close to my mother however he could. Following the divorce, Chris was now back in Mom's life.

Chris Mercer swooped into our lives like a hawk and made himself a part of our family from the get-go. He took us on trips to Windsor, Canada, across the Detroit River, as well as visits to museums, restaurants, and movies. He bought us gifts, gave us treats, and promised to love our mother until the day he died. I began to hear rumors of marriage as Chris firmly entrenched himself into the family unit, even leaving the priesthood. Being the young, naïve boy I was, I swallowed Chris's lies hook, line, and sinker, actually growing to feel true affection for the man. Unfortunately for me, everyone else in the family did the same, allowing Chris to have free reign of the household, a situation which he took advantage of as soon as he felt comfortable enough to pursue his true targets: my brothers and me.

My brother Michael and I shared a bedroom on the upstairs level of our home. Along with the bunk beds where Michael and I slept, there was a third bed in the room, a bed we referred to as the "guest bed." It was here that many different people would sleep when spending the night, occupied several times a year by the many friends of my brothers and me, as well as cousins, out-of-town guests — and now, Chris Mercer.

With my mother adhering to her strict rule of her boyfriends never sharing her bed when children were in the house, Chris now became a permanent fixture in the guest bed. Shortly after this new accommodation was put into practice, Michael and I realized that Chris had never intended to bed down with our mother in the first place.

We soon came to realize that Chris had other desires in mind.

I woke one morning on the lower level of the bunk bed, my usual sleeping quarters, and greeted the new day like a boy on a mission. Pulling back the bed sheets, I placed my bare feet to the floor and prepared to start my day. Out of the corner of my left eye, I saw Chris begin to stir. As I turned to look, I saw Chris lift his bedsheets as he called to me in a hushed tone.

"Come here, Larry," Chris cooed in a mellow voice. "Come lay with me."

Knowing no better, and being the trusting kid I was, I shrugged my shoulders, stood and walked to the bed. Once in the bed, Chris pulled the sheets over both of us and positioned me with my back to his stomach. Chris then wrapped his right arm around my torso, pressed his body firmly against mine and placed his chin on my shoulder.

Then, Chris's right hand manipulated the top of my pajama bottoms and worked his way down to my penis. Grabbing a firm hold, Chris began to masturbate me while grinding his own erect penis against my anus. As he did this, I could hear him breathe into my ear as he told me how beautiful I was and how much he loved me.

Being at a complete loss as to what was happening, I attempted to digest the situation, all to no avail, electing instead to release myself from the moment by submerging my mind into whatever my brain had to offer. There is no doubt that in that moment I released myself to the sweet sound of music in an attempt to remove myself from this horrendous experience. As had happened so many times in my life leading up to this incident, and infinite times since, music became a source of hope within a moment of darkness. I have no doubt that in this moment, music again became my savior.

As Chris continued with the steady rhythm of his assault, I instinctively removed myself and gave in to the sound. And I also knew instinctively that what he was doing was insanely wrong. But being a kid, I didn't have the tools to combat what I was experiencing, and being taught to not only respect my elders but to never question their actions, it never once entered my mind to resist.

Eventually, the experience came to an end, and Chris allowed for me to exit the bed and start my day. And as any young boy would do in that situation, I put the memories of what happened behind me and moved on with life. Unfortunately for me, this most recent voyage through stupidity was just the beginning. For days, weeks, and months to come, Chris repeated this act time and again, subjecting me to his sick ways whenever he pleased. He must have felt like a kid in a candy store, having free reign on a young boy whenever his heart desired. As time went on, I began to not only hate bedtime, but grew to fear the act of waking as well.

Upon sensing movement of any kind, Chris—like a calculating, creepy little spider—would lift his bed sheets and demand that I enter his lair. In total defeat, I would lower my shoulders, drop my head, and make the agonizing six-foot walk across the room to where Chris lay in waiting. While lying in front of him, Chris again would repeat the same act: embracing me, jacking me off while rubbing his penis on me, and whispering into my ear how much he loved me. If I had the understanding and comprehension of a young man twice my age, I would have taken a baseball bat and squashed his sleazy head like a melon... but instead I gave in to my fate while releasing myself to the sound of music.

Now, unbeknownst to me, my brother Michael had been subjected to the same disturbing scenario. And when we both realized that the other was being assaulted, we both acted accordingly. Waking one morning, I lay in silence while anticipating another odyssey into perversion. Suddenly, I heard Michael stir about in the bed above me and then jump to the floor. Feigning sleep, I peered through my partially closed eyes to see Chris lifting his bed sheets and inviting my brother to lay with him. Once Michael was situated, and Chris began his game, I popped out of my bed and ran for the exit. Michael, unfortunately, was on his own.

In the weeks and months that followed, Michael and I got wise and began to play a game ourselves. With both of us being young, healthy, energetic boys, we'd usually wake about the same time. But what we began to do now was try to out-wait the other. It became a contest of will to see who could outlast the other. I can remember lying in my bed for what seemed like hours trying to outlast Michael, even though several times my kidneys and bowels were about to explode. Whoever made a move first was inevitably corralled by Chris, allowing the other to run for safety. This was, for Michael and me, the only protection we had from the perverted ways of our molester.

After months of this insanity, Chris eventually disappeared from our lives. Years later, I would learn the reasons why. Out on a date one night, my mother and Chris were in downtown Detroit enjoying an evening together. As they walked along the streets, they came upon a woman who was being beaten by a man. My mother demanded that Chris intervene. Chris refused, leaving the woman to endure the beating on her own. My mother suddenly realized what a worthless piece of shit Chris was, and ended the relationship right there on the spot. Chris was now gone forever, and our tormentor released to the forgotten pages of history.

Many years later, while in my nineteenth year of life, Michael was dating a young woman he had met at a mall in Annapolis, Maryland, where I worked as a pizza chef. Michael and this woman began a relationship that lasted two or three years. As their relationship became more solidified, this young woman confided to Michael a dark secret: for years she had been horribly abused by her own father, having to endure sexual relations with the man who was supposed to embody comfort and security.

As he listened to her tale, Michael suddenly remembered his time with Chris Mercer and began to relive the experience.

Not long after, Michael came to me and asked if I had any similar memories. I clearly remember sitting in our apartment, talking it through with my brother; as we talked, unsettling memories began to arise. The content of these memories was now quite vivid; we were both blown away by the fact that we had blocked them from our minds. And we were both stunned by the realization that these things had actually happened to us. I remember the astonishment. I remember the overwhelming sense of disbelief. And I remember the memories as they began to sink in and take us right back to that time and place so long ago. It was pretty incredible.

Suddenly, the floodgates were opened and the experiences of Chris Mercer now crowded both our minds. Together, we sat and relived the experiences as one memory after the other poured from our minds. It was clear that we had both blocked the episodes in order to preserve whatever we had left of our sanity. And now, in Michael's twenty-first year and my nineteenth, we relived those times as if they had just taken place the day before. It's amazing how the human mind works, and it's incredible what the mind does when assaulted. Those memories were etched in my mind as clearly as the sun hangs in the sky; yet, to preserve my own mental well being, I had repressed them in order to forge ahead with my own dreams of a life steeped in hope and productivity. Man, what a world we live in.

Once Michael and I pieced the puzzle together, our brothers, Stephen and Paul, came forward with memories of their own, then our sister Katherine. This low-life Chris Mercer had had a field day in the Acquaviva household; the day he moved in, he must have felt like he had just won the lottery—having the pick of the litter at his disposal whenever he pleased. To this day, the memories of Chris masturbating me, rubbing his erect penis against my anus, and breathing in my ear like a man in love are disturbing enough. Whether or not there was anal penetration I cannot say for certain...but one thing I do know is this: if I had blocked those memories from my mind for more than nine years, there's no telling what that man actually did to me. What I do remember is bad enough. And truth being told, I don't want to remember anything more.

As I've gotten older, I, for obvious reasons, have grown to despise child molesters and those who take advantage of children in any way. A few times in my life I have reached the cusp of becoming a murderer of those I've suspected of doing as much, and cannot say for certain that if faced with the same situation today I'd be able to control my emotions. One thing I can say is this: it is best that I don't involve myself in such cases, and have learned that the best course of action is to allow the authorities and organizations dedicated to the welfare of children to handle them.

When all is said and done, I know myself too well to get involved any further.

Now, it took me decades to realize that the recurring Godzilla dream I had when I was nine and ten years old was, of course, about Chris Mercer. He *was* Godzilla, and I, in a very real way, could not escape this monster. It has only been in the last several years of my life that I have come to this realization. I was in my mid-40s when I first realized that this lying, low-life excuse for a human being was my worst nightmare. When I did come to this conclusion, a mystery had been solved and my mind and heart cleared of confusion. And the fact that this dream occurred in consecutive years on the night before Easter Sunday has not escaped my understanding either.

Here was a man, a priest in the Catholic Church, who was supposed to embody everything loving, giving, and caring about Jesus Christ. And he, a man fully aware and conscious, used his position of authority to take advantage of a situation that was obviously wrong and sinful. He simply did not care, and gave in to the lowest common denominator: that of selfishness, perversion, and lack of self-control. Easter Sunday is the celebration of not only the day Jesus rose from the dead to join his Father in Heaven, but also a day we mortals are supposed to realize that we are not alone in this fight against evil. It is a day of complete and total celebration of the triumph of good over evil, and a day we are to reflect on our own shortcomings. The fact that I had that nightmare on the eve of this joyous celebration makes complete sense to my adult mind now.

In place of Jesus coming to free my soul from the pain of this world emerged a monster, Chris Mercer, who embodied the form of a gruesome, terrifying beast from who I could not escape, despite my most powerful efforts to do so. I can clearly remember the fear I felt, the frustration I endured, and the horror that ravaged my entire being as I attempted to escape from this piece of shit. And now, understanding those dreams has not only answered some long-lurking questions, but even brought a semblance of peace to my mind: knowing that in my darkest hours, I have the power to release myself from the troubles of the world and the ability to bring light—the light of music—to the forefront whenever I am in need. This experience taught me that I can endure essentially whatever comes my way, and that I have the resources to combat my darkest fears, regardless of the circumstance.

Although Chris Mercer got off scot-free, I knew what he'd done. And this time I didn't forget.

In my 30s, my younger sister Katherine located the man living peacefully in San Francisco. Michael had employed the services of a private detective and was able to secure Chris's telephone number, which he gave to Katherine. Utilizing a three-way call, Katherine and I called Chris. When Chris answered, I told him who I was; I could practically hear the man shrivel to the size of a raisin. Although I had no intention of retaliation (I had come to terms with my rage years earlier), I did want to put the fear of God into him just the same. I told him that for the remainder of his life he had better look over his shoulder, and informed him that when he least expected it, I would jump from the shadows and beat him to within an inch of his life while ramming a hot iron up his ass. I also told him that he had better be ready to meet his maker—for when he did, he would be standing alongside some of the worst human beings the world has ever seen. The shattering fear in his voice was all I needed to hear, and the satisfaction I received from this—a man overwhelmed by his own demons—was fulfilling to the point of elation. I basked in the knowledge that he will forever reside, in his own guilty mind, among the worst humanity has to offer. A truly satisfying revelation...and one I can forever live with.

3. THE NEIGHBORHOOD

TWENTY YEARS BEFORE I WAS BORN IN APRIL OF 1965, DETROIT WAS known throughout the world as "The Arsenal of Democracy. " During World War II, the factories of The Motor City were cranking out tanks, jeeps, planes, half-tracks, troop transports, engines, and motors by the thousands every week, and all the supplies and materials needed to build machines of war. It could be argued, and rather strongly, that if it weren't for Detroit and the people who lived, worked, raised families, and manned the factories there, we'd all be speaking German right now.

Detroit has a proud history. Founded in 1670 by Antoine de la Mothe Cadillac as the French vied for supremacy in the New World, *le detroit*, or "the strait," was a vital location for anyone attempting to control the region. The city grew slow but steadily, and has always had a strong influx of not only Europeans settling in the area, but Native and African Americans as well. One of the jokes I heard as I was growing up, and one made famous by Lenny Bruce, was "Don't be offended; people in Detroit hate everyone equally. " If my childhood proved one thing, it was the truth of that statement. Detroit was a prime example of America's famed "Melting Pot" model.

The neighborhood I grew up in was located just west of where Gratiot Avenue (one of the main thoroughfares to downtown) intersected with E. McNichol's Road, more commonly known as 6 Mile. The neighborhood had sprung into existence, for the most part, directly after World War II. Back then, Detroit was attempting to deal with not only the large migration of workers flocking to the city to man the factories, but accommodating the hordes of GIs returning from the European and Pacific Theaters of War as well. Our neighborhood was one of dozens that came to life during this time and became—just like all the others—the quintessential example of sprawling Detroit.

These neighborhoods were packed tight with blue collar, single-family homes sporting small backyards; they were linked together by an intricate alley system and intersecting side streets. Each neighborhood had varied local businesses, a public—as well as a Catholic—high school and elementary school, and a nearby hospital to care for the residents. Everything about Detroit was logical and, looking back on it now, appears to be the perfect example of how a city should be built. The simplistic approach to the construction of these neighborhoods seems so logical to me now that I am not surprised such reasoning no longer exists. It seems that the further technology moves us into the future, the further we remove ourselves from logic.

Both my parents and my wife's parents grew up in or near downtown Detroit. The stories I have heard from both sets of parents pertaining to their neighborhoods conjure up even more images of logic and self-sustaining practicality. The location of the city, along the shores of the Detroit River, allowed for goods to be transported to and from other areas of the region with ease. My wife's father was actually born near the elaborate canal system of downtown, which allowed farmers, fishermen, craftsmen, and all others easy access throughout southeastern Michigan.

6 Mile, as the name implies, is located six miles north of downtown. When my neighborhood was formed, the logic that existed in the downtown neighborhoods was transferred to our neighborhood and

every other community that began to spring up. Our neighborhood literally had everything needed to sustain life and was built and maintained by the people who lived there.

If you walked out our front door, down to the street and turned right, you would have immediately crossed an alley. Several paces further and you would be at the intersection of our street, Goulburn Avenue and 6 Mile Road. Right there on the corner was Andy's Bakery, an old-school Italian bakery that was a slice of heaven. The aromas drifting through the streets were incredible. It was a daily routine to visit Andy's Bakery, and one was never disappointed.

Directly beside Andy's was a plumbing supply store—the name of which escapes my memory now, but was owned by a man who lived in the neighborhood. Right next door to that was the East McNichol Sausage Factory. Again, the aromas floating through the air were out of this world. My mother, a proud and beautiful woman, would receive bags of sausages from the workers every week, which my siblings and I devoured immediately.

Throughout my childhood, we always had cats as pets. When I was a little guy, I used to believe that the cats were there to entertain us; as I got older, I began to understand the practical reasoning behind having cats in a house when living directly beside a bakery and sausage factory. The rats occupying those places were as big as our cats—and our cats, in turn, were rather large animals. Coming home from school to see one of our cats gnawing on the head of a massive rat was not an uncommon sight.

Directly across from Andy's Bakery, on the opposite side of 6 Mile, was the Alinosi's Ice Cream Factory. Alinosi's was another old-school Italian establishment that had been in business for decades at that location. Boasting an old fashioned parlor in front, neighborhood residents could purchase everything from waffle cones and sundaes to milkshakes, banana splits, and gallons of ice cream in a variety of delectable flavors. That pistachio ice cream at Alinosi's was something special. The place was a dream. Alinosi's occupied half a city block and utilized the remainder of the building as a factory. They made their ice cream right there on the spot.

The remainder of the block was dedicated to Waltham Drugs, a pharmacy operated by a family of German descent. Waltham's was a mainstay in the neighborhood and was frequented by our family for as long as we lived there.

Further to the west were many more shops, including the candle shop, hardware store, a cobbler, a small grocery store, a couple of filling stations, and a park for neighborhood kids. There was even an airport nearby, the Detroit City Airport, opening its doors sometime in the 1920s. To the east of Andy's Bakery were a couple more filling stations, an Italian fresh produce market, a bowling alley (Ramona Lanes), a public library, several night clubs, and The Ramona Theater. I heard tales of my older siblings frequenting The Ramona Theater to see great rock and roll shows in the late '60s and early '70s. These bands included some of Detroit's greatest, like Grand Funk Railroad, Iggy and The Stooges, and The MC5. The likes of Deep Purple, Frank Zappa, and The J. Geils Band were rumored to have played there as well.

Once you reached Gratiot Avenue you could find everything you needed to live a full life: grocery stores, dime stores, pharmacies, head shops, florists, restaurants, night clubs, party stores, a barber college, an adult movie theater, department stores, a military recruiting station, and several pizzerias. Looking north from the intersection of 6 Mile and Gratiot, or to the left, and you would find the Assumption Grotto Catholic Grade School and Church on the right-hand side, the place I attended school from first through the eighth grades.

If you walked out the front door of our house and turned left, you would walk a full city block consisting of modest, working class homes lining either side of the street. These houses were so close to each other that you could see into each other's windows—and lives. Coming upon

Greiner Avenue, the initial intersection, you would find a mom and pop grocery store, the bar where my mother worked for a spell, and an electrical supply store. Turning right on Greiner and you could walk several blocks to the east and reach Gratiot Avenue, coming upon Assumption Grotto in the process. This street was mainly residential, as well as the side streets connecting to it, and was populated by many friends and their families we knew well. Left on Greiner, or west from Goulburn, there was more housing, several small businesses, and a public high school—Osborn High, which two of my siblings attended. There was also a public middle school, Von Steuben, and an elementary school, Fleming Elementary, in the vicinity. Connecting the three schools were baseball and football fields, and a spacious park. For all intents and purposes, our neighborhood had it all.

We lived at 17129 Goulburn Avenue. The crisscrossing streets of our neighborhood had names such as Westphalia Road, Dresden Boulevard, Waltham Avenue, Strasburg Avenue, Schoenherr Road, Hamburg Avenue and the aforementioned Greiner Avenue, all heavily influenced by the German culture. Although our neighborhood was populated mostly by Italians, there was a strong presence of not only Germans but also French, Irish, Polish, and others from all over Europe. Look through one of my old Assumption Grotto yearbooks from the mid-1970s and you'll find family names such as Balderama, Beaubien, Gardziola, Favara, Cassone, Gerling, Kopas, LaDuke, Mulrine, Loehnis, Nitz, O'Malley, Schulte, Papuga, Romenelli, Schoenhen, Kaiser, Woloszyk, LaBeau and Iafrate, just to name a few. There weren't too many Smiths, Joneses, or Davises around.

By the time I became aware in the early 1970s, Detroit was on the decline. The racial riots of 1967 had fractured the city in a monumental way, and the labor friction between workers and owners of the factories, machine shops, tool-and-die shops, and every other business dedicated to the auto industry was coming to a head. The ultra-corrupt city government, bilking millions of dollars every year from the citizenry, was doing a number on the city as well. Detroit was being primed for a total collapse.

Our neighborhood was hard-edged, populated by those immigrant factory workers employed by the auto industry. Most families in our neighborhood were large Catholic clans who cranked out kids like there was no tomorrow. It was not uncommon to walk down Goulburn Avenue and see those working class homes teeming with five to ten kids or more. Kids were everywhere in our neighborhood. Brawling, as in our household, was just as common on the streets. It was a rite of passage that no one escaped.

I remember one summer day when my brothers Stephen and Paul were walking down the alley behind the East McNichol Sausage Factory and two neighborhood kids challenged them to a fight. My mother, who was home at the time, caught wind of the melee and came out of the house to investigate. She then proceeded to direct all four boys to step on to the front lawn, pair up and fight one group at a time. She was not going to allow an alley brawl to ensue.

"If you're going to fight," she said sternly, "you're going to do it fairly."

Stephen fought one of the kids, and when it was over, Paul fought the other, fair and square as my mother policed the entire event. Again, total logic.

But most of the time, there was no one to step in when these incidences arose. Fighting in the alleys or on the streets was almost a weekly occurrence. I was not exempt. I had to defend myself numerous times while traveling the streets of our neighborhood, and learned to do so with proficiency. Although not a fighter by nature, I did have four older brothers who taught me well, whether I wanted to learn or not. Black eyes, sprained fingers, fat lips, and stitches were a common malady in our house and on the street. I was forced to be tough whether I liked it or not.

I remember another summer day, walking down 6 Mile with my brother Michael as we traveled to a friend's house. I was probably ten years old. Suddenly, a car occupied by two whacked-out, frenzied teenagers pulled alongside us. The kid closest to us — the one in the passenger seat — whipped out a gun and waved it wildly while laughing like a madman.

"Ever seen one of these, boys?!?" he cried as he pointed the gun directly at us.

Michael and I, as defenseless as newborn kittens, stood frozen like statues as both kids, obviously high as kites, continued to laugh like psychotics. They then peeled off while the kid continued to train the gun at our heads.

Our neighborhood, in my earliest years, still functioned as a thriving community, and we kids were free to roam and explore the environs whenever we wished. I always believed that our mother preferred it that way, and encouraged us to stay out of the house so she could enjoy some rare peace and quiet. Spring, summer, and fall were fantastic, with us traipsing around the neighborhood nonstop. Baseball games. Basketball games. Football games. Street hockey matches. Hours on end playing in the alleys, hours on end bicycling, hours on end running throughout the neighborhood, raising hell and stealing peaches from the old Italian man across the street (who somehow managed to nurture several peach trees on a small tract of land beside the alley). Threats from the old man to stay off his property came in the form of a phantom shotgun.

There were trips to Andy's Bakery, Alinosi's Ice Cream, and

Waltham Drugs, where we shoplifted candy and baseball cards. There were excursions deep into the neighborhood—often to one of the many houses that were rumored to be either haunted or the location of a horrific crime. The test was to sneak inside to see a ghost or remnants of a murder. Truly scary stuff. Following street sweeping machines and garbage trucks was a thrill as well, along with watching the airplanes above dispensing a toxic mosquito repellant across the neighborhood and screaming in delight as the chemical coated us from head to toe. It was not uncommon for us to leave the house in the morning and not come home until dinnertime. We even lived at a time when milkmen still delivered milk. The "milk chutes" on the sides of houses were proof.

Climbing trees, houses, and buildings was another favorite pastime of ours. There was even an old Italian man who pushed a vegetable cart through the streets, announcing his arrival with a melodic song; "To-ma-toes, cu-cum-bers, corn-on-the-cob!" Stealing from his cart would prove you were one of the best; the old man was a master at protecting his property.

Where Goulburn Avenue intersected Greiner Avenue, there was a section of sidewalk that had been deformed into a natural ramp, the result of a tree's roots forcing their way through the concrete. By the time I was six or seven years old, my brothers and I were experimenting with jumping ramps on our bikes. This was when Evel Knievel was a huge sensation in America, and we wanted to join in on the phenomenon.

When taking your bike to the intersection, the object was to ride as fast as you could towards the concrete ramp, hit it at full speed, and (theoretically) fly through the air like a little daredevil. Many times, I crashed violently upon landing. But there were many times I was successful, screeching in delight and bursting with pride as I skidded to a halt. The trick was, when approaching the ramp, you had to cross an alley. The house on the corner had a garage that completely blocked the view of the alley, and riding at full speed as you crossed was always a dicey proposition.

One day, my life was nearly ended when crossing that alley at sonic speed. When I got to the corner, I turned and faced the ramp; I was determined to jump higher than ever before. Peddling as fast as I could, I approached the alley with the ramp some thirty feet beyond, anticipating the jump of my life. However, as I began to cross, a car as big as a whale was motoring towards the street, hitting the intersection at the same time. Upon entering the alley, this car, obviously traveling at a high speed, slammed on the brakes as I slipped right in front.

As I passed, the car rocked to a sudden and violent stop. I could feel the hairs on my arm brush against the front end, I could feel the heat of the engine envelop my body, and I could see that I was a mere inch or two from being hit full-on by the entire mass of the car. Realizing how lucky I was, I continued to peddle like a maniac, hit the ramp at full speed and flew through the air as if shot from a cannon. When I landed, I continued to pedal with all my might as my heart pounded wildly in my chest—never once looking back or acknowledging that I had just avoided certain death. To this day, I often wonder what the driver of that car was thinking, and have thanked this phantom person profusely for displaying such keen and decisive actions in a moment of sheer terror.

And this was just one of many episodes in my life where I survived by the seat of my pants. Pfffttt, I've got your nine lives hangin', man. I think I'm on my thirtieth as I write this now.

Wintertime in Detroit was equally explosive, with a wide array of activities that were nothing short of magical. There were massive snowball fights that lasted for hours, tackle football games on the street, and backyard ice hockey games on small, homemade rinks. Latching onto the back fenders of cars was a riot as well, being dragged through the streets for blocks at a time before the driver got wise and chased us off. I do believe that the drivers of some of those vehicles knew exactly what was going on and would simply drive faster, giving us the ride of our lives.

Blizzards were also wonderful experiences, shutting the city down but not the kids. One of my favorite pastimes was dressing up as a Civil War soldier, or a Brit from WWI, or a G. I. from WWII, all of my own design, and recreating such epic battles as Fredericksburg, Verdun, or The Battle of the Bulge for hours at a time.

I would submerge myself into these experiences, hearing the sounds of battle, seeing the devastation of warfare, and absorbing the fear, all while subjecting myself to the harsh winters of Detroit for endless stretches. It was a test of will to be out in the elements for as long as I could stand it, just like the men who lived through those tragic events, and endure the pain in silence. By an early age, I had become hardened by the weather.

The houses in our neighborhood were extremely close to one another, usually separated by a thin concrete pathway. Back then, there were no air conditioners; in the spring, summer, and fall, you could hear the activity of your neighbors through the open doors and windows of their houses. Music, T. V. s, arguments, fights, laughter, beatings, dinner routines, and everyday household chores could be heard wafting from house to house. To the one side of our house was the alleyway separating us from Andy's Bakery and The East McNichol Sausage Factory. On the opposite side of our house were the Ladds, an old German couple.

The Ladds, who were easily in their 70s by the time I became aware, were a typical family unit in our neighborhood. We could hear them fighting almost every day. These episodes were hysterical, complete with screaming voices, shattering kitchenware, slamming doors, and an array of unmistakable body blows.

The Ladds' house was an exact replica of ours. The design was a perfect match, something rare in the neighborhood. My bedroom overlooked Andy's Bakery, the sausage factory and 6 Mile. When walking out the bedroom door you entered a small play area. To the right of our door was another bedroom where my brothers Mark, Stephen, and Paul slept. To the left was the doorway to the attic. Directly across from our bedroom was a window that looked onto the upper level of the Ladds' house, with a stairway to the lower level of our house directly to the right of the window.

When I was about nine years old, the Ladds turned the upper level of their home into a small apartment. The first people to move in were a young couple who appeared to be no more than twenty years old. The young woman was a beautiful, dark-haired girl with fair skin. She had long, straight hair that ran the full length of her back, a pretty face, and a slim, ample body. She was, to my young eyes, a dream. Shortly after they moved in, I was in my bedroom one night doing homework while listening to the radio. Suddenly, I heard the unmistakable sound of a man beating a woman. I could hear the young woman crying. I could hear her begging her young husband to cease with his assault. And I could hear the familiar sound of fists pummeling flesh. It was a horrific sound that caused me to cringe and hide in my bed.

When I finally heard a door slam, I knew that the young man had had his fill and was out of the apartment. Heading to the window in the playroom to investigate, I peered into the apartment next door. There I saw the young woman, dressed in shorts and a tank top, staggering towards the window to where a vanity sat. In silence, I watched as she slowly took a seat and attempted to gather herself. She was bleeding from her mouth, her eye was swollen, and her body was shaking. I then sat quietly and watched as she began to brush her hair in long, deliberate strokes while humming a simple melody in between bouts of sad, lonely tears. It was a heartbreaking scene. She was so young, so beautiful: to my mind, the perfect representation of womanhood. And now, here she was, alone and frightened, struggling to cling to a single shred of dignity in the soft light of her bedroom. I wanted so badly to run down the stairs, fly to her door and up the stairs to her apartment and take her in my arms, while telling her that everything would be alright. Instead, I continued to watch in confusion as she stroked her hair and whimpered in isolation.

This scene was repeated more than once in the months to come. Sitting in my room, I would hear a ruckus, the sound of the girl crying and her husband beating her. I would then see her stumbling around her apartment with fresh bruises and a bloodied face as she attempted to hold on to a sliver of hope. Unfortunately, this scene was all too common in our neighborhood, as women in my own family and those around us were subjected to male abuse. At a very young age, I became sickened by this ritual, and swore that I'd never raise a hand to a woman for any reason.

One day, I walked out into the alley behind our house to play with my toy soldiers. I was nine years old. Entering the alley, I looked to my left to see two teenage boys sitting behind our garage and leaning against the wall. One kid held a brown paper sack to his mouth and pulled in deep breaths of air. When he lowered the bag, his mouth was covered in what looked like soot.

The two of them were huffing glue. "Huffing" consists of filling a bag with airplane glue and breathing in the fumes to get high. For weeks to come I would see these same two kids repeating this scene numerous times. It never once entered my mind to invite myself to their party. The sight of them, although disturbing, was actually rather hilarious.

Drugs were prevalent in the neighborhood as I came of age shortly after the height of the Swingin' '60s. Having five older siblings, drugs were a mainstay in our house. Despite my mother's protests, I knew that my older siblings tried just about every drug under the sun, as it would have been impossible not to be exposed to them or tempted by friends.

Seeing whacked-out kids roaming the neighborhood was as common as spotting squirrels enjoying the tree-lined streets, and it became even more evident as I grew older. Partying—by adults or kids—was a daily routine and one could not escape this. Detroit was a breeding ground for escapism, and people in the neighborhood invented new ways of partying. We knew of several households that produced their own wine, old-world style, and others who produced European-style beer.

The bars in the neighborhood were constantly full, and the drug trade on the street obvious, even to a child. Life in our neighborhood was tough, unforgiving, and in a lot of ways, overwhelming. People needed ways to blow off steam and release their minds from the drudgery of factory work, screaming kids, angry neighbors, and violent streets. Drugs and drinking were one way of doing it. Life in the city dictated as much.

ASSUMPTION GROTTO

The focal point for our family and many others in the neighborhood was the Assumption Grotto Catholic Grade School and Church. But Assumption Grotto was infinitely more than just a church and school. It was a community gathering center that worked on numerous levels.

The Assumption Grotto Church—a beautiful, classically designed Gothic structure—was built in the 1870s and was the dominant feature in the neighborhood for many, many families. Several of my siblings and I attended school at Grotto from first through the eighth grades and were involved in many different aspects of the institution. Our lives, like so many others, revolved around Assumption Grotto.

Not only was it a privilege to attend school there, but you were infused with a sense of pride and historical awareness for being a part of its heritage. The school first opened its doors in the 1920s, allowing for generations of immigrant families to be educated. The long history enhanced the experience; it gave you a sense that living up to its reputation was not only a birthright, but expected of you.

Now, like any blue-collar city, Detroit—the Arsenal of Democracy—had an element to it that was strongly militaristic. Blue-collar cities have always been breeding grounds for the military, and specifically those who fill the "grunt" ranks of privates, corporals, and sergeants. Couple that with the Catholic dogma, and you're one step away from boot camp. Assumption Grotto proved this to me from the very first day I walked through her doors.

Discipline at Grotto was strict. Though I remember teachers who beat kids, and nuns and priests who used rulers and a swift hand as a means of controlling classrooms, my older siblings got it worse. As was the case in the rest of the country—and the entire industrialized world, for that matter—the early to mid-1970s was a time of political, cultural, and social change in Detroit. Life was beginning to move from the old-world ways to the new, softer ways that subsequent generations would come to know very well. To sum it up, I was a part of the last generation of children who were disciplined sternly before kids became soft.

It was not uncommon to address your teachers, faculty, coaches, and staff as "yes, sir" and "no, ma'am"; rather, you were afraid of the consequences if you did not. The most obvious manifestations of this discipline existed in team sports, which I played from the time I was allowed. The training rituals at Grotto were intense, and established immediately who could handle the abuse and who could not. I not only grew to love sports but also thrived during the training. I loved to push myself to the physical limits of endurance, and had the opportunity to do so from the time I arrived at Assumption Grotto.

Although Grotto was a Catholic school, I never bought into the religion or the strange (and, to my mind, sometimes bizarre) rituals that went along with it. My mother expected all of her sons to serve as altar boys, and I could not escape this fate. Although I served the shortest term as an altar boy in my family—less than a year—my tenure was far longer than I would have preferred.

One of the most difficult experiences to endure was the funerals. These ceremonies were morbid, dark, bleak, frightening; never a single hint of joy or celebration involved. This ritual always confused me: why, I would ask, were we celebrating the passing of a soul to be with their Heavenly Father in such a gruesome and terrifying manner? Serving as an altar boy during funerals was like being in a tomb as it was being sealed shut. Weddings, confirmations, baptisms, and everyday Mass were not much better either.

Although I was not much of a student, I did manage to be a pupil of average capabilities. Of course, writing, drawing, daydreaming, listening to music in my head, and chasing skirt were my real specialties. It was at Assumption Grotto where I blossomed into a true lover of females. To put it mildly, I tried getting laid from the moment I understood what sex was, and even remember masturbating in the third grade to "Jane" of the "See Dick Run" books. (Hey, what could I do? Jane was a hottie, and I was a Dick.) Those first tastes of the fairer sex were incredible, and fueled my very existence throughout my time at Assumption Grotto—all the while playing the field with every little girl who looked my way.

One of my strongest memories I have pertaining to young love was when the long, cold, harsh winters gave way to the sweet, warming sun and beautiful blossoms of springtime. There was nothing like it, catching the first glimpse of spring as you pined for the affections of some beautiful young girl who played coy and hid behind whispers of her hair. To this day, those memories make me swoon.

These rituals of young love were strongest in the spring and summer; Assumption Grotto blossomed right along with the trees, flowers, and fauna of the city. Looking at the 1870s Gothic-style church from Gratiot Avenue, you saw to the right the Rectory where the priests lived. To the left of the church was Building A, where kids in the first through fifth grades were educated. Further to the left of Building A was the Convent where the nuns lived. Behind Building A was Building B—where students from the sixth through eighth grades were taught—and the gymnasium. Directly behind the church was a parking lot, and beyond that, a beautiful, sprawling cemetery that ran the full width of the school grounds and spread more than a city block deep.

That cemetery was not only a place to test your manhood with excursions deep within, but it was also a place where young love blossomed. Not only do I remember sneaking in at night with the boys in search of ghosts and goblins, but I also have many memories of spending spring and summer nights courting the girls within its confines. The contrasts between being in the cemetery with the boys or a beautiful young girl were extreme.

A trip with the boys meant that everything became scary and uncertain—seeing sights and hearing sounds both frightening and otherworldly. Being with a fresh young female, however, it suddenly became a romantic journey through "Old" New Orleans. The headstones became works of art, the inscriptions poetry, and the statues of the Saints and Mother Mary protectors of the peace. That cemetery—smack-dab in the middle of the neighborhood—was a beautiful place to spend time in.

Nearing the end of the school year, as spring was in full bloom, a wonderful event was held every year that made a young boy feel the full measure of his growing loins: The Spring Fair. For weeks on end, kids prepared mentally, worked extra jobs for more spending money, grew their hair out to look cool, and behaved like little angels so as not to be grounded during this time. When the fair began, it was like unleashing your hormones into a tempest. There was nothing that could slow your romantic self down.

Suddenly, in the back parking lot behind the church, and upon every inch of available space of school grounds, there emerged gaming tents, food vendors, crazy, wild carnival rides, haunted houses—and every young girl in the neighborhood, Catholic or not, who descended upon the scene in glorious fashion. It was a young man's dream come true, and as long as you had cash in hand, the sky was the limit.

During the fair, which lasted more than three days and nights, a young man was free to do as he pleased. Although parents and teachers were present, as long as you kept your nose clean you had free reign of the joint. And of course, what that meant for me was exploring young love; I would spend all of my time and money trying to impress the ladies. This consisted of asking a young girl out on a "date," buying her treats, trying my luck at games of chance, purchasing a pocketful of tickets for carnival rides, and stealing kisses whenever possible. Those three days felt like an eternity, and if any one girl didn't work out, I moved on to the next in hopes of a better outcome.

I remember once, while vying for the attention of a beautiful young blond named Lynette Sun, my attempt at reaching romantic Nirvana literally blew up in my face. Lynette was a girl I fooled around with for most of my fourth and fifth grade years. At the fair during our fifth grade year, I saw Lynette enjoying the festivities with a group of friends. Gathering my composure, I asked if she would walk the grounds with me. To my surprise, she accepted. Coming upon the carousel in front of Building A, I pulled out my wad of tickets and asked if she wanted to take a spin. Again, she accepted.

Now, I've never been good with carnival rides that go round and round, for my stomach could never handle such motion. But this was a kid's ride for crying out loud: a smooth, revolving romp upon horseys and zebras. I felt confident that I'd be able to handle the experience while spending time with my chosen lady. I couldn't have been more off the mark if I had tried. Lynette and I were side by side as the ride began its continuous revolution around in endless circles. In a matter of seconds, I blew chunks, and had to hop off my horsey and lay on solid ground to stop the world from spinning. Lynette, obviously turned off by my weakness, simply walked away while giggling...and never spent time with me ever again.

When the fair came to an end it felt like the whole world had suddenly stopped, and it would take several days to recover from the endless excursions into romance. But what the end of the fair always meant was the beginning of summer vacation, a reality that softened the blow. And with the beginning of summer vacation came a whole new journey in to young love. You see, summer meant the beginning of festival season at Assumption Grotto—"Ethnic Festivals" to be precise.

Ethnic Festivals occurred almost every weekend during the late spring and early summer, and these events were nothing short of incredible. Each and every festival opened up an entirely new world for us kids, as just about every nationality at the school was represented during the season.

There was a German Festival, a Greek Festival, an Italian Festival, an Irish celebration, a Polish Festival—plus Spanish, Russian, Hungarian, and in later years, an African American Festival. These celebrations were wonderful, complete with authentic food, costumes, music, dance, and traditions that came to life with all the color, texture, and sounds of the old world, all saturating the school grounds for days. Again, this was the perfect setting to explore the fairer sex. If you couldn't get "lucky" during festival season, you might as well go to the cemetery, with shovel in hand, and end your life right there on the spot. Those festivals brought the neighborhood to life in ways that were impossible to deny, and created an energy that reached directly for every soul. Festival season was a slice of life unlike any other. It brought the entire community together in ways unimaginable today.

Detroit of my youth, and especially our neighborhood, was vibrant, vivacious, and—without a doubt—explosive beyond belief. Being lucky enough to experience the tail end of the city in its glory days, and just before its demise, is something I have been thankful for. As I've gotten older, I've come to appreciate it even more; our neighborhood was a child's dream, a gift I took advantage of every chance I got.

As I grew older, Detroit began its eventual descent into violence, decay, and urban chaos. Coupled with an unsettled family life, the older I became, the further into isolation I slipped—escaping into a world of music, creativity, and imagination that would encase my heart in a protective cocoon of light, sound, and exploration. The decline of Detroit had always been one of the saddest episodes of my life and one I would never forget, for how it has affected me is something I may never truly understand. To witness firsthand the fall of one of the greatest and most powerful cities the world has ever seen was a humbling experience, and one that may become all too common in this country the further we move into the future.

The logic and self-sustaining sensibility Detroit was founded upon has not only disappeared from The Motor City, but I can see it happening elsewhere in the country. One of the questions I continually ask myself is, "If we don't educate and employ our citizens properly, how can we expect to thrive as a country?" Unfortunately, I believe that we are about to find out. The rest of the country appears to be following suit. So, hold on to your hats, my friends. Hold on to your hats, for this ride is truly about to begin...

4. MY TENTH BIRTHDAY

LIFE IN DETROIT WAS AN ADVENTURE. I DON'T REMEMBER A SINGLE dull day in my entire childhood, and would be hard pressed to recall a single moment not steeped in nonstop activity. My mother, for one, would not allow for us to be lazy, unproductive, or sedentary. It was not an option to lie about idly while wallowing in self-pity. Our house was not only like "The Lord of the Flies," but was very much like a military encampment. Every morning we were expected to perform our chores, make our beds, cut the lawn, clean the basement, help prepare breakfast, shovel snow, and generally be responsible for our own lives at every turn. And if you were unwilling to do this, you suffered the consequences immediately. This was how every day began.

In those days, there were no video games, internet connections, smart phones or chit-chat rooms. Hell, watching television was restricted to evenings (following dinner) and Sunday nights (when the Walt Disney Hour was a treat for good behavior). As in every other aspect of our lives, we were expected to entertain ourselves once we had tended to our chores and homework. And I would have it no other way. This lifestyle allowed for my imagination to run free, and brought an understanding of life not realized by most children today. We were actually expected to take responsibility for our own existence, a mind-blowing concept that seems to have disappeared from the modern cultural landscape. What a notion: using your own brain to entertain.

Now, as I said, I realized early on that it was best for me to be by myself. Life in our household, and on the streets, dictated as much. As Woody Allen waxed so profoundly in the film "Zelig," and I'm paraphrasing here, "The family down the street beat us up. My mother beat my father. My father beat my brother. My brother beat me. I beat the kid down the street. " (What, did Woody grow up in our neighborhood?) Living in an urban setting amongst frustrated blue-collar workers created an atmosphere ripe for discontent on every level, and no one in our neighborhood was exempt. This tale—the tale of My Tenth Birthday—was, for all intents and purposes, just another episode wedged between so many others that boasted a similar flair. When all is said and done, it was just another classic example of everyday life in the city of Detroit as I grew into manhood.

Leo Fernette was a strange kid. It wasn't necessarily his appearance that made Leo an odd boy—Caucasian features intermingled with a slice of Asian, and possibly some extraterrestrial blood to boot—but it had more to do with his personality. Although we were friends for a few years, even going to Assumption Grotto together, I never felt a strong connection with him. Our friendship was born out of proximity; Leo lived only five houses down the street, and because of this (amongst other conditions) we were buddies.

I've always pulled for the underdog throughout my life. Being that I felt like an underdog myself, I generally gravitated towards those kids who were outcasts and loners—the kids who didn't quite fit in. Leo Fernette definitely fit that bill. Due to his strange personality, Leo had few friends and was bullied at school. So naturally, being the kid I was, I tried to be his friend. It was a strained relationship at best.

We did have some good times together though, Leo and I, playing army in the alley or chasing butterflies throughout the neighborhood, but there were conflicts as well. Leo was a possessive kid, a jealous kid who allowed his inadequacies to rise to the surface and dictate his actions. In early spring of my ninth year of life, these issues came roaring to a head.

Back in December, for Christmas, I was given a gift, one for which any nine-year-old boy would have sold his mother: the R-27 Power Rifle, complete with multiple attachments and a dizzying array of added implements of destruction. The R-27 was a thing of beauty. Made of stout plastic, the R-27 sat in your hands like a bazooka and had firepower that was mindboggling. It shot little Nerf rockets and tiny plastic balls, featured myriad buttons and switches, and generally had an aura about it that unleashed a child's imagination as freely as rain falls from storm clouds. From the moment I unwrapped it, the R-27 was a prized possession, and from the moment Leo Fernette saw it, he wanted it for his own. In early spring of 1975, Leo again allowed his jealousies to get the best of him.

One Saturday morning, in late March, I woke and decided that I wanted to rule the world. It was one of those rare mornings during this time when Chris Mercer wasn't around, and I took advantage of this situation with all I had. I wanted to control the planet and knew exactly what would allow for me to become the "King of All I See": the R-27 Power Rifle. Heading for the closet in my bedroom, I made a beeline to my secret hiding place, pushed aside the hanging clothes and reached for the rifle.

To my surprise, and pained disbelief, it was gone.

My heart sank, my palms became sweaty, and I swooned with the unthinkable. My precious R-27 Power Rifle was nowhere in sight.

Immediately, I ran to my mother and pleaded my case.

"Mama!" I cried. "My rifle, it's gone!"

"What rifle, honey?"

"My R-27 Power Rifle, it's gone! And I know who took it! Leo Fernette!"

"Now, Larry," my mother countered while grasping my quivering shoulders, "you can't make accusations like that without proof. Are you sure Leo took it?"

"I'm positive!" I fired back. "He's been jealous of me ever since I got it for Christmas! I know he took it!"

There was an investigation. There were accusations. There were threats of revenge and promises of a fat lip, but my mother would have none of it. She was determined to unravel the mystery before making a decision.

Now, I—like most kids—was known to stretch the truth from time to time. I had my issues with covering up the facts when my hide was on the line, but this time, I knew I was right. I knew that Leo Fernette had taken my R-27 Power Rifle, and my plea was so passionate that my mother believed me. Grabbing me by the hand, she led me out of the house, up the sidewalk and straight to the Fernette's. My mother would now lead her own investigation.

"Hello, Mrs. Fernette," my mother began as the woman calmly opened the screen door. "Um...there seems to be an issue, with a missing toy gun. My son believes that Leo took it."

Mrs. Fernette, a short, timid, and quiet woman, stared blankly at my mother through round, wire-rimmed glasses before finally replying: "Well, Leo and his father are at Cub Scouts. They won't be home for several hours."

We were suddenly at an impasse. I was forced to accept this unsavory turn of events but was certainly not happy about it. I believe my mother felt my pain.

"Well, Mrs. Fernette," my mother continued while still holding my hand, "do you mind if we have a look in his bedroom?"

Mrs. Fernette, a sad and lonely woman, paused for a few excruciating seconds before finally stepping to the side. Mom, taking advantage of the moment, silently brushed past with me in tow.

Leo's house was always an unsettling place to be. It was tomb-like, dark, and had a strange aroma to it. The energy was gloomy. Leo's father was a Vietnam Vet who suffered from Post-Traumatic Stress Disorder, and was a full-blown, angry drunk on top of it. And Leo's mother, beaten by life, had to endure her husband's frequent bouts of rage and endless drunken stupors. She was a dispirited woman. As we stepped through the front door, the cold, unforgiving energy of the house greeted me like an open hand to the face. But my mother and I were determined to get my precious rifle back, at all costs.

As we walked through the living room, I released my mother's hand and looked to the mantle. Resting upon it was the familiar display of Mr. Fernette's Army photos, several large bullets, and two or three hand grenades. I always wondered if those hand grenades were real and active, but concluded that now was not the time to find out. I put my curiosity to the side and followed my mother into Leo's room, just beyond the living room.

At first, my mother, like a seasoned pro, pilfered through Leo's closet only to come up empty. Then, it hit her. Leo, just like most kids, kept his prized toys under his bed. I watched in amazement as my mother dropped to her knees, crawled across the floor and lifted the bed sheet. And there it was, the R-27 Power Rifle. My suspicions had been confirmed.

My mother immediately grabbed the rifle, took me by the hand and headed for the front door. Not a word was exchanged between my mother and Mrs. Fernette and the jig was up. There was no need for words. I was never so proud of my mother and allowed for her to lead the way. The R-27 was once again in my possession and nothing, and I mean *nothing*, was going to separate me from it ever again. Over the next few weeks, not a word was spoken about the incident. I didn't bring it up: nor did Leo. But our friendship, from that point forward, no longer existed. I felt vindicated and allowed the relationship to fade into the passing memories of days gone by, where it belonged.

April 1975 was glorious. Spring was in full bloom and the weather was pristine. Mild temperatures and a bright, warming sun drenched the streets of Detroit. April was also the month of my birth. As my birthday approached, I was percolating with excitement at the prospects of what my special day would bring. The possibilities seemed endless.

My mother, despite our living conditions, always made holidays and birthdays memorable. Even the less important holidays such as Valentine's Day and St. Patrick's Day were marked with unique treats and interesting traditions. My mother desperately tried to make us feel loved, and went out of her way to ensure that we felt appreciated on some level. This birthday, I was certain, was going to be great. You see, as my birthday approached, my mother informed me that my father—a man who, by now, was as distant as the warming spring sun—was going to be present at my party. It was going to be one of those rare times following my parents' divorce that the entire family was to be together under one roof. I was ecstatic.

Sunday, April 20, 1975, was indeed a gorgeous day. The temperature was perfect. The sun, high in the sky, was as bright as my disposition. And I remember clearly, as the family gathered together, the usual friction and tension that permeated our home was as distant as my friendship with Leo Fernette. Not only were we celebrating my tenth birthday, but we had also gathered for my sister Maria's birthday as well (seeing as her birthday is only two days before mine), and it was a particularly notable birthday for Maria: her Sweet Sixteen. As per usual, we were to celebrate our special days together, a tradition I enjoyed. Despite the separation of years, I loved my sister Maria dearly. She was like a second mother to me.

The birthday dinner was spectacular: pizza from our favorite pizzeria, Mr. C's, a rare treat reserved for monumental days such as the one we now celebrated. The family was packed inside the cramped kitchen and situated around a kitchen table strewn with birthday cards, presents and overflowing pizza boxes. It was a wonderful sight. As all nine of us — my six siblings, my parents and I — gnawed on that pizza, my eyes were locked firmly on those presents.

What were in those shiny, colorful and carefully wrapped presents, I thought in anticipation? What unique gifts had my mother gotten for me? What kind of cool toys had my siblings purchased for me? And what did my father, a man who struggled to show affection, buy for me on my special day? I wolfed down my slices, knowing that the quicker we made it through the meal, the sooner the mystery of the presents would be solved. I was only moments away from gathering in my birthday booty and bursting at the seams...but as sometimes happens in life, that which we hope for is suddenly, and violently, taken away from us when we least expect it.

As my mother cleared the table of empty pizza boxes, as my siblings laughed and joked, as my father nestled in following the meal, my sister Maria and I prepared for the coupe-de-grace: the unwrapping of our presents.

The kitchen was probably no bigger than 12'x15', and was made even smaller by the stove, kitchen sink, refrigerator, and kitchen table that crowded the room. Entering the kitchen from the dining room, the table immediately greeted you from where it rested against the wall. On the opposite side was the doorway to the stairs that led first to the back door, then down into the basement. Across from the table was the sink, with the stove set against the wall, perpendicular to the kitchen table, and the refrigerator opposite that. The nine of us in that room made for tight quarters—but it was a peaceful, celebratory scene.

And now, finally, it was time for cake and presents. As my mother turned out the lights and lit the candles on the cake, I was so excited that I couldn't sit still. Following the Birthday Song, Maria and I blew out the candles and awaited the distribution of gifts. It was now the moment of truth.

Then, suddenly, we heard the unmistakable sound of someone stumbling through the screen door at the front entrance of the house. A sudden wave of silence enveloped the kitchen as we all looked to one another in confusion. We then heard heavy, uncoordinated footsteps approach, first through the living room, then across the dining room. It was then that my brother Mark, who was sitting at the doorway where the dining room greeted the kitchen, said, "Hey Mr. Fernette, how are you doing today?" Mr. Fernette, Leo's father, had unexpectedly appeared in the doorway of the kitchen. There was a moment of silence, a sliver of confusion...then, a sudden burst of violence.

Mr. Fernette—dark, unkempt and stinking drunk, with a bottle of rot-gut booze in his greasy, gnarled hand—looked around the room through sinister eyes and mumbled something indecipherable. He then turned to my brother Mark, grabbed him by the throat with his free hand, lifted Mark out of his chair, and pinned him violently against the wall with a force of power that was astonishing. That's when all hell broke loose.

Now, as I've already disclosed, my father has always been a mystery to me. He was distant, to say the least, when my parents *were* married. Following the divorce, he became even more elusive. Because of this, I never knew much about him. I had heard stories—like how when he was a young man, he and his brothers ruled the neighborhood they grew up in with iron fists. I had also heard that he had ties to the Detroit Mob, being a strong-arm soldier who collected debts, enforced mob policies, and busted heads for various reasons. I had, at that time, heard of yet another story: of one of my sisters being violently assaulted by an ex-boyfriend, and my father and one of his "associates" showing up at the kid's house with baseball bats in hand to "even the score." I had heard rumors that my old man was a fighter, a street kid who could scrap with the best of them and put the fear of God into his enemies. I never knew if his reputation was a series of tall tales, exaggerated truths or straight-up lies. I never knew the truth about my father until Sunday, April 20, 1975. That's when I realized the stories I had heard about my father were, without a doubt, dead-on balls-accurate.

As my brother Mark struggled to breathe and free himself from the fierce grip of Mr. Fernette, as my siblings and I screeched in horror and attempted to grasp what was happening, as my mother howled in agony at the sight of her son being violently assaulted, my father—the pride of the Kercheval neighborhood in downtown Detroit—sprang into action with the dexterity of a cat and the fierceness of a lion.

From where he sat on the opposite side of the kitchen table—directly across from where my brother Mark struggled to free himself from a madman's wrath—my father, in a single bound, flew across the table, grabbed Mr. Fernette forcefully, threw the drunkard violently to the floor, clamped him by the throat with his left hand, and raised his right fist to pummel his fresh conquest into submission.

As my father threw his fist forward to deliver the knock-out blow, my brother Stephen—in a move that most likely saved Mr. Fernette's life—wrapped both his arms around my father's powerful paw and pulled back with all his might to prevent the fatal blow from making contact.

"I'm sorry! I'm sorry!" I heard Mr. Fernette call in a slurred tone. My father continued to pin him to the floor. My brother continued to cling to dad's arm.

Through the chaos, through the insanity, through the energy of the situation on the verge of mayhem, my mother fought her way through her screaming children to reach for my father.

"Please, Angelo!" she cried while grasping his shirt. "It's over! Please don't hurt him! Please let him go!"

My father, to the great fortune of Mr. Fernette, complied. He slowly released his grip, pushed himself off the beaten man and got to his feet.

"You ever assault my family again," my father said in a tone that, to this day, frightens me when I think of it, "you'll be a dead man, do you understand me?"

As Mr. Fernette slowly got to his feet and attempted to gather his composure, he straightened out his shirt, smoothed back his hair, then silently and sheepishly turned and shuffled towards the front door. Any memories of what transpired at the birthday party following that episode are wiped clean from my memory. I'm sure that my mother tried her best to bring order to a chaotic scene. I'm sure that my sister Maria and I relished our presents, even though I can't recall a single gift I received. And I'm sure that my tenth birthday party was a happy occasion on some level, but the one thing I know for certain is that we all sat around the kitchen table and attempted to figure out why Mr. Fernette thought that it was a good idea to walk into our house, a house populated by six healthy and vibrant males, and act the way he did. And I'm certain that we all relived the moment when dad flew over the kitchen table like a superhero, pinned the drunkard to the floor and nearly ended his life.

From that day forward, whenever I saw Mr. Fernette, he was usually on his front porch, drowning his sorrows in a bottle of booze and mumbling indecipherably. Whatever spirit the man might have had before my tenth birthday was now gone forever. He was reduced to a shell, an empty man who not only had to carry around the horrific memories of Vietnam in his head, but also the memory of my father nearly ending his life on that fateful day in April of '75. Despite the trauma of that incident, I've always looked fondly on that day, for it is the day I realized that the stories I had heard pertaining to my father's exploits were probably true—a reality confirmed by my mother years later, and a realization that brought me, on some level, a little closer to him. And it was also the day that I realized that Leo Fernette and his father would never be a part of my life ever again, an understanding that brought true comfort and a release of tension in a neighborhood that bred tension on a daily basis for as long as I lived there. My tenth birthday is the day I learned to never live in fear again. And I have followed that lesson, as powerfully as I can, to this day.

5. THE BATTLE OF GREEN MOUNTAIN

WHEN I WAS IN MY TWENTIES, I HAD A RARE CONVERSATION WITH MY father. In the conversation, my father shared with me his experiences of being drafted into the Army at the tail end of the Korean War. Two things stand out in my memory about that conversation. The first was that my father's drill sergeant—a crazy Turkish man who had seen horrific combat in a war most Americans have forgotten, or care little about—did whatever was necessary to prepare the new recruits for certain hell. My father told me that the man was ruthless, never caring how his actions affected those beneath him. He was preparing those boys for an experience of pure horror and had free reign to bring his point home however he saw fit. The man literally beat the shit out of my father and his fellow draftees—and no one, including the top brass, prevented this from happening.

The second thing I remember about that conversation was this: my father told me that in the Army, the boys from Detroit had reputations more fierce and intimidating than any other city in the nation, including those from New York. He told me that the New York boys stood to the side when my father and his mates from the Motor City passed by. They, in a very real way, ruled the roost. Growing up in the city of Detroit has made me understand why.

Not only are those born in the city products of the harsh and brutal conditions — themselves a by-product of the gritty, industrial complex gone wild — but they are also products of the anger, frustration, and insidiousness these conditions breed. Everyone — and I mean *everyone* — I knew while growing up had a hard edge to them. Coming of age myself at the end of the Vietnam War, I heard numerous stories of young men from the neighborhood who were drafted into service and never came back home, or returned either horribly disfigured or forever mentally unstable. As I've stated, Detroit was a breeding ground for the fodder that fed the guns of the American Military Machine, from the madness and carnage of the Civil War all the way to the stupidity and greed of Vietnam.

The area where 6 Mile Road and Gratiot Avenue intersected was a great place to experience and explore. Just down the street from Assumption Grotto on Gratiot Avenue was a military recruiting station.

Almost daily, while walking home from school, a recruiting officer dressed in his military best would be out front of the station casting his net over the endless waves of children and young men passing by. He would appeal to our strong sense of adventure and curiosity about all things military. And he would not be shy in trying to convince us that life in the military was what we needed to become honorable, patriotic men.

"Hey boys," he would say while puffing on a smoke, "want to learn how to become a real man? Just step inside and I'll show you how."

I bought the spiel hook, line, and sinker and spent many, many afternoons in the recruiting office listening to stories, reading literature and dreaming about becoming a military hero. In my youth, my mind was entrenched in all things military and historic. The neighborhood, and city, pounded this into my head every day.

The tale I am about to share now, the Battle of Green Mountain, not only describes my fascination with all things military but it also sheds light on the state of mind my siblings and I were dealing with on a daily basis.

A child's imagination is truly a force of nature. A child's imagination can travel across the galaxies. It can create new worlds. It can swim in the oceans, walk on the face of the moon and dream a new day in the light of the morning sun. A child's imagination is limitless, fearless and free. A child's imagination is priceless. As a child, I had the freedom to allow my imagination to roam to the furthest reaches of inspiration and explored these opportunities every chance I had. My childhood was steeped in a wide-open imagination: the adventures I had were boundless, seamless, and chock-full of color, texture, light, and sound. I chose to live every day to the fullest.

I was a quiet kid who, due to circumstance, learned to keep to himself and walk alone. Being the second youngest of seven children, and the youngest of five boys, I learned early on—through trial and error—that the best opportunity for survival was to stay as far away from the turmoil and upheaval of a broken home as I possibly could, and learned to do this with great proficiency. I was a kid on a mission.

One of the most appealing aspects of our neighborhood was the labyrinth of alleyways that crisscrossed the city streets in every direction for as far as the eye could see. Those alleyways ran behind, and in some cases alongside, the endless rows of box houses that lined every street in every neighborhood. They were a child's fantasy in every definition of that word. But these alleyways also served a practical purpose. One-car garages, usually constructed of wood or brick, housed the vehicles those factory workers drove to work in every day; these were accessible only through the alleyways. In Detroit, the Motor City, every house had a detached garage. The alleyways also allowed garbage trucks, utility workers, linemen, and telephone repairmen passage to the inner workings of every neighborhood. These alleyways were mysterious, enticing, and even a little bit frightening. There was an element of danger that was undeniable. Because of this—regardless of the season—I spent most of my time exploring, creating, and playing deep within them. I loved those old alleyways. Their possibilities were limitless.

One Saturday in my eleventh year of life, as summer dawned on the city of my birth, I was prepared to spend my day in the alley that ran behind our house. The night before, I had discovered an exotic collection of plant life that had sprung into existence behind the fence that enclosed our backyard. Walking through the gate that provided access, I looked to my left and noticed this new growth, immediately deciding that it was the perfect location for mounting an epic battle with my toy soldiers. The following morning, I put my plan into action.

When I woke on that Saturday, I felt like a kid on Christmas morning. A large portion of my childhood was dedicated to the re-creation of one historic battle after the other; this day would prove to be no different. In fact, this new collection of exotic plant life provided an entirely new palette for my adventures. I had never seen plants like this before. Their long, firm stalks towered above the little plot of soil like massive trees. Their flowers fanned out like fingers and created a canopy of texture and fragrance unlike any I had ever encountered. These plants were jungle-like, unusual and very exciting. I put my plan into action shortly after downing my morning bowl of Cheerios.

I then gathered my implements of destruction: several companies of German and American World War II toy soldiers, and a cache of recently discovered bottle rockets, firecrackers and M80s. With these in hand, I made my way to the alley. This day was going to be great, I just knew it. The sun was bright and warm as I walked the concrete path to the alley, just like a sun in the wilds of Guadalcanal, and my imagination was just moments away from being unleashed. I couldn't wait to begin the epic Battle of Green Mountain, and settled in as the sun continued its ascent above the city.

The one thing you need to understand about my approach to playing army was that I *lived* the experience. Not only did I completely submerge myself into the reality of warfare, I *became* the reality. From my earliest memories, the study of what mankind has done to itself was not merely all consuming, but a permanent state of mind. I didn't read books about baseball players, comic book heroes, or presidents. I read the biographies of George Custer, "Black Jack" Pershing, and George Patton. I wrote short stories about Civil War battles, World War I catastrophes, and blunders in the jungles of Vietnam. When it came to playing army, I did not fool around; I lived it.

Green Mountain, a vital defensive position on Mystery Island, was of great strategic importance to the two battling combatants. On this day, the German Brandenburg Regiment held the high ground and was being challenged by the American 101st Airborne Division who had parachuted in the night before. The stage was set for vicious, brutal warfare.

The commander of the German Brandenburg Regiment, Col. Wilhelm Kliendorf, was a seasoned veteran who had survived numerous campaigns in the past. He was cunning, elusive, and highly determined. Orders from the German High Command directed Col. Kliendorf to hold Green Mountain at all costs, and he had no intention of relinquishing the stronghold to the dreaded American Dogs of War, now surrounding him on three sides. Col. Kliendorf knew that if his supply route to the south was cut off, he was dead meat.

The commander of the American force, the cigar-chomping and chiseled Captain Thomas "The Rock" Murphy, was as determined to blow the Krauts off the mountain as they were to hold it. Capt. Murphy knew that at some point, the flyboys in the 5th Fighter Squadron of the Army Air Corp were going to offer support from above, but he didn't know when this was going to happen—and to wait would have been suicide. Capt. Murphy knew that he had to cut off that German supply route to the south or all would be lost. At 1030 hours, Capt. Murphy began his maneuvers to take Green Mountain. By the end of the day, Capt. Murphy thought, an American flag would be fluttering freely in the winds or his command would be lost and all his men dead. The stakes were high, and the morale low—but it was now time for Capt. Murphy to become a man.

Sending two squads of his men on a reconnaissance mission to the south of Green Mountain, Capt. Murphy began his conquest of the German stronghold. Shortly after deploying his men though, the two squads of American fighter men were met with stiff resistance.

The battle had begun.

Col. Kliendorf countered the Americans' move by sending three companies of crack troops to block the American advance. A wicked firefight ensued. Using mortars (firecrackers) and bazookas (M80s), the Germans pushed the Americans back, with both sides suffering heavy casualties. The battle was now in full bloom.

Capt. Murphy employed a diversionary tactic, sending several companies of his most seasoned troops on a search-and-destroy mission to the west, in hopes of pulling the German troops away from the southern outpost. The plan worked to a T. As wicked fighting erupted on the western slope of the mountain, Capt. Murphy sent the bulk of his remaining forces south, even as the main body of the German forces headed west to thwart the threat there. It was a textbook maneuver. As mortars flew, as bazookas spit fire and flame, as machine guns, rifles, and small arms fire erupted on both flanks, the phantom squad of American flyboys suddenly whisked into view.

In an instant, the American fighter squad unleashed a torrent of bombs (bottle rockets) into the thick canopy of jungle protecting Col. Kliendorf and his men. In a series of attacks from above — and as the American ground troops continued with mortars and bazookas from below — Green Mountain was set ablaze. Ka-pow! Ka-blam! Ka-bloosh!

The mountain and the German stronghold were being obliterated by the relentless American assault. German toy soldiers were being blown apart, the jungle-like plants were being decimated, and the soil that housed them was being annihilated, as one American assault after the other reduced Green Mountain to a heap of shattered lives and limp, broken jungle life. It was pure carnage. That's when Capt. Murphy prepared for his final assault...and the safety of my own life suddenly came into question.

As I lay another two or three rows of firecrackers and M80s on Green Mountain for the final, total destruction of the battlefield, I heard a sudden commotion. Peering over the fence and looking to the back door of the screen porch, I saw one of my brothers running down the concrete pathway and straight for me. He was not happy. Through ceaseless cursing and relentless name-calling, I soon gathered that my battlefield, Green Mountain, was of vital importance of another kind — the smoking kind.

"What the fuck are you doing to my pot plants, motherfucker?!?" My brother screamed as he was now only seconds away from assaulting *my* position.

Pot plants? I thought in a panic. *Holy shit, this ain't good.*

Even though I was only eleven years old, due to the fact that I had five older siblings, I knew what marijuana was and the importance some people put on it. What I didn't know was that you grew it.

Until now.

In an instant, I realized that my brother did not care in any way, shape or form that I had so convincingly recreated an epic World War

II battle in such striking fashion. It became immediately apparent that my brother could have cared less about the formidable German stronghold I had built, the impressive American counterstrike on the German defenses, or the effectiveness of the Air Corps' airborne assault on Colonel Kliendorf's men. My brother was not impressed by Captain Murphy's textbook maneuvers, the swiftness on his men's actions or the courage it took for both sides to endure the brutality of modern warfare. My brother cared for one thing and one thing only: the fact that I had destroyed, in a very convincing fashion, his prized pot plants.

As I stood before the remnants of Green Mountain, I slowly looked over what remained of the marijuana plants, then peered up at my brother—just as he lunged for me, face ablaze. Instinct then kicked in; I needed to make a move, and make a move quick. As one hand grabbed my shirt, I turned, ripped my shoulder free, and ran as fast as I could down the alley, screeching as I did. My brother, like a German Storm Trooper, was hot on my tail.

Fortunately for me, I was a pretty fast kid. Back in the spring, I had even won the class 100-yard dash, and knew that I now needed my talents more than ever. As my brother cursed—spitting venom and swearing vengeance—I, and my Chuck Taylors, were in the midst of setting the neighborhood record for the 400-yard dash. In fact, I didn't stop running until I was a couple of neighborhoods to the west, even though my brother had ceased his pursuit several blocks after he began. All I could see in my mind's eye was my brother's rage ravaging me. When I finally did stop running, it was out of pure exhaustion...not due to the fact that I was free of my brother's wrath. I'd run as fast as I could, for as far as I could—and now, to top things off, I was in a foreign land, an entirely different neighborhood with alien kids to contend with. It was a no-win situation.

Setting foot in unfamiliar neighborhoods was always a dicey proposition. You soon found that you had to deal with a whole new set of kids, kids who didn't care who you were, and who were most likely on the lookout for fresh meat to beat into the ground. Every neighborhood was loaded with kids who loved to brawl, and if you were in foreign territory, you had to deal with the rules of engagement set forth by the laws of the street. Kids knew instinctively who was a foreigner and who was a native; no matter what you did, if you didn't belong, you stuck out like a sore thumb. Your demeanor and appearance gave you away immediately.

As I took in my new surroundings, I knew that I was in over my head. And I also knew that my only option for survival was to stick to the alleyways and off the streets. I was suddenly a lone combatant, lost behind enemy lines.

I understood now: I had to resort to covert operations.

Making my way through the alleys, I hid behind garbage cans, scanned for enemy patrols, and moved on to the next garage. While making sure the coast was clear, I sprinted for freedom until spotting more enemy movements. Ducking behind a fence, I crawled along the alley floor until cleared, got to my feet, and ran for my life. Coming upon a parked car, I hesitated, studied the lay of the land, weighed my options, and took my chances. I repeated this maneuver over and over until finally, mercifully, I reached the cusp of our neighborhood. Even then, I feared for my well-being. My brother was out there, somewhere, searching for me and hell-bent on revenge.

The closer I got to our alley, the more fear enveloped my world. My senses became sharper, my hearing clearer, and my vision as fine-tuned as an eagle's. Inching my way closer to our alley, every sight, every sound, every gentle breeze caused me to quake in my shoes. *Where is he?* I asked as my breathing intensified. *Where is my brother, and when will he strike?* I couldn't take it any more, I couldn't handle the uncertainty. I knew that, despite my worst fears, I had to eventually meet my fate.

In due time, I did make it back to our alley, many hours later and in one piece. It was so late, in fact, that I could hear the distant peal of church bells marking the noon hour as the sound drifted through the byways and trailways of the alley system of our neighborhood. By now, I was tired, hungry, ready to accept my fate, and not at all concerned about the outcome of the Battle of Green Mountain. All I wanted now was to be home and in the comfort of my normal surroundings. Fortunately for me, when I did reach the gate leading to our backyard, I saw my mother hanging laundry amidst a scene that was serene and peaceful.

"Hey, Mom," I called while scanning for my brother, "is...um... Paul home?"

"No, honey," she replied in an easy tone, "he's at work."

I released a lifetime of tension as I quickly realized that my sworn enemy was blocks away and chained to the grill of The Clock Restaurant, where he worked as a line cook. To my relief, he wouldn't be home for hours.

Lost in elation, I looked to my right to where the Battle of Green Mountain had taken place. My toy soldiers were scattered to the wind. My firecrackers, M80s, and bottle rockets were ripped apart and lay in heaps of twisted paper, worthless gunpowder, and fizzled wicks.

And there on Green Mountain were what remained of my brother's pot plants.

He had, in his misery, attempted to piece his prized garden back together. It was a pitiful sight. I had done quite a number on his precious plants; only a few remained. The ones that still stood were tattered, ripped apart, and barely able to remain upright. I knew that when I saw him again, I would have to pay the price for being so ignorant.

The next day I did take a beating, but it was far less severe than what it could have been in the heat of the moment that previous day. And despite the pain, I knew that I had gotten off easy, and took that beating with the glorious memories of the great and colossal Battle of Green Mountain dancing freely in my head. I had pushed the limits of exploration, I had reached the threshold of glory, and I had brought myself to the edge of greatness, only to have my dreams shattered once the harsh reality of life came crashing home like a P-51 Mustang slamming into the devastated wastelands of Green Mountain.

    I had lived to see another day.

6. THE NIGHT MARK CAME A KNOCKIN'

MY BROTHER MARK HAS ALWAYS BEEN A MYSTERY TO ME. IT WAS PARTly due to the separation in years (Mark was nine years older than me), but it had more to do with his personality. Mark was a strange cat—dressing differently, talking differently, acting differently, and most assuredly thinking differently. Mark has always impressed me as a guy who embodied a lot of pain. In a lot of ways, it was like I didn't even know who he was.

My mother once told me that the family life my older siblings understood and lived through was far different from the family life my younger siblings and I experienced. This holds true for any large family, and ours was no exception. The family dynamic Mark had known was infinitely different than mine. He knew both of his parents, had the run of the house, had an entirely different set of rules and expectations, and watched as one kid after the other entered his world. He understood life on a totally different level and grew up in a time far removed from my own. But there always seemed to be something else about Mark that made no sense; there was always something about Mark that was not quite right.

Through conversations with many of my family members in later years, I grew to understand that Mark may have been dealing with a lot of emotional issues. According to these older family members, Mark had unrealistic expectations, issues with anger, was confused by life, and ultimately had trouble dealing with the family. He felt slighted, unfulfilled; he was suspicious, paranoid, aloof. For these and other reasons, he never submerged himself fully into the family unit. In light of this, I can't say that I blame the guy. By the time I became aware and was able to grasp the reality of family life, I was, to say the least, confused by what I saw. I could only imagine what Mark witnessed.

If my childhood was any indication, the things Mark experienced must have been mindboggling. He saw first-hand what he perceived to be the demise of the family and couldn't escape it. For several years, he and my sister Maria *were* the family, and to have their world invaded by an endless stream of screaming kids must have been unsettling. And to top it off, Mark had a front row seat to the debacle my parent's marriage had become. Again, I couldn't imagine the things he saw or the sounds he heard. In a very real way, I feel very fortunate that I came around when I did. I caught the tail end of my parents' marriage, and what I saw was confusing enough. Mark was in the belly of the beast and couldn't have escaped the worst of my parents' marriage, even if he had tried.

I've heard stories that as soon as the opportunity arose, Mark simply removed himself from the home, disappearing from sunup to sundown—and sometimes never coming home at all. He spent a lot of time with friends, a lot of time playing music, and a lot of time partying at an early age. Mark started high school in the early 1970s, at the height of the drug explosion. What he got into is anyone's guess, but being a kid who explored the drug culture during my own adolescence, I could only surmise what Mark and his friends got themselves involved in. I'm sure that Mark, just like me, felt fortunate to have lived through his youth.

By the time I became aware, Mark was in the final phase of high school; I have few memories of him ever being around. And Mark was not the kind of guy who appeared excited about having six younger siblings in his life. The kids that came directly after him, Stephen and Maria, I think he tolerated to some degree. The rest of us—Michael, Paul, Katherine and myself—he chose to ignore as best he could.

I remember once when I was about seven years old, as full of life as a young man could be, when I ran through the yard to get to the back entrance of the house. In my excitement, I swiftly opened the door and felt the handle hit someone on the opposite side. It was Mark...and he was not happy. Suddenly, Mark yanked the door open and began pummeling me with a barrage of punches. Astounded by their ferocity—and being a kid with half a brain—I simply turned and ran for my life.

This was about the extent of my interactions with my brother Mark during my youth.

Shortly after graduating from high school, Mark married his girlfriend Anne. They had met as students, dated for a few of years, and then—as so many kids did at the time—married immediately following graduation. The wedding was a happy affair, with several of us kids being a part of the wedding party. At the time, I had no reason to doubt that their union would be anything but happy and carefree. Mark and Anne appeared to love one another, enjoy one another, and care for each other. They seemed to laugh a lot and have fun; they played music together, and lived life as if they truly appreciated one another's company. Their union, in a comforting way, brought a certain level of stability to the entire family, something I welcomed with open arms.

Shortly after they married, Anne announced that she was pregnant, news that delighted the entire family. Along with a happy marriage now came the realization that a child was on the way—a child that, as far as I could tell, was conceived in love. This should have been a moment steeped in all things good and positive, but what I began to see was something different, something toxic. As seems to be the case in a lot of marriages when youth, uncertainty, instability, and jealousy mix with the coming of a child, the union of Mark and Anne began to strain under the pressure. Things began to sour.

During this time, I was dealing with issues of my own, and had already reached the point where I began my descent into isolation. By now, I had witnessed the end of my parents' marriage, a marriage that, in my eyes, never existed in the first place. My father offered little guidance and was, for all intents and purposes, out of my life. My mother was overwhelmed, and my relationship with my siblings was one long, continuous brawl. There was no way of escaping the chaos of the house, no way of escaping the harsh realities of the neighborhood, no way of escaping the insecurities ravaging my soul. And to add to my confusion, the experiences with Chris Mercer, a. k. a. Godzilla, were either still going on or had just recently ended. (You see, you've got to understand that by this time in my life I was so confused, I was lucky if I even knew what day it was. Keeping track of exact dates and events is impossible, but what I do know for certain is that during this time, all these things were coming together—with more still to come.) The combined psychic discord had reached a fevered pitch; in response, I instinctively set about removing myself from my reality. It seemed like every day offered a whole new set of troubling circumstances. And even worse, there appeared to be no light at the end of the tunnel.

To add to this mess, one of my sisters had recently run away from home, hitchhiking out to Colorado for several months, and had come home a changed girl. She had been abused in a horrific way by an ex-boyfriend, was dealing with a volatile home life, was confused herself, and needed to get away. Concurrently, my mother was dating a series of men who drifted in and out of our lives. In the thick of such turmoil, it's no surprise that my siblings and I hated each other, and there was nothing holding us together as a family. Mark and Anne may have been living in the house at this juncture, but I'm not certain. What I do know is that they were around most of the time, and when they were, their relationship grew progressively worse by the day.

This was the point in my life at which I had completely removed myself from the family dynamic. For hours on end I kept to myself: writing, drawing, and play-acting; spending long afternoons on my bike, searching the neighborhood for solace; escaping to the backyard and alleyways, playing army, throwing baseballs, climbing buildings, and creating my own world—anything to remove myself from the chaos. At this point, I wanted out...and did whatever I had to in order to maintain my sanity.

Thanks to a fertile imagination, solitude posed no problem when entertaining myself by playing traditional team sports—especially my favorite: baseball. When by myself, and playing America's Pastime, I had two ways in which I approached the game. One was by using the side of the garage where a strike zone was etched out in tape. Using a firm rubber ball, I would spend my afternoons pitching full-length games as I imagined I was playing for the mighty Detroit Tigers. I'd have the entire Tiger team behind me and in the field: Al Kaline, Jim Northrup, Norm Cash, Mickey Stanley, Willie Horton, Aurelio Rodriguez, and my favorite, catcher Bill Freehan—all of whom were there rooting me on. My old friends and I would play full games, and sometimes double-headers, against some of baseball's best: The Amazin' Oakland A's of Reggie Jackson, Catfish Hunter and Bert Campaneris; the tenacious Baltimore Orioles of Brooks Robinson, Boog Powell and Jim Palmer; and of course, my nemesis, the Big Red Machine of Cincinnati, featuring the great Johnny Bench, Pete Rose, and Joe Morgan. Those games were epic, and became a staple throughout my childhood.

The other way in which I approached solo baseball was by viewing it from the offensive side of the field, at the plate. From this perspective, I would stand at home plate with bat in hand, and hit the ball while running the bases. I'd even recreate strikeouts, getting thrown out at second base while trying to stretch a single into a double, or barely making it home following a bang-bang play at the plate. *"SAFE!"* the imaginary umpire would cry, and my teammates would carry me off the field as I howled in triumph.

Such was my child's mind as I tooled through life. But despite my best efforts, I could not entirely escape what was happening around me...and found myself having to deal with the family whether I liked it or not.

Many months into Anne's pregnancy, I once again found myself out in the backyard playing baseball with my imaginary friends. On this particular day, I was playing a game from the offensive side of the plate. The Tigers were facing the dreaded Boston Red Sox in a showdown for the American League Pennant. It was a hotly contested game, surging back and forth, with great hitting at clutch moments throughout. It was the top of the ninth inning with the game tied at 8-8. I was now Jim Rice, the power-slugging Red Sox DH who embodied menace, digging in at the plate (which was located just several paces from the screen porch and back entrance of the house). I was preparing to tear the hide off another fastball when I suddenly heard a commotion that halted the game.

I heard my brother Mark yelling, I heard his bride Anne crying, and I heard the jarring sounds of random objects being thrashed about. Suddenly, Anne—more than eight months pregnant with a large, protruding belly—burst out of the back door, zipped through the screen porch, and ran for freedom. Hot on her tail was Mark—fuming, reckless, and full of rage. Catching up to Anne, I watched in stunned silence as Mark began to beat her, reaching around and pounding her in her swollen belly while informing her that she was a worthless whore who deserved what she got. I couldn't believe my eyes.

As Mark continued to hit her, as Anne continued to cry, as the scene unfolded like some absurd dream — I, to put it sharply, had had enough. I immediately dropped the ball and bat, raced for my bike, jumped on, and pedaled with all my might. I couldn't stand it any longer, and rode my bike for hours on end, wanting to escape the stupidity that was now crashing down all around me. I didn't come back home until well after dark, and when I did, I simply slipped inside the house, made a beeline to my bedroom and hid in my bed, wondering what tomorrow would bring. I wouldn't have to wait long to find out.

Again, as I said, at this point in my life I had removed myself from the daily goings-on in the household. I was in my own world. But the next thing I do remember about the relationship between Mark and Anne was that the volatile union had now hit the boiling point. Coming home one evening following a full day in the neighborhood, I walked into a house teeming with uncertainty. Nighttime had already fallen. Anne was there, frightened and sobbing. My sister Maria and my mom were there, consoling her. There was an air of panic dominating the entire house. I remember my brother Stephen running from room to room, locking doors and closing windows, something never before seen in our household. Not only do I remember never locking the doors of our home, but I don't even remember seeing a key to any of the locks at any point in my life. (To this day, I don't think any of us ever carried a key, nor had any clue as to where one was.) We had never before locked any doors — and yet, here was my brother Stephen, bolting them shut while we were still *inside*.

So this, to my dismay, was the situation I walked in on, on that fateful evening, and this was the reality that greeted me as I attempted to grasp an incredibly confusing state of affairs. Fortunately for me, this was just another day in the Acquaviva household, and by now, I had learned to deal with these scenarios in a professional and silent manner. Everyone was frantic, everyone was scared, and everyone was preparing for the worst. Yet I — a ten-year-old boy — accepted this as innocently as I had every time in the past.

My mother, upon seeing me walk through the door, told me to stay close and help Maria when the time came. All I could do was make an effort to absorb what was happening and do what I was told. There was no escaping the intensity of the moment, and in reality, I didn't even try. Suddenly, the phone rang, causing everyone to be on high alert, and causing me to sink even further into confusion. As I stood silently nearby, Stephen answered, listened intently for a few seconds, and then hung up.

"The car will be here shortly," he said while looking out the kitchen window. "When it comes, take Anne to Mom's bedroom window and get her to the alley. He told me that he'll be waiting there in his car."

My head was now spinning. Who was "he"? Where was he taking Anne? And for what reason?

This is the point where things got out of hand.

"Oh God, Mark's here!!" I heard someone cry from the living room.

With Anne, Mom, Stephen, Maria and me in the kitchen near the back of the house, we instinctively sprung into action. I followed Stephen and my mother through the dining room and into the living room, where another brother (I'm not certain who) peered out the front window.

"He's running for the door!!" he cried. "He's running for the door!!"

That's when Stephen and Mom ran straight for the front door and placed their bodies firmly against it.

"Larry," Mom ordered as she braced herself for the inevitable, "help Maria get Anne to the alley!!"

Still not certain what to do, I stood at the entrance of the dining room while straddling the living room. Looking to the kitchen, I saw Maria with her arm around a sobbing Anne.

And that's when I heard Mark come a-knockin'.

Maybe "knockin'" is a bit of an understatement; he announced his presence with a full-fledged kick to the front door. I turned to face Stephen and Mom as they barricaded the door, while Mark continued to kick full-on, causing them both to reel from the intensity. I remember Stephen struggling with all his might; I remember my mother grimacing in pain. Mark's assault was relentless.

"Larry, get Anne out now!!!" Mom cried once more.

Without hesitation, I turned and ran for Anne, who was now being escorted through the hallway by Maria, towards the back bedroom where my mother slept. Slipping around them, I got to the window, punched out the screen, jumped down and waited for my sister-in-law. Maneuvering a large, pregnant woman through that small window was a challenge, but with Maria hoisting her down, I wrapped my arms firmly around Anne and managed to help her to the ground. As Anne and I ran for the alley, Maria was close behind, encouraging us to move faster. Approaching the alley, it felt as if my heart was about to explode. I still had no idea why this was happening.

There in the alley was a waiting car, with the engine running and the headlights turned off. Assisting Anne into the passenger's seat, Maria and I shut the door and the car peeled off, spitting rocks and dirt in the process. It zipped around the corner and into the adjacent alley as it disappeared into the dark of night. Suddenly—with the swiftness of a knockout blow in a back-alley brawl—this latest excursion into stupidity was over.

The reasons for this particular descent into violence I have never known, even to this day. I certainly didn't understand it then, and have no desire to figure it out now. It was, like so many other scenarios I experienced as I grew into adulthood, just another day in the neighborhood. Any attempt at figuring out what was at the source has never been pursued by me. I simply acted according to the circumstance, despite my confusion, and did what any other kid would have done in that situation. Whatever happened for the remainder of the night I truly don't remember, and most likely have blocked from my memory.

One thing I remember for certain—when we got back to the house, Mark was still on the front porch attempting to kick the front door in, and Stephen and Mom were still in the entranceway trying to keep him out.

What did I do for the rest of that evening? Maybe I jumped back on my bike, headed to a local park and spent the night under the stars. Maybe I crawled under the front porch and spent the night in one of my favorite hiding places, as the turmoil of the family unit teetering on its last legs erupted above me. Or maybe I retreated to the basement and hid in the pantry as the world exploded. "The Night Mark Came A-knockin'" was just one of many episodes from my childhood which I simply buried deep in my heart. What I do remember is more than I care to. The one thing I know for certain is that I never—not then, and not now—had any desire to speculate on what the scene was like once we got Anne to that waiting car. That night, I'd had my fill of violence, chaos, and blind rage from the moment I'd walked through the door, and I refused to acknowledge any more of it once it was over. Most likely, the only thing crowding my mind at that moment was my next baseball game, some young girl I couldn't shake from my memory, or a sweet song that never left my head.

Needless to say, the marriage between Mark and Anne did not last long, and may very well have ended shortly after this incident. I remember my niece Shelly being born and Anne staying with us for a while, a situation which put an eternal wedge between Mark and my mother.

Again, Mark felt slighted by my mother "siding" with Anne, and never quite recovered from this sharp indignity. Sometime later, Anne moved to New Mexico to be with her family; Mark began a relationship with Anne's best friend, a situation that opened up an entirely new set of issues. As was my standard practice at this time, I simply removed myself from the entire mess. From this point forward, I could not stand the thought of being with my family, and merely tolerated it (to the best of my ability) whenever I was forced to.

Whatever concept of family there might have been before this incident, it had now been shattered into oblivion. My mother, to her credit, fought with all her might to keep the family together and in one piece... but all to no avail. My focus now became my own sanity, and clinging to my dreams at all cost. As I forged on into the future, I would do so alone, and happily so. And so I retreated, despite my mother's desires to maintain a stable home life—something that was now completely unrealistic and painfully unobtainable—as we all moved further into the future, and the great unknown of life.

7. CAMP OZANAM

IT WAS, IRONICALLY, DURING THIS TIME OF COMPLETE AND TOTAL UPheaval of the family unit that my mother presented me with a gift unlike any other. Partly motivated by her desire to get me out of the city and into a healthy environment, and partly motivated by the need to preserve her own sanity, my mother bestowed upon me a gift that was to prove nothing short of magical: Camp Ozanam.

Ozanam was a camp for boys, located just south of Port Huron, along the shores of the Great Lake. Situated upon a sprawling tract of land in rural southeastern Michigan, the camp was no more than 50 miles from our house—but might as well have been on the other side of the moon, given its extreme contrast to our neighborhood. Camp Ozanam was owned and operated by the St. Vincent DePaul Society; it catered to poor and indigent Catholic boys in need of stability and guidance and was (to our great fortune) free of charge. Camp Ozanam was an experience that altered my life from the moment I arrived, bringing a sense of security I never knew existed. Some of the happiest moments of my childhood were spent there—small wonder that I looked forward to those trips to Lake Huron all year long.

The camp restricted their operations to summertime, and each trip lasted a mere two weeks, but that short period of time felt like an eternity. The amount of fun we packed into those two weeks was nothing short of astounding. To be allowed to not only escape life in the neighborhood, but the reality of my family as well, was nothing short of a dream; it liberated me to pursue my journey of becoming my own man. Upon arrival, I felt as if I had the freedom to live my life according to my own desires, far from the interfering eyes of my family. From the moment I submerged myself into the culture, my mind was lost in it.

I clearly remember the first time I went to camp, and the feelings of fear that dominated my heart so powerfully as that time approached. I was nine years old and as scared as I could possibly be. I felt my mother was a tyrant for making me go, and remember being consumed with anxiety as a host of other kids and I were loaded onto buses at the embarkation point. I was with other first timers, and not a word was spoken as we began our journey to Camp Ozanam.

The trip itself was terrifying, the landscape changing from the familiar sights of Detroit's gritty neighborhoods and teeming cityscape to the softer views of sprawling suburbs in the outer reaches of the city. Beyond the suburbs, the landscape changed even more; now we saw distant clusters of homes surrounded by fields and trees. Finally, as we approached the camp, I began to see farms: actual, working farms, complete with cows, horses, and barns, surrounded by freshly-cut fields that appeared to fade into the distant, rolling horizon.

I was struck silent with fear, as was every other kid on that bus with me. *Wow*, I thought in wonder, *it's like we're in the wilderness out here, man. What have I gotten myself into?*

Pulling into camp was even more unsettling. Buses from other parts of Detroit and the surrounding areas were unloading hordes of alien kids; as they disembarked, they were separated into different groups by camp counselors. These counselors looked like drill sergeants to me:

everything was uniform, organized, exact, and precise. I began to secretly fear that I had been surreptitiously drafted.

Stepping off the bus and straight into a line, the new recruits were then given a welcoming speech by the head counselor. This speech was highlighted with warnings that ill-behavior would send you home immediately, news that perked my ears and instigated thoughts of open rebellion: after all, home was where I wanted to be, so why not misbehave?

Once matriculated, we were assigned to a cabin. My cabin, one of two designated for "Giants" (the youngest campers) was near the entrance of the camp; it was named the "Yankees." The other was called the "Rebels," with both names being an homage to the American Civil War, an aspect that immediately put me at ease. Once situated, we were allowed to roam the grounds for an hour or so to soak in our new environment. I was still terrified as I walked those grounds like the lost little boy I felt I was. I wanted so badly to be home.

Soon, I found myself on the opposite side of the camp, and near the "Junior" and "Senior" cabins of the older boys, when something happened to me that altered the experience immediately. On this same trip were three of my brothers—Michael, Stephen, and Paul, who were enjoying camp life as well. Stephen and Paul were staff members and Michael was a Junior. As I stumbled around the sea of kids, I ran into Michael, who was on his second trip to Camp Ozanam in as many years. Michael, having possibly seen the fear in my eyes, and having most likely experienced those same emotions the year before, walked up to me and pulled me to the side. Michael then said something that shattered all my worries in the blink of an eye.

"Hey, man, you'll feel uneasy for the first day or two...but before long you'll never want to leave."

Michael's words were not only kind and prophetic, but without a doubt, the definition of accurate. From that point forward, due to my brother's insightful words, I immersed myself into Camp Ozanam with every fiber of my being. And as Michael had promised, I would never want to leave. My time at Camp Ozanam, and my life, would never be the same from that point forward.

One of the greatest aspects of Camp Ozanam was its size. It spanned eighty acres or more, and was populated with forests, ravines, open fields, an ample beachfront, and numerous trails. There were two Giant cabins, six Junior cabins, and two Senior cabins, housing in the vicinity of 400 to 500 kids. There was an arts and crafts building, a PX, an assembly hall, a large dining hall and kitchen, a chapel, counselor cabins, guest cabins, an administration building, and a medical center. They were all constructed in a uniform fashion—wood buildings painted green with pure white trim—and spread generously throughout the grounds. There were baseball fields, basketball courts, latrines, an archery range, and a large field surrounded by woods where a massive teepee stood, known as Indian Village. A ghostly bridge crossing a mysterious ravine connected both sides of the camp. There was so much room, so many wide-open spaces, that you felt you could get lost at any moment.

Due to this liberating feeling, and even though I would spend most of my time there with my brothers, I rarely saw them—and didn't really care to. And I'm certain that my brothers shared this sentiment. Camp Ozanam allowed for all of us to spread our wings and enjoy life without the friction, anger, and frustrations of being near each other. Hell, most of the time I didn't even realize they *were* there, and rambled through my days as if I were alone. My time at Camp Ozanam initiated a period of adventure that I have pursued to this day. Being alone, I was free to become who I wanted to be, spared from the disapproving glares of my family. Consequently, my time at the camp gave me the tools I needed to become my own man. This annual excursion, though brief, would become the complete release of tension I needed so badly.

It's amazing what a sliver of hope can do to a single life.

And so, every summer from the ages of nine to fourteen, I spent two weeks at Camp Ozanam. It was at Camp Ozanam that I first experienced positive male influences; it went a long way towards proving to me that the world could be a hopeful place. Every year I had counselors who took me under their wings, talked to me, encouraged me, and more importantly, listened to me. They listened to my fears, my dreams, and my aspirations. These men were inspirational and went out of their way to make me feel safe. Several of these men maintained relationships with the family and became a part of our lives throughout the remainder of the year. I have numerous memories of counselors taking me to the side and spending time with me in a wonderful and gentle manner, while subtly preparing me for life. And none of them, and I mean *none* of them, ever did anything inappropriate, or aggressive, or confusing—another aspect of camp life that put me at ease.

Most counselors were in their twenties and thirties and had attended the camp themselves in their youths. I met several older cats who were among some of the first campers to ever attend, as the institution first opened its doors in the 1920s. Most counselors were educated, wise and street-smart, coming from situations not unlike my own. Some were ex- or current military men. All were kind, fair, and forgiving. And none were pretentious or arrogant. These men were the definition of "cool" and had good intentions that were pure and righteous.

Most campers were an exact mirror image of me: young, confused, and coming from broken homes. Most had no fathers, were abused in some way, and were outcasts—just like me. There was a feeling that we were all in this mess together, and together we'd find a way out. These kids came from similar environments, from every ethnic background, and all pined for positive male influence. At Camp Ozanam, we all received everything we needed. There was no violence (kids showing a violent side were sent home immediately), no abuse, no molestation, and no verbal insults. I not only felt safe at Camp Ozanam, but felt as if the place was encased in a protective cocoon where nothing negative could touch or harm me.

Fellow campers, I would come to see, embraced the experience of camp life as lustfully as did I; they submerged themselves into every aspect of the camp dynamic with as much gusto and enthusiasm as I would. Kids came alive at Camp Ozanam, breaking free from the restraints of broken homes and unstable lives. We searched together, explored together, and flourished together, drinking in every nuance of camp life to the furthest reaches of possibility. And to our delight, camp life was like a dream come true, appealing to those aspects of boyhood that are impossible to ignore.

There were physical challenges, mental challenges, artistic challenges, and spiritual demands of a most appealing nature. There were experiences that were inspiring, powerful, enlightening, and liberating; every day provided a new palette upon which to explore our own capabilities. There was a sense of freedom that ran rampant and unchecked, but all skillfully encouraged within the comforting confines of structure and order. Each morning we woke to the sound of a bugle, announcing Reveille. We would then have to make our beds and form into lines in front of the cabin for "inspection." This was followed by the daily routines we all grew to love and anticipate.

There were scavenger hunts for breakfast, where the counselors hid single-serving boxes of cereal and buckets of iced-down milk in the woods for us to find. There were games of Capture the Flag in these same woods that allowed me to explore my fascination with all things historic; in an instant, I'd be transported back to 1916 France and the

Great Battle of Verdun, crawling along the forest floor as I searched desperately for my sworn enemy, probing the landscape for that damned, elusive foreign flag. Capture the Flag was an incredible adventure.

There were excursions into the mystic ravines where we searched even further for more hidden treasures, and trips to the beach to locate ancient fossils and exotic wildlife. There was a "ropes course" with ladders, zip lines, and catwalks constructed of wood, rope, and wire. The ropes course was a true test of your manhood and challenged us in ways never before realized. There were archery lessons, swimming competitions, and baseball games. At the Arts and Crafts Building, we learned to work with lace, paints, plaster, and needle and thread. There was a PX where candy, sodas, and treats were available; all paid for with the "allowance" our mothers gave us. (My own allowance came accompanied by letters from my mother, telling me how much she loved and missed me. I absolutely cherished receiving those letters.)

The camp had cool and interesting traditions passed down from year to year that made every day appealing and unique. One of these traditions was "Backwards Day," a custom based in the absurd. Backwards Day began with yet another bugle call—but one normally reserved for bedtime, that of Taps. Upon waking, we'd walk to the dining hall in a backwards, single-file line where dinner awaited us for our morning meal, usually consisting of hot dogs and chips. All the normal routines performed on any given day were reversed, including wearing your underwear on the outside, shirts turned inside out, nighttime activities in the day, and pancakes and sausages for dinner at night. Backwards Day was a gas.

"Suckers Creek" was another adventure ripe for a camp full of growing, adventurous boys. Suckers Creek was a muddy, rustic creek located a few miles north of Camp Ozanam. Traveling through the ravines, back roads, forests, and streams to get there was, in itself, an exciting time, but once there, all hell broke loose. This area of the creek, like I said, was thick, muddy, and wild. The challenge was to submerge yourself as deep into the muck as you possibly could, followed by a trip down a natural water slide formed into the side of a cliff. This was done in hopes of emerging covered from head to toe in not only the mud but with leeches as well, which clung to every part of your body—hence the name "Suckers Creek." Though I personally loved this part of camp life, some kids understandably couldn't handle it. These kids hid in the shadows as best they could, but even they were eventually forced to accept their fate as imposed by the rest of us, who forcibly submerged them deep into the mud. Later, in order to free yourself from the leeches sticking to your body—and sometimes finding their way into every crease and crevice of your head, torso, arms, legs and feet—salt was applied and the leeches simply fell off.

In this current world of pacifiers of every kind, and political correctness of a most shameless kind, I doubt that such an activity would thrive today. A true shame if you ask me, for the fun had at Suckers Creek was hard to top.

At Camp Ozanam there was even an evening dedicated to courting the ladies, if you can grasp that concept.

Oh, yes...I said courting the ladies.

You see, a few miles south of Camp Ozanam was Camp Stapleton, a girl's camp also operated by The St. Vincent DePaul Society and catering to the female of the species. (My youngest sister, Katherine, attended camp there for several years.) That night spent at Camp Stapleton was hysterical, and—for obvious reasons—a night each and every one of us anticipated with extreme giddiness.

Every kid at Camp Ozanam was familiar with the stories pertaining to Camp Stapleton, said to be teeming with wild, boy-hungry vixens who would eat you alive while having their way with you if given the chance. And every camper had also heard the stories of counselors and staff members who had a bevy of girlfriends at Camp Stapleton whom they courted nightly, actually kissing and fooling around with them, girls who would do anything at a moment's notice (or so the rumors went).

The evening at Camp Stapleton usually fell on a Saturday night midway through the trip. Every boy dressed in his best clothes, which inevitably consisted of dirt-soiled pants, stinky, muddy shoes and a t-shirt with the fewest holes. Driving down the highway in our bus with the stars hanging high above and lighting the way, we would sing songs and fantasize about meeting the girl of our dreams once we arrived. What we didn't fully comprehend was that this was a *Catholic* girl's camp, and would be chaperoned by pretty female counselors who would not allow for romantic contact of any kind. In fact, upon our arrival, the girls of Camp Stapleton might as well have been wearing body armor for as "lucky" as any of us got.

The music at the dance usually consisted of incredibly bad mid-1970s pop songs. Counselors were everywhere and strict rules enforced at every turn. Hell, even at Assumption Grotto dances you could at least get away with "feeling up" a girl, squeezing some ass, and maybe exploring some early attempts at French kissing. Not at Camp Stapleton though. No matter how hard we tried, we were blocked at every turn, and not by the girls themselves (who wished for as much experimentation as we did), but by those damned, meddling female camp counselors. They were like "Dance Nazis," putting the kibosh on every advance we made.

To this day, I believe that the Camp Stapleton Summer Dance was a means of torture performed by both the male and female counselors from each camp, and their demented way of entertaining themselves. Many a hard-on melted away on that long, tortuous drive back to Camp Ozanam, and many a bed rocked about wildly in the dark confines of the cabins as young boys released the tension of unfulfilled dreams. Hey, what did you expect? We were healthy, young boys denied a romp through romance in a harsh and deranged manner.

One of my favorite traditions at Camp Ozanam was an excursion into history, and an experience that allowed my historian's mind to explore Michigan's colorful past. This tradition was called Indian Lore Night. Having been a student of Michigan's history from the time I can remember, I was very familiar with my home state's vibrant past. I was well aware of the many Indian tribes living in the region for centuries, and was well versed in the history of the Indians and the French colonist's ability to live with one another. I understood the place in Michigan's history numerous Indian tribes have held. Hell, look at a map of Michigan and you can clearly see the influence these tribes have had on our culture.

Names such as Huron, Chippewa, Washtenaw, Tecumseh, Newaygo, Macatawa, Pontiac, Shiawassee, Osceola (just to name a few) cover the map of Michigan from north to south, east to west, and across the waterways surrounding and dissecting the state in every direction. A true Michigander is proud of this Native American influence and shares a sense of sadness and loss for their tragic demise. Even before my Camp Ozanam experiences, I was familiar with many Indian tales, from the numerous Native American Confederations and their relationship with the French and English, to the many wars fought among the tribes. Studying the French and Indian Wars was a constant pursuit in my younger years. It fueled my imagination for hours on end as I rambled through the snow-covered alleys of our neighborhood, pretending to hunt down the bloody English Limeys with guidance from my imaginary Indian Scouts.

Indian Lore Night at Camp Ozanam was dynamic, explosive, and passionate, allowing for a young man's imagination to be unleashed to the wilds of exploration. While gathering before the imposing teepee of Indian Village, circled around a massive bonfire exploding with fire and flame, the counselors dressed in traditional Indian garb and had us all mesmerized from the opening salvo. These counselors would unleash one Indian tale after the other, sharing stories of bravery, courage, adventure, and romance in ways that made us light-headed with promise. There were tales of Indian boys who fought for their tribes—sometimes saving beautiful young women from certain death; sometimes dying proudly in combat against the white man. There were stories of hunting down ferocious game, battling spirits from the netherworld, and communing with the great gods of earth, fire, water, and sky.

As the bonfire roared, as the teepee danced in the shadows of soft, flickering light, as the distant trees surrounding Indian Village came alive with ghosts from the past, our hearts and minds were whisked away to another time and place. Counselors danced with fire, performed ancient rituals, reenacted glorious battles, and summoned the ancient Indian spirits to lift our souls to the heavens. On occasion, counselors and older campers dressed as braves would emerge from the woods to sneak up on us with all the stealth of true Indian warriors, and then scare the ever-living shit out of us. If you couldn't lose yourself and become engrossed in Indian Lore Night, you might as well make your way down to Lake Huron and give up your soul to the Great Water Spirit while calling it a life.

You could not deny the power, you could not escape the passion, you could not release yourself from the spirits of the past crowding your soul. We were alive, we were *alive*, and the ancient Indian spirits were guiding our restless souls while pointing the way to becoming men. This night, Indian Lore Night, was awe-inspiring in ways that were natural and true.

As I became a seasoned veteran of the camp, I was invited to participate in Indian Lore Night myself. I would dress as a young Indian brave and reenact epic battles, perform ancient dances, and even become one of those silent warriors who emerged from the shadows and unleashed their power upon unsuspecting campers. Indian Lore Night was beyond magical; it entered the realm of surreal, as you could feel the ancient spirits dancing all around you. The feeling was real, palpable, all-encompassing—and absolutely inescapable, as those ghosts of Michigan's past came to life right before our eyes. Indian Lore Night was a journey into hallucinatory exploration years before I understood what that concept was, and it prepared me for my own spiritual odysseys as I grew older. Indian Lore Night was like a dream, and an experience that is still firmly entrenched in my heart.

THE LEGEND OF THUMPDRAG

Now, without a doubt, the most memorable, frightening and long-lasting tradition of Camp Ozanam was "The Legend of Thumpdrag." Just like any other camp story in the nation, "Thumpdrag" was the quintessential tale of horror unleashed upon young, impressionable minds, solely intended to scare the crap out of us. And I'm here to tell you: it worked like a charm. The first time I heard the story I nearly soiled my shorts, and had a hard time convincing myself that it was fictitious every time after.

At the time of my first trip to Camp Ozanam there was another legend, a story I believe entitled "Carl the Cook," that had been banned because of the fear it instilled in the campers' minds. My brothers caught the tail end of the "Carl the Cook" storytelling era, and from what they passed down to me, it was truly horrifying. It had something to do with a crazed, psychotic cook who snuck into the cabins at night, stole campers from their slumbers, and integrated their flesh into the daily meals he served to the kids. Just the premise of the story caused me to rattle in my Chuck Taylors, and I'm glad that I never heard the entire tale. But I'm here to say, "Thumpdrag" was bad enough, especially when hearing it for the first time.

My first year at Camp Ozanam, when I was nine years old, I exploded with every emotion held within my excited body, and I explored every one of those emotions to the furthest degree of possibility. But I could have never prepared myself for The Legend of Thumpdrag and the fear that it would grind into my soul. Even though my brothers tried to prepare me for the legend, there was no way their words of warning could have protected me from what I was about to hear.

The counselors gathered all the campers into Kennedy Hall, which abutted the "Capture the Flag" forest, and sat us down. The hall was alive with energy as the older campers taunted us, promising endless nightmares and perpetually wet beds. We attempted to show no fear and shook off the verbal attacks while hiding behind defiant faces as the hall lights quickly fell silent.

Suddenly, upon the darkened stage, there appeared several soft lights. The head counselor, Mr. Andy Saunders, then emerged from the shadows. Upon seeing Mr. Saunders, the hall became uncomfortably still. I held my breath as he walked confidently to the edge of the stage and looked down on us.

Mr. Saunders—a large, robust man with a big, protruding belly, rounded face and thick, red beard—was an imposing figure. When I heard his voice, I was frozen in my seat.

"Friends, campers, and skeptics!" Mr. Saunders bellowed. "We are gathered here tonight to share with you a tale...this tale is a story based in absolute truth, and is offered to you as a message of warning from beyond. For as you travel the trails, ravines, and forests of our beautiful campgrounds, be aware that we are not alone! Understand that we are merely strangers in a foreign land, and that the true master of these environs lurks in the shadows...hides in the dark recesses of madness...and wanders the bleak caverns of fear and uncertainty every single night! This tale is true; this tale is real; and this tale is not for the faint of heart. If you have the courage, you will take this journey with me and follow it until the end of reason! Come my friends...come with me to The Legend of Thumpdrag!"

I was mesmerized to the point of hypnosis. Time ceased to exist, fellow campers faded into the woodwork—and I alone sat before Mr. Saunders as he paced back and forth upon the stage, harnessing the ancient spirits of Pontiac, Tecumseh, and Michipichy. There was no turning back now.

Mr. Saunders began The Legend of Thumpdrag slow and steady, as any great storyteller would do—and Mr. Saunders was a master storyteller. He began the tale back in the innocent days of the mid-1950s, when a counselor named Reginald Barnes worked the same grounds we now found ourselves enjoying. Reginald—or Reggie, as his friends called him—was a typical counselor of his day. He was young, fresh, intelligent, and carefree, spending his summers working with the kids of Camp Ozanam as he made his way through college at Western Michigan University.

Reggie was bright and caring, perfectly suited for his job as a counselor. And like so many other young men, he was a die-hard romantic. Reggie had a longtime girlfriend—his high school sweetheart, Penelope Caldwell, a pretty girl who swore to love him until her dying breath. Penelope was equally bright, vivacious, and proud, and worked as a counselor at Camp Stapleton so the two could be close to one another during their summer vacations. Their relationship was strong and pure, and was on a natural path towards marriage and family. But during the summer of their junior year, their relationship took a sudden and unexpected turn down a dark and deadly path. There were rumors that Penelope was falling out of love with Reggie, and that she even began secretly dating another young man who was a member of the staff at Camp Stapleton. Despite Penelope's passionate pleas of loyalty and faithfulness, jealousy began to ravage Reggie's soul.

Stealing away to Camp Stapleton one night, Reggie stumbled upon an unsavory scene. As he peered through a window of the counselor's cabin, Reggie saw Penelope and the young man poring over activity schedules for the following day. In the muted light, Reggie saw Penelope laughing at the young man's jokes, smiling brightly, addressing him sweetly; and once—*once*—Reggie saw Penelope place her right hand playfully on the young man's shoulder in a manner that instantly sent Reggie over the edge. This was all he could take. Reggie was now out for revenge. There was no way he was going to be played for a fool. The following day he put his plan for Penelope's downfall into action.

Under the guise of burying the hatchet and convincing Penelope that all was well, Reggie invited Penelope and the young man to a late-night, picnic-style dinner inside Kennedy Hall...the very place we now sat listening to the tale. But Reggie had other plans. Reggie—perhaps, some say, possessed by a demented Indian spirit—was out for blood.

When Penelope and her young friend arrived at Kennedy Hall, they stepped inside to see a single white candle, flickering upon a lone wooden crate in the dark shadows of the room. Confused by this, they stepped deeper inside; immediately, they heard the door close behind them, followed by the sound of it being locked from the outside.

It was then that they heard Reggie—laughing, like a madman. Struck blind with panic, Penelope's young friend raced from door to door and window to window, trying to find an escape route. Every one of them had been locked tight.

Outside, Reggie put the final act of his plan into effect and began soaking the wooden building in gasoline as Penelope and her young friend cried out in desperation. Striking a match, Reggie let the flame fly...and Kennedy Hall erupted. For several minutes Reggie watched in delight as Penelope and her friend burned alive. Reggie had now crossed over into madness. Wanting to ensure Penelope's ultimate demise, Reggie picked up one last can of gasoline and began to disperse it. In his haste, Reggie's feet became entangled in a cluster of vines, causing him to fall—spilling the gasoline can and soaking him in the combustible liquid. In a flash, Reggie was now burning alive.

Reggie thrashed about manically, Reggie spun like a top, Reggie threw himself to the ground in a desperate attempt to extinguish the flames. Kennedy Hall burned; Penelope and her friend clawed at the doors, and the night sky erupted with the intensity of an inferno. Miraculously, Reggie doused the flames searing his skin but suffered horrific burns over most of his body, and lay beside Kennedy Hall as it began to fall to pieces. A large beam broke free from the roof and fell directly on Reggie's right leg, crushing it in the process. Crossing over into the realm of insanity, Reggie was suddenly infused with the power of ten men.

As counselors, campers and staff converged on the burning building, they saw the smoldering image of a man staggering about wildly in the light of the raging fire. Drawing closer, someone called to the man. Reggie turned, lifted a burning beam high above his head, and slung it at the approaching group like a twig in the wind, forcing the crew to scatter in every direction. When they looked up again, Reggie—now a raving lunatic—howled like a beast and disappeared into the forest... dragging his shattered leg behind him.

"Thump...Drag!! Thump...Drag!!" Mr. Saunders bellowed from the depths of his lungs.

I must have jumped five feet out of my chair.

"Reggie was no longer a man!" Mr. Saunders cried. "Reggie was now a monster! And this monster...he still lives to this day! As you walk these grounds, children, especially at night, search your surroundings deep and wide for a pair of dark, seething eyes that may be following your every move. And beware! Beware! For at night, while you sleep, Thumpdrag roams, Thumpdrag breathes, and Thumpdrag lives! You cannot escape this truth, for these grounds...this sacred place we call Camp Ozanam...they now belong to Thumpdrag! And no one can escape his wrath!"

Mr. Saunders then related that, following the fire and the death of Penelope and her young friend, there was a posse sent out into the ravines to search for Reggie and end his troubled life. Finding him after an exhaustive search, the posse shot the monster several times as he tried to escape. Wounded but alive, Reggie stumbled through a drainage tunnel that stretched beneath the main road running alongside the camp. That tunnel — still in service, and forever known as Thumpdrag's Cave — remains smeared with the blood of Thumpdrag and serves as proof positive of his existence.

"Following the long, cold winters," Mr. Saunders went on, "staff members arrive to find kitchen doors ripped from their hinges, cans of food torn apart, and rotting carcasses of deer, rabbits, and bears strewn about! He is out there, my friends, and he roams free! From the shadows he comes, announcing his presence with his familiar, deadly calling card...Thump...Drag!!! Thump...Drag!!! And into the future he roams!!!"

I thought I was going to have a freaking heart attack. Even though the tale had suddenly, and mercifully, come to an end, it did nothing to stop the fear from seizing my heart. Upon making our way back to our cabin (and now perceiving mysterious, disturbing sights and sounds in the distance), we were now forced to go to sleep. And as was the routine every night, we slept with the doors and windows wide open, with only flimsy screens to prevent any unwelcomed entry. And of course, as if all of this was planned years before, my bunk was located right next to the front entrance of the cabin. I lay awake as long as I could that night, thinking of Thumpdrag and scurrying into a sitting position in reaction to any sound that broke the silence of night. I was convinced that Thumpdrag was out there, and dead-set on ending my life.

To make things worse, the following day, we were informed that we were to take a field trip to Thumpdrag's Cave. On the way, and as we walked through the ravine running beneath the bridge connecting both sides of the camp, someone called to us from above. It was my brother Paul; he had a quick question for one of our counselors. The counselor answered and Paul went on his way. We thought nothing of it.

Upon entering the cave, there on the walls—just as Mr. Saunders had promised—was Thumpdrag's blood, clear as day and glistening in the bright light of the afternoon sun. As counselors continued to share the tale of Thumpdrag, a man covered in a sheet appeared from out of nowhere and ran through the tunnel while howling like a monster, causing all of us to scream like little girls and run for cover. As the man ran through, however, I happened to look up to see a familiar image: my brother Paul, peeking through the bottom of the sheet. It was a sight that put my heart at ease with the sudden realization that all of this—the legend, the panic, the fright—was nothing more than a ruse designed to make us crazy with fear. At that point, I began laughing hysterically, nearly falling over while screeching like the nine-year-old boy I was. It was an absolutely hilarious scene. And so ended The Legend of Thumpdrag.

The two-week stay at Camp Ozanam always ended with a bang. Fourteen days of mayhem, adventure, and pushing the limits of freedom culminated with the annual Camp Ozanam Summer Olympics. What pure and unfettered joy. For two days, we tested our skills, sharpened our talents, and fought to prove that we were the best. The Camp Ozanam Summer Olympics, in all their glory, were a blast.

These events were plentiful and varied: long and short distance swimming races; archery contests; horseshoe competitions; volleyball matches; arts and crafts face-offs; a baseball tournament; a ropes course throw-down; a basketball tourney; and my favorite, the Camp Ozanam Marathon—just to name a few.

When I was ten years old, I suddenly realized that I could run like the wind. Because of this, the neighborhood instantly became a cross-country course, complete with puddles to jump, garbage cans to hurdle, fences to leap, walls to scale, hedges to hop, and freshly mowed lawns to tumble upon. I would run through the labyrinth of alleys and down the streets, across the wide, bustling avenues, and cut through yards with the greatest of ease. I would run as fast as I could for as far as I could, pushing myself to the edge of endurance time and again. By the time I got to Camp Ozanam, I had perfected my craft, and during my first Senior-year stay at Camp Ozanam, I was allowed to show off my talents. And show off I did.

The Marathon, which was no more than three to four miles in length, covered just about every inch of the camp grounds and became a test of will of the highest degree. The previous two years, the kid who bested me was my own brother, Michael.

This year, I was determined to be the champ.

We started in a field overlooking the shores of Lake Huron, where the course twisted and broke, meandering through ravines, dense forests, and vast fields, through Indian Village, and past Kennedy Hall. It skirted along the ropes course, shot across the bridge, encircled the cabins, and pressed the edges of civilization. My time training in the neighborhood had paid off, and I soon found that I held the lead—with my brother Michael hot on my tail.

Rather uncomfortable with the thought of losing—especially to his younger brother—Michael pressed, and began to gain on me. The final test came during the long stretch that ran along the beach. Earlier in the trip, in preparation for the Marathon, I would steal away to the beachfront and practice running through the dense sand. Again, my preparation had paid off; as we hit that final stretch, I dug my feet in and churned up that sand like I was a pro, pulling away from Michael as he struggled to keep pace. And when I crossed the finish line, I was infused with pride and soaked up my victory.

That's when Michael walked up to me, shook my hand, and offered congratulations.

I was floored.

Again, his kind words meant the world to me, and were the perfect ending to the wonderful experience that was Camp Ozanam.

Now, as I said, we maintained several relationships with camp counselors throughout the year, and formed friendships with a number of these men that lasted for years. The strongest relationships we had were with two counselors named Tim Dolan and Rick Manning. Tim and Rick were great guys. They were fun, honest, straightforward, and sincerely cared for our well-being. Not only did they look out for us during the camping season, but they also made themselves a part of our lives year round.

For three years in a row, before moving on to greener pastures, Tim and Rick presented my brothers and me with yet another gift: the gift of experiencing Camp Ozanam in the wintertime. If I thought Camp Ozanam was a riot in the summer, I had no idea what awaited me in the winter. Camp Ozanam in wintertime was a frozen paradise.

In the middle of February—in the heart of long, cold, and painful winters—Tim and Rick would arrive at our house, load Paul, Michael, and me into their cars, and head to Camp Ozanam. Along the way, we'd pick up three or four other kids selected for the trip, and arrive at Camp Ozanam for a long weekend of wintertime fun.

Upon arrival, we'd load our gear into one of the guest cabins reserved for adults and honorary V. I. P.'s. These cabins were glorious. We'd each get a room to ourselves in a rustic, wood-paneled chamber tricked out with comfortable beds and cozy surroundings. The guest cabins also had kitchens, warm showers, and roaring fireplaces. Spending time in a guest cabin was an entirely new perspective of Camp Ozanam. You felt like a rock star at a slumber party, being allowed to experience camp life from an adult perspective. It was wonderful.

Once settled in, we would run absolutely wild, for Tim and Rick were like kids themselves and let their hair down just as we did, free from the restraints of daily counselor responsibilities. Although they maintained a certain level of discipline and order, they cut loose right along with us, enjoying the experience as much as we did.

The campgrounds were perpetually covered in a thick blanket of snow, desolate and free of the hundreds of kids, counselors, and staff present during the summertime. We were the only souls there and had free reign of the joint. We had massive snowball fights, excursions through the ravines and forests, and journeyed to the polar wastelands of the lake, where we fished through the ice for our dinner. We'd take a car to one of the large, open fields, attach a toboggan to the back with a long, firm rope, and buzz around the grounds like madmen.

Those toboggan rides were hysterical and took up a generous portion of our time. One or two kids would jump on the toboggan and Tim and Rick would pull us along at 30-40 miles per hour. It would feel like you were moving at 100 miles per hour behind that car, hanging on for dear life as the landscape whizzed by in a blur. The key, of course, was not to wipe out. Inevitably we would, teetering on the side of the sled as the car took a sharp turn or careened around an arching slope. I do believe that the ultimate goal of Tim and Rick was to *make* us crash—and inevitably we would, losing our grip, falling off, and spilling out onto the ground, bouncing, rolling, and tumbling before finally coming to a rest. In a heartbeat, we would shake off the pain and be ready for more, begging for another ride atop the frozen earth of Camp Ozanam. Toboggan time was a stitch.

One of my favorite experiences of Camp Ozanam in the wintertime was traipsing through the grounds by myself, which I did often. The fear and sense of adventure I felt while traveling alone was astounding. Of course, there were isolated times during the summer when I felt the desolation of Camp Ozanam, like when walking to the latrines at night or when the entire camp was in Kennedy Hall and I was late for arrival. But those experiences were few and far between. During wintertime however, I could not escape it, and in all reality, never wanted to.

I would spend hours at a time walking through the ravines, through the forests, along the icy shores and in the open fields. I would make my way to the sacred grounds of Indian Village, and Thumpdrag's Cave, sometimes in snow more than thigh-high deep. These experiences were otherworldly and allowed for my imagination to run wild while testing my endurance. The fear was undeniable; and the fear, without a doubt, was the exact reason why I put myself through these experiences.

As I walked the grounds, I could hear a pin drop; the snow-covered trees stood like silent warriors in a breathless wind. The only disturbances on the ground were the prints left behind by deer, rabbits, and squirrels. Were these the same animals that kept Thumpdrag alive during those cold winter months, I wondered? Was Thumpdrag watching my every move now?

Making my way through the ravines and across the frozen streams, I could feel the ancient Indian Warriors walking silently beside me, as I imagined a secret British patrol of The King's Army out in the distance. Suddenly, it would be February 1761, and I was a French Scout, leading my party on a raid of Fort Defiance. My Indian scouts would give a hand signal to halt all movement, scan the top reaches of the ravines for enemy soldiers, and quietly move on. I could feel the past come to life; I could sense the deep history of the region swirling all around me, and could breathe the same air as Count Frontenac and the tribes of the Huron and the Iroquois. My senses would sharpen to precision, and my movements would become natural and strong.

"Nakawa," I would whisper to my faithful Indian scout, "what do you see?"

Nakawa, crouching low, would perk his ears with the intensity of a hawk. He would slowly scan the ravine as his eyes grew as big as saucers, and then, in a flash, he would cry; "Holy shit, man, it's Thumpdrag! Run motherfucker, run!"

Screaming like a banshee, I'd run as fast as I could with my imaginary firearm in hand, jumping over felled trees, across the frozen streams, and up the banks of the ravine to where the British camp lay in full view out in the distance. Dropping to my belly, I would crawl along the forest floor, leading my men forward as we closed in on the dreaded Limeys—now alerted to our presence and calling for reinforcements. Suddenly, musket fire would pierce the stillness of the forest, ringing fiercely in my ears as I gave rabid commands to my troops, urging them to forge a strong defensive line and retaliate with extreme prejudice. Musket balls would hit all around me, British troops would appear from behind trees, and a wicked firefight would explode across the region.

Men would die, men would get cut down, and men would rise to heroic heights as I urged my troops onward and to victory. Then suddenly, as I rallied my troops for the final assault, a random musket ball would slam into my chest, dropping me to the ground in a bloody, broken heap as I writhed in pain and held on to life. Nakawa, my faithful Indian friend and fellow warrior, would howl in despair as he'd run to my side, place my limp head on his lap, and seethe with revenge.

"Nakawa," I would whisper, placing a trembling hand to his cheek. "Nakawa…" I would say again, drawing my final breath as my hand fell silently to my side, and Nakawa shed tears of grief for his slain brother. My war, in the blink of an eye, would suddenly be over.

Camp Ozanam, to sum up this tale of wonder, was an absolute gift of freedom coming straight from my mother's heart. Camp Ozanam was a paradise, Camp Ozanam fueled my engines, and Camp Ozanam gave me everything I needed to become a man. When the experience came to an end during my fourteenth year of life, it was, without a doubt, a bittersweet moment. Suddenly, I realized that childhood was now a part of my own history. The road ahead was most certainly laced with all the trappings of manhood and fierce adult ways, but those things now appeared obtainable and far less scary to me. As I would move forward in life, I would do so with a newfound confidence, a newfound awareness, and a newfound sense of pride. And the sense of adventure that now seized me would be forever entrenched in my heart, and would help to protect me as I grew. Camp Ozanam, as my brother Michael had promised, would never fade—and has never faded—from my heart. I have carried her in my soul all these years and have cherished her memories as powerfully as a dying man would his final breath. Camp Ozanam, in a very real way, has *become* my life.

8. THE WORKING YEARS

WHEN I FIRST SAT DOWN TO WRITE THIS CHAPTER OF MY LIFE, I INItially struggled to find the proper way to approach it. I felt unsettled, anxious and uncharacteristically uninspired. To put it mildly, I felt confused.

Then suddenly, I remembered an incident I had when I was with Widespread Panic and my time working for them as a roadie. At first glance, said incident appears to be nothing more than an excursion into unrestricted partying—but it was actually a very poignant moment.

By the time I began working for Widespread Panic back in October of 1987, the confusion swirling through my head had become overwhelming and, at times, downright debilitating. I've often wondered what those guys thought of me back then: a wild, crazy, whacked-out kid from Detroit who just showed up one day, barely speaking, working extremely hard, and rocking even harder...then never going away. I will forever be thankful for my time with Widespread Panic for numerous reasons, but one of the most important was the fact that those boys accepted me for who I was, never busted my balls, and allowed for me to work through my confusion on my own and within the comforting confines of the band. It was a beautiful gesture on their part, and one for which I will always be grateful.

One night, while out in Anywhere, U. S. A. following a gig in the late 1980s, I was sitting with Bill "Gomer" Jordan, Panic's soundman, in our hotel room inhaling one nitrous hit after the other and getting wild. I decided to kick things up a notch and tripled my dosage while inhaling deeply. Now, as anyone who has experimented with nitrous knows, the high can be intense at times, and the hit I had just taken became a little more potent than what I was prepared for.

Suddenly, I lost touch with my body, became unaware of my surroundings, and found myself transported back in time. I was now having a hallucinatory trip. In the trip, I found myself in the basement of our house in Detroit, confined to the pantry; I could feel all the familiar sights, sounds, and smells enveloping me. It felt as if I were about ten or eleven years old; I was crouching on the floor, the door was closed, and it seemed as if it was either locked from the outside or that I was hiding inside. The energy was uncertain, tense and undeniably unsettling, and I was *not* in my happy place. I felt as if I was put there against my will, and was attempting to digest the reasons for why I was being confined.

Nitrous highs are short-lived, and as I began to come out of the experience and drift back into my body, I saw Gomer staring at me and laughing as he attempted to dissect where I had just gone.

"Mmmhmmm," Gomer chuckled in his familiar, Southern drawl, "that was a good one, wasn't it?"

It took several minutes to gather my composure and shake those raw images from my mind, and as I write this now, I've come to see that my hesitation—my lack of inspiration, my overpowering anxiety about writing this chapter—comes from the fact that when all is said and done, writing about many of my childhood experiences is extremely difficult. It is draining, it is unsettling, and it is oppressive—and that, I have come to see, is only because it so intensely reflects what my childhood was actually like.

But the experience of writing about those times is equally liberating.

It acts as therapy and allows for me to work through some bitter pain and confounding disillusionment that has hounded me my entire life. For that, I am also eternally grateful.

That nitrous trip, I have learned (through my beautiful wife, who has worked in the dental field for most of her adult life, and has experienced similar scenarios with her patients), took me back to a random day in my youth that was not carefree; just another day in my troubled youth, and one which I had blocked from my mind. This kind of memory suppression has probably occurred more times than I'll ever even know, but what I do remember is quite enough.

I don't need any more reminders.

Now, again, I can't place blame on anyone for what went on back then, and I certainly don't hold any grudges. To do so is not logical. And by this time in my life, things were so out of whack that no one in the family—myself included—had a firm grip on reality. What I do know is that we all tried our best to survive, and did whatever was necessary to maintain some shred of sanity. With this in mind, I am now prepared to move on with documenting this next phase of my life, while keeping those sinking feelings in check...as I now describe what I refer to as "The Working Years."

The work ethic in the Acquaviva household was pounded into our heads from the time we could all walk. Detroit was the definition of "blue collar" and no one was exempt. There were no trust funds, no rich relatives, no offshore bank accounts, and certainly no free rides. In the city of Detroit there was just work, day in and day out, and the sooner you accepted this, the better off you were. And for us kids, that time—the time to wake up and go to work—came at age twelve.

Again, I would have it no other way. It prepared me for life.

Shortly after I turned twelve, my mother came to me and said:

"Honey, it's time for you to get a job, and you'll have to start paying room and board every week. If you want something that I can't supply, you'll have to pay for it yourself."

Sounded fair enough to me. After all, every one of my older siblings had done the same at age twelve, and now it was my turn. And the fact of the matter was that we all had been working since the day we could walk, so making the jump to an actual "job" was no big deal.

Since I could remember, we were all expected to do numerous chores around the house and take care of ourselves in every imaginable way. There were no free passes in our home, and our mother ensured that we all pulled our own weight. From the time I was five or six years old I was doing yard work, cleaning windows, clearing gutters, raking leaves, shoveling snow, and finding other ways to make cash throughout the neighborhood.

I even have a clear memory of when I was about eight years old; my mother informed me that old lady Baumgartner was looking for someone to cut her lawn, and that she would "make it worth my while." With my eye on a new set of official G. I. Joe walkie-talkies, I jumped at the chance. Making my way to Mrs. Baumgartner's with my tools in hand, I began the job on a gorgeous spring morning.

After more than four hours of mowing, clipping, trimming, and raking with nothing more than our old-timey, non-motorized push mower, hand-held clippers, and a rake, I tidied up, swept the sidewalks clean, and made everything look nice and sharp. Now it was time to collect my fortune. I then headed to the front door, knocked respectfully, and waited in anticipation for the big payoff. Old lady Baumgartner answered, thanked me for my hard work, opened her change purse and handed me two shiny, brand-new 1973 quarters while patting me gently on the head. As I walked down the steps, I cursed that old woman relentlessly for tossing me two measly, worthless bits for an entire morning of busting my hump and headed home in defeat. It was that day that I clearly saw the injustices of the world, and realized that the lifetime of work that awaited me was going to be one long, tortuous road fraught with endless disappointments. And it was also the day I realized that those official G. I. Joe walkie-talkies were nothing more than a distant pipe dream, now appearing forever out of my reach.

The first official job I had at age twelve was one in which I followed my brothers' footsteps. Every one of my brothers delivered newspapers for The Detroit Free Press, and now it was my turn to join the team. Back in those days, Detroit had two newspapers in circulation, and as a paperboy, you either worked for *The Free Press* or *The Detroit News*. There was no flip-flopping: you were either a Free Press man or a News man.

To us, the distinction was clear: to work for the News meant you were a pretty boy who needed beauty sleep. Your mommy drove you around your route after school, and you softly meandered through life along with all the rest of the pansies.

But to work for the Free Press meant waking at 5 A. M., braving the elements to deliver your papers before most kids even woke. Working for the Free Press meant you were a man, hardened by the weather and the ways of the streets.

Working for the Free Press was a badge of honor.

On the night before I was to start my big job for the Free Press, I was consumed with anxiety and uncertainty: *Can I handle the responsibility? Will I be able to manage waking at 5 A.M. and dealing with the psychotics, drunks, pedophiles, and late-night cruisers roaming the streets?* As I lay in my bed I felt like I was having a panic attack; my heart beat wildly in my chest. In one of the few times I have ever asked my mother for advice, I got out of bed, went downstairs and saw her reading on the couch in the living room. Swallowing my pride, I expressed my concerns and shared my doubts. Never looking up from the book she was reading, my mother offered her sage advice.

"Pray to Jesus, honey, that will put your soul at ease."

I stood in front of mom as her words hung in the air and she continued with her reading ritual. I somehow felt curiously unfulfilled by her insights.

What, is Jesus going to deliver my papers for me? I thought as I made my way back up the stairs. *The guy can't even free the world of disease, poverty, war and hunger, and now he's going to magically appear and work my route for me?*

Even more confused, I went to bed and prepared for my big day.

I eventually learned the ropes of my paper route and became a model paperboy, even embracing life on the streets in the early morning hours. There were several scary incidents I had to deal with that made the experience of working a morning paper route interesting, such as the day I kept seeing the same car appear the further I went into my route. This car would sit silently on nearly every street I worked, and I could see the silhouette of a man puffing on a smoke inside. Recently, there had been a series of kidnappings of young girls in the city, and seeing that car shadowing my route made me certain that I was next on the list.

Fortunately, I made it through the morning and never saw the car again. I guess I wasn't pretty enough for the guy.

Dogs were a real treat—if you were seeking to test your manhood on a daily basis. If you were simply trying to do your damn job, they were just short of a nightmare. These hounds would appear out of nowhere, usually seeking to rip you limb from limb: big dogs, little dogs, wild dogs, cute floppy lapdogs...they came in all shapes and sizes. Some were looking for nothing more than friendship, but even those were a constant nuisance. It was not uncommon to have a crazed pooch chase you up and down the street, nipping at your ankles as you tried desperately to pedal away from the rabid beast. Dogs would tear around corners as you approached a house and attack you like you were a milk bone. Kicking, punching, slapping, and growling at those animals were a common defense throughout the route. I eventually learned to go straight for their balls and give them a swift kick to the crotch to ward them off. I believe that it was my time as a paperboy that soured my taste for canines. Wild, angry, vicious mutts roaming the streets were a constant distraction, and I grew increasingly weary of dealing with them as time went on. Going straight for the canine family jewels, however, became a very effective tool in the War of the Pooches, and established me as a world-class tamer of beasts. Stupid freaking dogs...

One morning, in the pre-dawn darkness, I approached a porch cluttered with hanging plants, dangling wind chimes, and random knick-knacks, all serving to effectively obstruct the view of the street. When I stepped up the small concrete stairs to deliver the paper, I could make out the form of a man, passed out cold on a chair and surrounded by numerous empty beer bottles.

I paused, unsure of whether to advance.

Without warning, the form suddenly sprang to life, popping into a sitting position. "Huh? Who the fuck is there?!?" he yelled. "I've got a gun!!!"

I almost had a heart attack. I dropped the paper, turned in fear, and ran for my life. Eventually, over time, the man and I developed an understanding and became comfortable with the arrangement.

"Good morning, Mr. Bellagio," I'd say while stepping to the porch.

"Uh...good morning kid..." he'd respond, knocking over beer bottles as he sat up, rubbing his throbbing head. "Uh, you have a good day."

Working a morning paper route ensured that you got to know your neighbors well. Guys passed out in their cars following a long night of boozing; remnants of a major fiesta strewn across lawns; seeing people in the throes of early morning passion through partially drawn blinds—these were not unusual sights. Arguments, disagreements, and pretty ladies traipsing through their houses in their birthday suits were common as well. Shut-ins were a real pleasure, those individuals who never left their houses and saw the paperboy as their only connection to the outside world. This would inevitably lead to long, tortuous conversations about school and the state of the family as Fido humped your leg like a little Casanova.

Now, the most troublesome aspect of an early morning paper route in a Midwestern city was, without a doubt, the weather. Fall, winter, and spring presented challenges that were astounding. The tool available to carry my papers was a 1960s monster of a thing known as a Schwinn Deluxe American bicycle, a model handed down from my brothers. I affectionately referred to it as "The Tank." These bicycles had no speed shifts, no hand brakes, and no features to make for an easy ride. These contraptions were made of stout metal, extremely heavy, and completely utilitarian. You didn't take these bikes out for long joy rides; the only power feature they had was your own two legs.

Peddling the Schwinn Deluxe American bicycle through a driving, early-morning downpour was bad enough; I would curse God as endless sheets of rain soaked me to the bone. But this, unfortunately, was not the worst of it. What took the cake were ceaseless amounts of snow and freezing temperatures that ravaged my body while pushing The Tank from one house to the next. Attempting to pedal through snow, while weighted down with sixty papers or more, was an impossibility. Inevitably, I'd be encouraged to walk my entire route while forcing my way through four, six, sometimes ten inches of snow or more. Even through blizzards, people expected their morning papers, and rare was the day when the snow prevented the paper trucks from dropping off your allotment at the hardware store. And asking mom to assist with the old family truckster was never an option either. It never once entered our minds to seek such a reprieve — for it would never have materialized in the first place, even if Hell had frozen over.

I guess I was a rather heavy sleeper in my youth, because one of my brothers (who had a paper route at the same time I did) discovered a unique way of waking me from my slumber. In the middle of January, as a healthy snowfall descended from low-flying clouds, and as I'd be as snug as a bug beneath my warm, cozy blankets, my brother would nudge me awake in a manner as soothing as the torrid weather raging outside my window.

"Get up motherfucker!!! Get up!!!" he would serenade while unloading a maelstrom of punches to my head and body.

As if reaping the rewards for a lifetime of ill-choices and deplorable sins, my reveille came in the form of a barrage of pain reserved for the condemned. It was a normal routine to be woken this way, and made me understand that mine was not a normal life. (Or was it?) Following this ritual, I'd enter the street where either a torrent of bone-chilling rain would greet me, or a frozen landscape of thigh-high snow awaited my arrival. Hopping onto The Tank, I'd pedal, push, and strain in disillusionment as I thanked Jesus for beginning my day encased in his loving protection. Ah, such was my life as a young entrepreneur.

The one part of the morning paper route I never quite grasped was the business side of things. Truth be told, I have always been a horrible businessman who has forever been confused by the concept of money. Talk to my beautiful wife about this one and she'll tell you that I'd be happy just to accept a pat on the back for a full day's work, and give away the money I'd earned as a tip for good service at a restaurant. Money, for whatever reason, has always slipped through my fingers. It's a true phenomenon. In light of this, and although I was in all respects a great paperboy, I never seemed to make the same money as my brothers.

I would simply give it away, spend it on baseball cards, or lose it from my pockets. I was one stone-cold knucklehead when it came to holding onto cash. Still am for that matter.

Friday afternoon was the day I would go around the neighborhood and collect from my customers. Inevitably, when I'd return home, my pockets would be devoid of money as I'd simply lose track of it or share it with a neighborhood friend.

One Friday afternoon, when arriving at the house following school, my father was there waiting for me. I was deeply confused by this. Not certain as to what was going on, my mother informed me that Pops was going to take me around my route and show me the ropes. So, I shrugged my shoulders and hopped in Pops' car.

I'm telling you now, I should have listened to my instincts, which screamed for me to jump on my bike and ride to freedom as fast as I could upon seeing my father waiting for me. Because the first thing I realized about my adventure with Pops was that he was not happy about being forced to spend time with his son. That entire time I drove around the neighborhood with the old man was an absolute waste of time. His *and* mine. He sighed a lot, shook his head in disgust, and never once offered a single shred of advice on how to approach not only my paper route, but life in general. No more than ten minutes into the experience I was so uncomfortable that I simply walked along the sidewalk as the old man followed close behind in the car.

Whenever I did get back in the car, the old man continued to express his dissatisfaction and showed me that I was not among the favorite of his children. I always felt that my father thought of me as a bit of a dandy, a weak kid, and this episode seemed to prove it. (Understanding where he came from, he may have been right.) When Pops finally did speak, he mumbled something about having enough of this bullshit—then immediately headed back to the house, dropping me off in a huff. The guy even pulled away before I had the chance to close the door; I stood in his wake wondering what the hell was going on. And this, to sum it up, was about the extent of my "alone" time with my old man during my entire childhood, formative, and teen years.

By the time I was thirteen, I had two jobs that I worked seven days a week. Besides my morning paper route, I also had a coveted busboy job at The Clock Restaurant on Gratiot Avenue. The Clock was another gig I picked up due to my brothers paving the way: Paul, Stephen, and Michael had also had tenures there, and now it was my turn to enjoy the experience. And I'm here to tell you, The Clock Restaurant was not just another greasy spoon diner slinging hash and offering free refills. Oh no, it was much more than that. It was, in reality, a magnet for every freak, degenerate, drug addict, pimp, whore, and late-night whacko the neighborhood had to offer.

My shift was every Friday and Saturday night from midnight to 8 A.M., when the pretty, gentler side of the city opened itself up to my delicate, fresh mind. Drug deals went down, not only in the parking lot but also in the restaurant itself, creating a comfortable and friendly atmosphere for everyone to enjoy. I do believe that just about every drug known to man circulated through that restaurant, and that just about everyone there indulged in them.

Grown men would settle their disputes in a most gentlemanly fashion while women did the same: pulling hair, scratching out eyes, and screaming like psychotics as they beat the shit out of each other in the parking lot. These simple misunderstandings were settled in a gracious and amicable manner and taught me at a very young age just how wise it was to mix booze, drugs, jealousy, and blind rage together in a bubbly, toxic cocktail for all to enjoy. Late-night revelers would pour into the place for hours at a time, stumbling blindly through the doors and staggering to their tables while announcing their arrival in joyous, boisterous salutations. Patrons who were served meals to their disliking simply inquired if a change of fare was possible: "Tell that fucking moron that I wouldn't serve this shit to my dog. Now go get me a fucking hamburger...."

The Clock Restaurant was frequented by an endless wave of colorful characters, those who approached life from a different point of view. One of my favorites was a gal I nicknamed "Trixie." Trixie would come see me just about every weekend as she and her unique friends sat down for a well-earned meal following a long, strenuous night of hard work. One of her pals was a dashing, sharply dressed lad in six-inch disco shoes. This gentleman would spend his time counting wads of cash while discussing with the girls where their next "party" would be. And those gals seemed to attend a lot of parties, for their dance cards always appeared full.

Trixie, a classy and well-dressed gal herself, would drop her silverware on occasion, forcing me to bend over to pick up the errant items. Somehow, her hand slipped *every time* and found its way to my backside as she explored my nether-regions. My little Trixie was not a shy girl.

"Oh, sorry sweetheart," she would say in a breathy tone while looking me up and down, "I don't know *how* that keeps happening..."

I too, was confused by this recurring dilemma. Just about every time I saw her, Trixie made it painfully clear that she would love to treat me to my own "party." She would share interesting and engaging sentiments such as "I'd devour you honey," and equally enlightening statements such as, "There'd be nothing left of you when I finished." That was usually followed by the entire table agreeing with Trixie, as the rest of the girls offered even more unique ways of entertaining me. Trixie was a sweet girl, with a bubbly and vivacious personality...and she scared the shit out of me.

Life at The Clock Restaurant was a perfect example of late-night Detroit, and showed me the true character of the city in bold fashion.

I've always been appreciative of the experience and really did enjoy my time there, for it was a clear and unfettered view of life in the city of my birth. Other kids who worked there were as tough as the city that raised them, and exposed a side of the neighborhood that was pure and untainted. Some of these kids had incredibly tough lives, and were able to maintain a measure of dignity by fending for themselves as they worked at the restaurant. One kid I worked with, a cat named Devon, was a few years older than me and so subtly strong and silently wise that I grew to respect him in short order.

Devon and I would walk home from work almost every day following our shift, and he eventually began to share his life with me. His mother, whom Devon loved dearly, died when he was twelve years old. His father, broken and angry, ceaselessly beat the shit out of Devon to the point that he finally had enough and moved out on his own at age fifteen. By age sixteen, Devon had impregnated his girlfriend, and both were living in a trailer somewhere in the neighborhood. Despite this, Devon was determined to provide for his kid and was hell-bent on offering her a better life — no matter what it took.

Devon had few options, fewer opportunities, and a future steeped in the unknown. Yet despite the odds against him, Devon was tough, street-smart, and funny, with a positive attitude that was humbling. And Devon, to me, was the quintessential example of the average, working-class Joe that Detroit had produced for generations. Devon was rock-solid, with an undying spirit and a tireless work ethic that would put most people to shame. Following our shift at The Clock, he'd clean up and start his day as a mechanic at his cousin's garage.

Devon was the kind of Detroit native that I grew to respect and admire — the kind of guy the city was built upon. I never heard Devon complain, never saw him drown in his miseries, never saw him miss a shift.

And I never saw him give up.

One of my favorite aspects of The Clock Restaurant was, without a doubt, the music saturating the dining hall. You see, every booth at The Clock had its own private jukebox loaded with a seemingly infinite number of Motown songs, each of which rang clearly through the air. Moving from table to table, an entirely new tune would enter my sphere and make those long, grueling nights pass by just a little more easily. If you couldn't get excited, inspired, and moved by those unforgettable, powerful, and catchy songs, you might have wanted to check your pulse to see if you were still alive.

Tunes like "Please Mr. Postman" by The Marvelettes, "Where Did Our Love Go" by The Supremes, "My Guy" by Mary Wells, "The Way You Do The Things You Do" by The Temptations, "Heat Wave" by Martha and The Vandellas, and countless other homegrown hits slipped across the restaurant twenty-four hours a day, bringing a true sense of understanding of where you were, where you came from, and the potential the city still had—even in the mid-1970s. Motown was, and still is, a source of pride that has withstood the test of time…one of the few things Detroiters could hold on to as the city began its descent into chaos.

I have numerous memories of swinging to those incredible sounds with men and women, both black and white, rich and poor, beggar and thief, as we would get lost in a song and forget about race, creed, religion, politics, or gender for a sweet sliver of time and submerge ourselves in the pride of being fellow Detroiters. This music would break down walls, open minds, make people genuinely happy, and cause them to dance in their booths as its power helped us to forget all the worries, all the concerns, and all the doubts of a dying city, if only for a minute or two, and fused us together whether we desired it or not. Sometimes that feeling was undeniable, sometimes it was unavoidable, sometimes it was warmly welcoming.

Often I'd walk to a table to fill coffee cups while singing along to one of the tunes, and gradually become aware that some of the patrons, too, were singing along to the same song; though strangers, we'd always acknowledge each other with a binding nod.

The music of Motown still makes me swell with pride.

My time at The Clock Restaurant and my tenure as a morning paperboy for The Detroit Free Press instilled in me an ethic that I still honor to this day: that of good, honest, hard work. I've always been proud of my blue-collar roots, and have carried those lessons in my heart my entire life. No matter where I have gone, I have always had that foundation of a strong work ethic deep inside me, forged by the factories, machine shops, auto plants, refineries—and, most assuredly, The Motor City people themselves. It's a quality that has allowed me to roll up my sleeves, dig in my heels, and make my mark on the world like the Motown man I am. Even though this phase of my life was just the beginning of my work experience, it set the table for the future, and offered a foundation upon which to stand and create my own dreams, my own voice, and my own reality as I grew. There would be no turning back now, for as I moved into the future I would do so knowing exactly where I came from, despite the nagging confusion ravaging my soul. And wherever I would go, and no matter what would happen in my life, I would move forward with the sweet sound of the music of Detroit, The Motor City, forever resounding in my ears.

PHOTOGRAPHS

Mom and me

Pops kissing his boy

Ready to motor

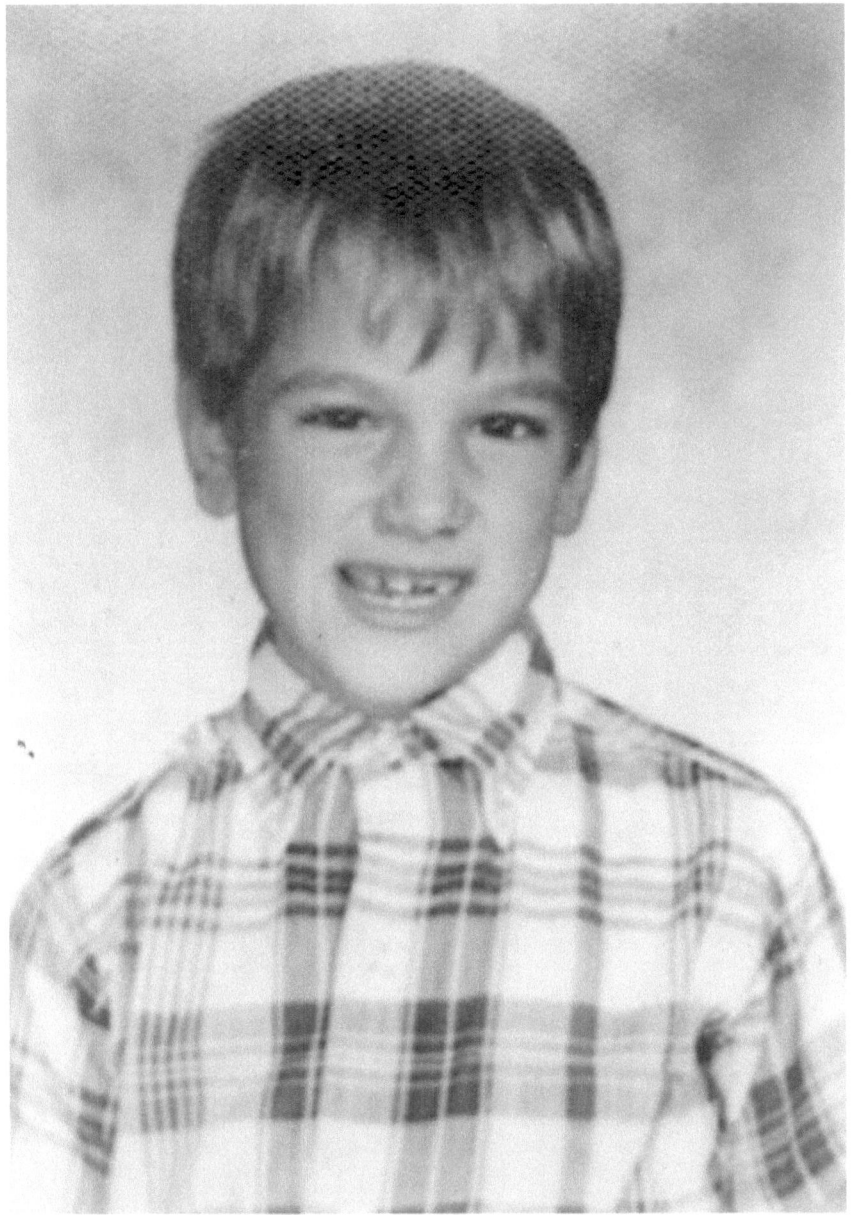

The kid

Ridin' that board

Too cool for school

Andrea and me at the Goulburn house

Running for my life

Andrea and me at her house

Fighting for that rebound

The Goulburn house, late 1980s

Graduation picture, 1983

Can't believe that I graduated.

Rugby days

The family in West Virginia

Heading back to school

Joe the Plumber

9. SCHOOL DAYS

IN THE FALL OF 1979, I STARTED HIGH SCHOOL. AFTER EIGHT YEARS OF walking the halls, gracing the classrooms, courting the girls, and exploring the neighborhood of Assumption Grotto, it was time to move on. But I'm here to tell you, if Grotto had offered a high school, I would have spent all twelve years being a Panther and loved every second of it.

But to my dismay, fate would have something more in store. As summer gave way to the cooler temperatures and dynamic colors of fall, I would experience the first of many culture shocks that would enter my life over the next few years, making for interesting experiences and unusual times. And the first of these shocks to the system was named Bishop Gallagher High School.

Now, I'm a pretty old-school guy who has always taken pride in approaching life in a simplistic manner. I've never needed much to survive. Give me a decent job, a place to hang my hat, and a cold beer from time to time—I'll get along just fine. I've never been one for fancy duds or extravagant trappings. And I'm certain that this aspect of my personality has everything to do with my childhood and how I grew up. So walking through the doors of Bishop Gallagher for the first time was a bit of an eye-opener, and an experience for which I was not quite prepared. To sum it up, I hated everything about Bishop Gallagher from the moment I arrived.

Bishop Gallagher High School was located in Harper Woods, Michigan, nearly three miles from our house and bordering such ritzy areas as Grosse Pointe Woods, St. Claire Shores, and Grosse Pointe Farms. I couldn't have been more out of my element if you had dropped me on the hostile surface of planet Mars. But at least on Mars I would have been on a level playing field with whomever else was there with me. Not at Bishop Gallagher, though. At Bishop Gallagher, I felt like a man without a country, a child lost in the Black Forest, a kid walking blindly through the dark of night. I felt about as uncomfortable as a young man could feel.

Bishop Gallagher was large (nearly 2,000 students), clean, modern, and populated with kids from "the right side of the tracks." These kids were white—"preppy," if you will—and came from stable, two-parent homes. They owned cars that their daddies had purchased for them, had gaudy bank accounts, and frowned upon work. To be a kid like me, who *had* to work, was the equivalent of being poor and uncouth. These kid's fathers were executives for Ford, G. M., Chrysler, and the like; they were college graduates and members of the elite. Their stay-at-home mothers were "proper," and raised "proper" kids. There was a lack of culture and diversity—everyone looked the same. To act differently, and to actually think differently, was to be considered not only an outcast, but also someone who was on the lunatic fringe. It felt as if I had walked into my worst nightmare. Trying to connect with those kids was nearly impossible.

The fact that I was already the definition of confused when I walked through the doors didn't help the situation in any way either. Trying to find kids I could actually relate to was a journey into disappointment. I was surrounded by a student body that was being primed to become the lawyers, politicians, and executives of the future, and the energy of the school reflected this. Most kids came across as pretentious, conniving, and ruthless; automatons that had already embodied greed, avarice, and personal self-gain. There was a lack of soul at Bishop Gallagher, and my time there would prove to be an excursion into loneliness, frustration, and self-doubt.

Besides writing, drawing, and the never-ending song playing in my head, the only thing I had to hold on to during my time there was my ability to run at great speeds for long distances. Because of this, I naturally gravitated towards the cross-country team, joining the squad shortly after my arrival. This would be the only thing keeping me sane as I listlessly meandered through my days at Bishop Gallagher.

One of the greatest aspects about running is that it is a solo activity; you don't need anyone else to do it. It's one of the main reasons I loved it. And training for the cross-country team at Bishop Gallagher involved little more than that— running.

And so we ran. And ran, and ran, and ran. We ran through the streets, up hills, along streams and creeks, across the interstate, and through just about every area accessible to the public. And as I ran, I had one wonderful song after the other roaming through my head, filling my mind with rhythms and melodies that fueled me from the time I woke until the time I lay down to sleep. You see, I was one of those lucky cats who was born with a "radio head," a never-ending internal jukebox that has always been with me and will never go away.

As I trained, and even during competitions, I'd go through all my favorite albums, starting with song 1 of Side A and straight through until the last song of Side B hit its final note. Bands like The Beatles, The Who, Blondie, The Cars, Van Halen, The Police, The Clash, The Knack, The Stones, and infinite others inspired me like nothing else, giving me a sense of freedom and self-confidence unobtainable in any other way. My mind would explore these songs, hearing every nuance of every composition as clearly as if speakers were permanently wedged in my ears. Pffft, I got your IPod hanging, man. I was, and still am, a walking iPod, decades before they ever existed.

Those days of running cross-country at Bishop Gallagher were the only positive aspects of my time there, and kept me moderately sane, on some level, as I walked through life. However, every single remaining facet of school life was a complete mystery to me. I didn't understand the kids' motivation. I didn't understand their direction. I didn't understand their intentions or purpose, except their endless pursuit of money—that aspect was as clear as day.

I didn't understand their lingo, their culture, their fashions, or their dreams. Hell, I didn't even understand the girls. Those young girls looked at me—a rough-edged cat from Detroit who actually had to work for a living, wore hand-me-down clothes, and possessed an artist's soul—like I was from the other side of Planet Crackers. Those chicks never gave me the time of day, another reality that had my head spinning. It was obvious that these broads didn't give a shit about a guy unless he had a brand new Camaro and a trust fund at his disposal, another aspect of school life that made me sick.

Despite this, my freshman cross-country campaign was relatively successful. I broke a couple of freshman records, two J. V. records, earned a spot on the Varsity team, and even received my Varsity Letter. My coach loved me, and my work ethic, and was certain that by my junior year I'd be All-State. But, unfortunately for him, following the season, two things happened that would change my life, convincing me that my time at Bishop Gallagher was coming to an end. I could not have been happier when these episodes unfolded, and accepted them with a grateful heart as a whole new world opened up to me in a manner that was both welcoming and, without a doubt, needed.

The first thing that occurred was simple enough, but put me on the path to reconsider my time at Bishop Gallagher. My brother Michael, a junior at Gallagher, began tossing around the idea of transferring to a small school on Detroit's east side called Servite High. He eventually decided to go for it, and did everything in his power to make it happen. This move perked my ears, but the thought of following Michael to Servite made me uneasy—at this point, I was trying to stay as far away from my siblings as I could. However, Michael's move became even more enticing following the second incident—the one that completely soured me on Bishop Gallagher.

I was a well-rounded athlete who thrived in a number of sports. I had been running, jumping, climbing, riding and tumbling since I could walk. At Assumption Grotto, I excelled in everything from football, baseball, basketball, track, and more. Sports were as natural to me as breathing, and became an activity that silenced the demons in my head as I grew older.

Following the cross-country season, when the long, cold winter months began, I tried out for the freshman basketball team. Bishop Gallagher had numerous good athletes but I was confident that I could make the squad. Basketball was one of my favorite sports and I played often, spending countless hours dribbling, shooting, and jumping at school and at home. I simply loved the game.

The try-outs for the freshman basketball team at Gallagher were intense, but all my years of training on my own and at Grotto were paying off. I could hang with the best the team had to offer. As final cuts approached, I was certain that I'd be a Lancer for the Bishop Gallagher freshman basketball team. But sometimes, the harsh ways of the world smack us in the face, reminding us of the true nature of man. And sometimes this reality proves to us that things are not on the up-and-up, and likely never have been ever since the day our first ancestors harnessed the power of fire and withheld it from others. In short, those with the upper hand have always held onto it, and always will.

On the final day of cuts, I went to the locker room, changed into my shorts and Chuck Taylors, and made my way to the gym. As I was shooting baskets with the guys before practice, the coach called me into his office. Sitting down, I settled in as I prepared to hear the good news that I had just made the squad.

"Larry," the coach began, "You're a great player with a solid work ethic and I'd love to have you on the team." He fidgeted in his seat as he spoke. "The final spot on the roster has come down to you and Jonathan. You're the better player...but you see, Jonathan's father is a booster, and because of this, we're going with him."

I was speechless. It was that day that I had my first lesson in politics: it doesn't matter how good you are, it's who you know. With this information firmly in my mind, I then made my move. I immediately made plans to follow my brother Michael to Servite High and could not wait to leave Bishop Gallagher behind. Shortly after Christmas break, and as the New Year dawned, Michael and I became students at Servite High on Detroit's east side. No one at Bishop Gallagher shed a tear, and no one wished me well. Hell, I doubt that anyone even knew that I had left. They just carried on in their argyle shirts, penny loafers, and khaki pants as if it were just another day. My time at Gallagher was over and I could not have been happier. Adios to Bishop Gallagher and hola to Servite High, the place I was destined to be.

SERVITE HIGH

Sometimes there are things in life that unfold like a dream; moments in time that put us on the path we are destined to follow. No matter what we do, we cannot escape this, and to deny it would be tantamount to turning your back on whom you truly are. Such was the case when I left Bishop Gallagher for Servite High in January of 1980. I soon found that the decision to transfer would change my life in ways impossible to calculate, and would put me on my own path of destiny. The move to Servite High, I would soon come to see, would ultimately save my sanity.

Servite High School—home of the Panthers—was on Coplin Avenue on Detroit's east side, about three miles from our house, and prophetically in the opposite direction of Bishop Gallagher. Servite High was itself three miles closer to downtown and smack-dab in the middle of the city of my birth. This neighborhood had character; it was old school, and struck me as very familiar. It was the definition of blue collar, and was as welcoming as a cool breeze in the throes of a hot summer. It was a real, genuine Detroit neighborhood, just like our neighborhood—no pretensions, no gimmicks, no game playing. What you saw was what you got, and if you didn't play by the rules, you suffered the consequences. I once again felt at home.

Servite High was built in 1946 by Catholic craftsmen returning from World War II. Back then, every neighborhood had its own Catholic grade school and high school, which catered to the residents surrounding these institutions in numerous ways. The 1940s, 50s and 60s were the heyday of these schools, when they flourished, and had great teachers, a strong community spirit, and reflected the character of every neighborhood perfectly. By the time I arrived at Servite in early January 1980, however, these schools were on a decline. They, like the city, were dying.

I can clearly remember walking the halls of Servite for the first time. The contrasts to Bishop Gallagher were enormous. Bishop Gallagher was modern, clean, and had a feel about it that was antiseptic, as if it had no soul. The student body was overwhelmingly white and embodied the definition of pretentious.

Servite was old, run down, almost neglected. The student body was 70% minority: African American, Latino, and Filipino. There were

Irish kids, Slovakian kids, Polish, and Italian kids. There were no more than 500 kids in the entire school. There were no football fields, no athletic fields, and no "campus" grounds surrounding the school. The building was hemmed in by busy streets and residential homes bustling with activity.

Behind the school was an asphalt parking lot where kids lucky enough to own a car parked their late 60's and early 70's models: Ford Pintos, Dodge Darts, and Chevy Impalas, all proudly displayed, earned by the sweat of their brows. You could feel that the school had seen better days, that the "glory" days had passed it by. It felt as if Servite High was populated with underdogs, outcasts, and those who would never be accepted by the Bishop Gallagher's of the world—and in truth, would never want to be. There was an independent spirit and a sense of pride that was palpable. The kids at Servite, for the most part, were there because they wanted to be. I immersed myself into the culture from the moment I walked through her doors.

Those early days at Servite were glorious. Despite my shyness, confusion, and independent spirit, I made fast friends and felt a connection with just about everyone there. I felt like Ferris Beuller at a Friday night mixer; I became friends with the sportos, geeks, freaks, motorheads, dweebs, knuckleheads, and whackos, all in short order. It was at Servite where I learned the valuable lesson that the only way you can stand independently is to stand with those who also embrace the independent spirit. Servite was a microcosm of democracy; to be free one must stand with those who do the same. It was a lesson I never forgot.

Shortly after my arrival, I was walking down the hall when I saw a man, possibly a teacher, heading towards me. His eyes grew as big as saucers as he stopped before me, looked up, and grasped me by my shoulders.

"Tell me that you're a football player," he said, smiling a devious smile.

"No, sir," I replied. "I'm a cross-country runner."

"Not at Servite you're not. We don't have a cross-country team! You're going to play football. Come see me in my office after school."

I was now a football player at Servite High.

In my childhood, I used to dream of my future wife: a beautiful, Dark Haired Angel who would spend the rest of her life with me as we explored the ways of love and romance. I could see her, in my dreams, walking hand in hand as she rested her head gently on my shoulder. I could smell the sweet fragrance of her hair; I could taste her skin and could see the light of love dancing in her eyes. We would talk, laugh, play, and love together, as one. This "phantom" love was as real to me as the sun in the sky, and by the time I entered Servite High my romantic self was in full bloom; unfortunately, so were my shyness and confusion. But I had an artist's soul, a romantic soul, and knew that love and romance were somewhere on the horizon.

Servite High, like most Catholic high schools at the time, had a grade school attached to it — St. John Berchman's. Late in my freshman year, as springtime blossomed on the streets surrounding Servite, I caught a glimpse of a beautiful Dark Haired Eighth Grade Angel. I even remember fighting through my shyness to say a few words as she stood surrounded by her girlfriends. What I said is anyone's guess, but I'm certain that it was smooth, debonair, and timeless. (If you believe that, I've got some prime real estate I can sell you in the tundra of the Upper Peninsula.)

For the remainder of the school year and throughout the summer, I could not get this girl out of my head; I envisioned spending time with her, enjoying her, and loving her forever. As summer crept on, however, a sinking feeling in the pit of my stomach told me that I would never see her again. I figured a girl like her would end up at Bishop Gallagher or some other fancy school far away from my beloved Servite High, and that I would never cross paths with her ever again. Reluctantly, I attempted to block her from my mind as I moved on with life.

During the summer of 1980, several things happened which altered my life. The first was when three major car factories shut their doors and laid off tens of thousands of autoworkers over a period of several weeks. Detroit would never be the same from that point forward. This period initiated the beginning of the end for not only our neighborhood, but for the city itself. Things began to spin out of control in a way that was shocking and hard to comprehend. The things I began to see were mindboggling.

In a matter of weeks, people in our neighborhood began a mass exodus out of the city to find work, and the rapidity of the flight was astounding. Families we had known our entire lives suddenly disappeared, with no fanfare or grand send-offs, leaving empty houses that suddenly appeared everywhere. Taking over these houses, now being offered at rock-bottom prices, were people from deeper within the city who were fleeing the urban decay and political malfeasance erupting all around the factories and industrial wastelands that now spread through the city. These new residents, familiar with a certain lifestyle prevalent in their old neighborhoods, brought with them ways not in tune with our pride and strong, self-sustaining work ethics.

Members of a biker gang moved in down the street, followed by an element that was equally criminal. Stabbings, beatings, robberies, and neighborhood neglect fell upon us in a manner that was instantaneous and surreal. There was suddenly a feeling that life in the city had become a battleground where anything was fair game and that the concept of hard work no longer mattered. Life on the street suddenly became a free-for-all, snatch-and-grab, frantic blowout. I began to feel like an unwelcome guest in the neighborhood I grew up in, helped nurture, and cared for from the time I could remember. I began to feel like an outcast within a city of outcasts while attempting to deal with a family life that had now spun completely out of control. The confusion in my head increased, sending me to the edge of sanity time and again as I attempted to grasp the concept that our old school Italian family was now a minority in a neighborhood that was quickly slipping through our fingers.

Within months, the electrical supply store, wedged in between Andy's Bakery and the East McNichol Sausage Factory, closed its doors forever, followed by the sausage factory itself. The owner of the factory, an elderly Polish man who lived above the establishment with his wife, was stabbed in the alley behind our garage and suffered wounds that he never quite recovered from. The factory was gone shortly thereafter, and with its passing came the true downfall of the neighborhood. I would never have one of those tasty sausages ever again.

The Ramona Theater was torn down, only to be replaced by a parking lot. The hardware store closed and the cobbler shop, owned by an old German man, simply disappeared, as did several other businesses. The streets became dark, scary places to be; that old-world feeling of our neighborhood was gone. Being a confused fifteen-year-old young man, there was no way I could grasp what was happening, and simply accepted this change for what it was: the end of life as we knew it.

I felt as if the walls had come crashing down, that the foundation of the neighborhood was destroyed, and the familiar faces of those we knew and trusted relegated to the ancient pages of history. It felt as it the city had been given a knockout blow that was impossible to bounce back from, and in reality, that is exactly what happened. From the summer of 1980 onward, Detroit began a long, tortuous downward spiral into urban decay, unprecedented in the history of the nation, never to rise again amidst the greed, corruption, and political tomfoolery that now characterized Detroit. And my family and I were in the heart of it. We could not escape it.

In light of this, I sallied forth like the Detroiter I was, fighting on—just like everyone else I knew, including my family. As fall time approached and the new school year dawned, another event came to fruition: that of being a member of the Servite High junior varsity football team.

The man I'd encountered in the halls of Servite who had inquired if I was a football player was Mr. Jim Hanson, the 26-year-old varsity football coach. Mr. Hanson was an intense, fiery man who loved the sport of football and coached his kids as if it were life itself. Being a member of the J. V. team kept me in close contact with Mr. Hanson, as my coach, Mr. Jim Bangor, was his protégé. Our training rituals were an exact replica of the varsity squad's, and put us in close contact with Mr. Hanson on a daily basis.

In fact, on occasion, the J. V. squad would scrimmage against the varsity as a part of the training regimen. Now, the one thing you need to understand about this situation is that by the time I arrived at Servite High, the school—just like the city—was on a fast track towards doom. By the late 1980s, Servite, like so many other schools in the city, would close its doors for good. With this in mind, the 1981 senior class was the last class that flourished, blessed with a strong school spirit unmatched by subsequent classes. My brother Michael was a part of this phenomenon as a member of the varsity squad. His team would be the last great team Servite would field, loaded with talent from top to bottom.

One day at practice, we were informed that our J. V. squad was to scrimmage the varsity team, news that made us all cringe. Another aspect of the situation was the fact that the J. V. team lacked potent talent of any kind. In fact, we had less than twenty guys on the team, and I was one of the biggest kids on it. We were a weak squad. Having to face this powerful varsity team simply meant we were to become nothing more than a punching bag for juniors and seniors who were ready to have us for lunch. With no way out, we strapped on our helmets and accepted our fate.

As we lined up on offense, the boys of the J. V. team and I looked across the field at a bunch of hungry, crazed maniacs who were moments away from knocking our heads off. Gathering in the huddle, Coach Bangor gave us our play when suddenly, Coach Hanson entered the circle.

"Coach Bangor," he began in a greedy tone, "run a fullback isolation on our linebackers. I want to test our defense."

My heart sank. I was the fullback, and a strong, nasty cat named John Brenneman—a monster football player known to ingest cocaine during games—was the varsity linebacker I was now set to oppose. As we broke the huddle and I got in to my stance, Coach Hanson spoke up once again. Calling across to Brenneman, the man left nothing to the imagination.

"Brenneman, Acquaviva's coming straight for you!"

Again, I about soiled my shorts. Not only was it my responsibility to take out this coked-up maniac (who, not incidentally, would become All State that year), but now he knew that I was coming straight for him. When the ball snapped, the line opened like the Red Sea to expose Brenneman, who ran directly at me with the power of a locomotive. Running as fast as I could, I lowered my head and made full contact. I might as well have been running into a brick wall. *Kapow!!*

I remember a flash, like a lightning bolt, and a sudden loss of hearing. There was a feeling that I had just lost contact with my body as everything went numb. I remember seeing clouds; puffy, grey clouds that crowded my vision, and a feeling that I was floating. When I began to once again gather in my surroundings, I saw Coach Bangor standing in front of me as he grasped my shoulders and looked me dead in the eye. I was still on my feet. Brenneman had not knocked me down. A small victory for the price I paid.

"I think we better get you to the hospital," I heard Coach Bangor say on the fringes of comprehension. "I think you have a concussion."

This would be the first of several concussions I would suffer throughout my life and this would be an ominous start to the J. V. football season of 1980. I do believe that our undersized, under-manned team of misfits lost every game that year, while the varsity squad went 8-2 and became the pride of the east side. As I would move on with my football experience at Servite High, I would come to see the true nature of Coach Hanson, as the following year, my junior year, he would be my coach and bring with him even more pain and confusion that I never knew existed.

In the fall of 1980, as my sophomore football fiasco was unfolding, something else happened. Upon walking through the doors on that first day of classes, I saw, to my utter surprise, my Dark Haired Eighth Grade Angel walking the halls of my school. She was now there with me and I was suddenly struck blind with fear and all-encompassing shyness. I couldn't believe my eyes and began to put into action the plan to make her mine.

Also during this time, my lifelong fascination with all things military and martial had become altered as well. I had recently become engrossed in the history of World War I, that brutal European struggle known as The Great War and The War to End All Wars. Reading about the carnage was horrific and terrifying, and began to alter my view of the world. I had, like a knucklehead, been considering making the military my chosen profession at this time, once I finished high school, and felt that in some way it was my destiny to become a military man who would die honorably upon the field of battle. All that changed, however, and changed in a monumental way, in the fall of 1980.

I was having a hard time finding books dedicated to the history of World War I, other than encyclopedias, so my history teacher, Mr. Rolland, suggested that I go to the library and check out two of his favorite books on the subject. The books, "Johnny Got His Gun" by Dalton Trumbo, and "All Quiet on the Western Front" by Erich Maria Remarque, instantly knocked some sense into my head pertaining to the killing, maiming, and destroying of other people simply because one was told to do so. Upon reading them, I would never look upon the military in the same light ever again.

Both of these books were brutal, uncompromising views of warfare that brought the true nature of man to life in a manner that sent my head spinning. Both books showed me that the men who fight and die on the battlefields of the world are never the ones who start these wars, never propagate them, and never solicit them. The men who fight and die are merely pawns in some twisted, global chess match designed to make the few at the top even richer while those at the bottom carry out these policies simply because they were ordered to do so.

I had been hearing the adage "Rich Man's War, Poor Man's Fight" all my life, and now, I began to understand what that statement meant. I had been groomed to be the perfect military killing machine, being born and bred in a city that was ground zero for the grunts who fought and died in wars since the early 1800s, and was on the path to follow blindly in my ancestors' footsteps. But now, my views had changed. Reading those two books had my head reeling in disillusionment.

I can clearly remember sitting on my bed absorbing the horrific tales of carnage being heaped upon young men who could have cared less about the reasons for war but who died in them just the same. None of it made any sense, and none of it remained appealing to me once I finished reading. I was suddenly a young man who would die to preserve peace rather than kill others simply because I was told to do as much. I would never again consider a life in the military in the same light, and I would never view the ways of the world in the same way. Thank God for books and reading, man, for without them we'd all be fucked. And that is exactly why the military gets them when they're young, so they can brainwash them into becoming machines of death well before they have the sense to figure out that what they are doing is horribly wrong and goes against the doctrines of Christianity in every possible way. But life just isn't fair now, is it?

DECEMBER 19, 1980

The power of music, the freedom of expression, the pursuit of dreams at all cost. Where does this muse come from? Where does this gift from the gods originate? Is it inward? Is it outward? Is it simply ourselves, or is it a combination of self and some power not for us to comprehend? In the winter of 1980, these were the questions I unknowingly pondered, and these were the questions that became the foundation for my life from that point forward. It was a foundation constructed on breaking free from all that caused immobility and fear. It was now time to shed my demons and come face-to-face with who I wanted to become, for better or for worse, as the world came more into view.

It was now time to become a man.

December 19, 1980 was a glorious, sunny winter's day and Servite High was alive with energy. You see, December 19 was the last day of school before Christmas break, and the kids were crazy with excitement and giddy with the welcoming call of freedom. My final class for the day was Mr. Lemay's religion class, an experience akin to a single man attempting to block out the sun. I remember Mr. Lemay sitting on the edge of his desk with no intention of subduing us; he simply spent the hour asking us to share with him the hopes and dreams that we had for the Christmas season, all the while playing his guitar and serenading us with songs. A smart man was he.

I, on the other hand, was discombobulated for another reason. Over the previous few weeks, I had let every opportunity to talk to my Dark Haired Angel slip through my fingers. I had given in to my fears and allowed my shyness to get the better of me. I felt as if I had lost the battle to become a man. And now, here it was, D-Day, the Hour of Reckoning, the dreaded "do or die" hour. If I did not seize this moment it would be one long, tortuous holiday break, and my Dark Haired Angel would be gone forever. I figured that if I didn't make the move now, I never would. Zero Hour was at hand and I had to either stand up and be counted, or allow the girl of my dreams to fade into the fleeting memories of days gone by. As I sat at my desk, the energy of the classroom swirled about me like a tempest and the image of my Dark Haired Angel danced in my mind, hovering before me like a phantom.

Then it happened. The class bell rang and every kid in the room sprinted for the door. I remember slowly standing up on wavering legs, barely able to maintain my balance. I remember Mr. Lemay bidding me a great holiday as I looked to the clock above the door. It was 1:10 P. M. and I could barely move forward, hounded by the ghosts of indecision. I mumbled something to Mr. Lemay, walked through the door and looked to my right. And there she was, my beautiful Dark Haired Angel, down the hall and standing at her locker. She was adorned in a white blouse, grey Catholic schoolgirl skirt and white, knee-high socks. I was stopped dead in my tracks. She was absolutely glorious.

Then something amazing happened; I began moving towards her. It felt like I was floating, being drawn to her as if a magnet to metal. I felt that it was beyond my control, as if I had no say in the matter. From the moment I saw her, I knew that I would spend the rest of my life with her. Our connection was that strong. Then suddenly, I was upon her, standing next to her as she turned and raised those gorgeous green eyes to mine and smiled a beautiful smile. I became lost in those pools of light and swallowed hard. There was no turning back now.

It's funny how memories become solidified and constructed in a way that best serve our own wishes and desires. It's as if, in order to maintain our sanity, memories shield us from our own inadequacies and inner pain. Such was the case on December 19th, 1980, for my memories of that day are far from what my Dark Haired Angel remembers. I recall standing before her and becoming consumed with all things manly and macho. I remember flipping my shirt collar up, slipping into a relaxed posture that defined "cool" and nodding my head while chomping on my gum like Marlon Brando in "The Wild One." I remember smoothing out my eyebrows with my thumb, looking deep into her eyes and saying in a street-wise, ultra-smooth tone; "You...me...now. Let's go." I remember her swooning, letting out a breathy sigh and falling into my arms as I laid a big, wet one on her quivering lips. I remember embodying the definition of smooth and debonair. And I remember overcoming my shyness and insecurities and blossoming into Errol Flynn right there on the spot. I remember becoming a man. My, how memories can deceive us.

The reality of the situation, according to my Dark Haired Angel, was far different from what I remember. According to her, I stood before her like a lost, little boy who barely had the courage to ask, "You got a name?" while looking as uncomfortable as a calf in a slaughterhouse. She remembers that I asked if she was going to attend the basketball game that night, a game in which I was schedule to start. She remembers both of us being overcome with shyness and insecurities. And she also remembers me fidgeting about like a child while inquiring if it would be ok if I called her later.

Regardless of how it happened, I finally did break through my shyness to meet my Dark Haired Angel, and as it turned out, we would have the remainder of my days at Servite High to relive that day and tell tall tales about how we met. My Dark Haired Angel, Miss Andrea Marie Saylor, would be by my side for the next two years and would explore the ways of love and romance with me in ways that, to this day, make my head swoon.

Andrea and I instantly fell in love and submerged ourselves into each other from the moment we began hanging out. And boy, did we have fun. Our time together would be one long excursion into passion and playfulness. I would spend nearly every minute of my free time with my Dark Haired Angel. Those days with Andrea were incredible. I soon found that spending time with her silenced the confusion in my head like nothing I had ever encountered, and the way Andrea did this, the way she brought my fears to a silent end, was simply by loving me, and loving me in a purely natural way, and nothing more.

Being a young man of few words, my time with Andrea would be spent looking deep into each other's eyes, loving one another for long, passionate stretches of time and laying in each other's arms until it was time to go home. Andrea's family, to my delight, accepted me as one of their own, and time spent at her house was a journey into security and nurturing. Andrea's family had their issues as well, but the contrasts to my family were extreme. Despite any problems they might have had, I always felt that Andrea's family truly cared for one another and enjoyed being around each other. A far cry from my family. I loved spending time in their little box of a house; it was smaller than ours, and housed seven people. But there I felt safe, comfortable, and an undeniable sense that I could be myself once I walked through the door. And as long as I didn't act the fool, I could do as I pleased. A truly refreshing reality. Knowing Andrea and her family was one of the happiest periods of my life up to that point.

Early in 1981, Coach Bangor pulled some strings and found a position for me at The Colonel's Restaurant on Mack Avenue, a mile or so north of Andrea's house. My home on Goulburn Avenue was three miles from Servite and three and a half from Andrea's, making The Colonel's a full four miles, or more, from home. Back then I either walked or ran everywhere I went. Traveling the streets between school, Andrea's and The Colonel's—regardless of the weather—consumed much of my time over the next two years. Despite some moments of fearing for my life, I loved every second of it.

The Colonel's Restaurant was an interesting place to work. Being more in tune with people from Bishop Gallagher than Servite, I kept my mouth shut and realized that if I worked hard I'd make a decent living, especially for a fifteen-year-old kid. And that is exactly what I did. I worked hard and made cash. I would grow to love my time at The Colonel's. The environment was perfect for my state of mind.

In January of 1981, I began training for my first year as a varsity football player at Servite High. Even though I was still a sophomore, my fellow J. V. teammates and I began workouts for our junior year football campaign that winter. Those training rituals would become some of the most strenuous I ever encountered and prepared me for what lay ahead in life. They were not for the weak minded.

Waking before the crack of dawn, I'd dress and make the three-mile walk to Servite through the worst weather Detroit had to offer, passing by the bums and early morning drinkers who stood on frozen street corners looking for handouts. Upon arrival, my teammates and I would make our way to "The Dungeon," the basement level of Servite, where we would begin our training regimen.

As I said, Servite High was constructed in 1946, and by the early 1980s began to suffer from old age. Money was tight, and upkeep of the school not a priority. The workout room, lockers, and shower area were in the dark, damp basement level of the school, and featured no windows, no ventilation, and bad lighting. It felt like we were in a freaking cave.

The first thing we'd do upon our arrival was turn the showers on full blast in preparation for when we finished our workout. Inevitably, by the time we got to the showers, cold water would still be pouring out of the showerheads as the heating system, just like the school, had seen better days. Standing under a cold shower deep within The Dungeon on a brutally frigid day in January was truly a test of our manhood, but became a challenge one had to endure. (After all, I had to be fresh and clean for my Dark Haired Angel didn't I?)

Now, the training rituals were nothing short of ridiculous, as Coach Hanson now had us in his hungry sights. He knew that the best team he would ever field in his short tenure at Servite was out the doors come springtime, and that the current ragtag group of misfits and knuckle-heads was his only shot at glory. He had to whip us into shape.

To put it bluntly, our weight room was a shitbox. Twenty of us kids would surround the single weight machine, consisting of a bench press, squat machine, leg press, chin-up bar, and dip bar. We'd rotate around the machine continuously as Coach Hanson barked out orders and encouraged our development. He'd give stirring speeches and spew insightful sentiments designed to build our confidence, often referring to us as "niggers and rednecks" who "couldn't carry his sister's jockstrap."

Following an hour or so in the weight room, we'd stumble up to the gym for a cardio workout, which consisted of endless wind sprints until we reached the cusp of vomiting.

"You're all a bunch of pussies! My mother's got more balls than you do, you pansies!!" Coach Hanson would cry.

I'm telling you now, the cat had a way with words.

Following the workouts and a nice, refreshing shower, I'd begin my day by cleaning and sweeping the boys and girls locker rooms, bathrooms, hallways, and lunchroom, all in the basement level of the school. I did this as a way of helping to pay for my tuition. Now, somewhere along the line and during this period, Coach Hanson would spend quality "alone" time with me while encouraging me to become a better young man.

We would load into his car, where I'd sit in the passenger seat as Coach Hanson drove around the neighborhoods surrounding Servite. In his inspiring manner, Coach Hanson would then serenade me with his words of encouragement.

"Acquaviva," he'd begin while looking at me with disdain, "you're one of the biggest pussies I've ever met. You've got no balls and you'll never amount to anything. I know little girls who are tougher than you are. And that girlfriend of yours, you don't deserve her. She needs a real man and you're not him. How you're going to make it through life is beyond me because to be a man you need balls, character, and intelligence, three things you lack in spades. You're gutless, worthless, and weak. My six-month-old son has got more heart than you'll ever have and how you're going to...blah, blah, blah..." And on and on he'd go until we finally arrived back at school.

This scene unfolded more times than I care to remember throughout the remainder of my sophomore year and straight through my junior year, as Coach Hanson enlightened me on my many strong attributes. Like the dutiful kid I was, I'd sit next to him and take his bullshit in silence. I was still in the state of mind that you never back talk your elders, especially coaches, and it never once crossed my mind to retaliate. And I'm here to tell you that his gentle words of praise were nothing short of confounding, only adding to my feelings of confusion, self-doubt, and worthlessness. At the time, I was thoroughly convinced that my mother had gone to Coach Hanson and told him that I was in need of strong, male influence, and that this was his way of approaching the matter. However, when I asked her about it many years later, my mother told me that she had never once talked to the man. Coach Hanson had done this all on his own...a tidbit of information that has confused me even more.

The Colonel's Restaurant was owned by the family of the coked-out linebacker who presented me with my first concussion, John Brenneman. The Brenneman's boasted some ten children, all older than me, and most of whom worked at the restaurant. I believe that there were six boys and four girls in the Brenneman clan, and all the boys were former or current football players who were nothing short of intimidating.

One night, shortly after beginning my employment working as a dishwasher, one of the Brenneman boys—a strapping lad in his 30's with a mustachioed, chiseled face, and equally powerful disposition—introduced himself to me. Being the quiet, shy kid I was, I must have crossed a line and acted out of turn in some way, because walking behind the bar with a tray of clean glasses this guy stepped right in front of me and said hello.

"You better lose that fucking attitude, motherfucker," he began, staring me down. "I'll fucking knock your teeth out, you fucking cocksucker. What, you think you're a tough guy? I'll show you who's tough, bitch. Keep up with that attitude and see where it gets you."

In all honesty, I had no idea what I had done to provoke such frightening actions—but believe me, from that point forward I walked around that place with a permanent smile plastered on my face. I needed no more encouragement to do so. Growing up in Detroit, it seemed like every time I turned around, someone was there to remind me that I needed my ass kicked. It was a phenomenon that left me perpetually confused.

Now, despite this episode, I slipped into a nice, easy rhythm at The Colonel's, soon becoming a pizza chef of the highest degree, almost running the pizza kitchen by myself. The restaurant offered seafood, steaks, prime rib, and burgers, and had a full bar as well. There was a second kitchen that produced some of the best old-world pie I've ever had. Even in a city loaded with old-school Italian pizzerias, The Colonel's was some of the best. I quickly came to all but control that kitchen.

The Brenneman's, and Pops himself, knew how to have a good time, and as I became a more trusted employee in their family, I also began to be exposed to their partying ways. Drinking during and after shifts was common, and other extracurricular activities opened my eyes to a whole new world, as some of the Brenneman boys sold cocaine out of the basement of the restaurant. I would spend many a late night in that basement or at one of the Brenneman's houses, playing poker and partying until the wee hours, having my first exposure to the world of booze and drugs. Those were fun times.

Playing poker during the summer of 1981 became a regular routine, for not only did I spend time at The Colonel's exploring this world, but at home as well. During that summer, my brother Michael and several of his friends played poker several times a week, and I found myself involved in these escapades more than I cared. That summer I lost more than $300 to poker, a large sum for a fifteen-year-old kid back in those days. The summer of 1981 proved to me that I was not a gambler, and rare was the time following that I have involved myself in that world — something that continues to this day. I learned my lesson, and realized early on that you can never beat the house, no matter how good you are, and to try is a fool's game.

One night, following a long shift at The Colonel's, I closed the restaurant down and began my walk home nearing 2 A. M. Feeling especially tired on this night, I decided to treat myself to a reprieve and take a city bus to alleviate the pain of walking. My ride approached within a matter of minutes. When the bus pulled in front of me, the doors opened and I stepped aboard. Immediately, I realized why I had rarely taken city busses throughout my life.

When I looked to the back of the bus, the only other passengers aboard were five or six young black males who thought they had just died and gone to heaven. Electing to take a seat directly behind the driver, an older black man, I prepared for the worst as the bus pulled off. Immediately, my new friends introduced themselves to me.

"Hey mothafucka, what you doin on our bus, bitch?" One of the fellows inquired. "This ain't your bus mothafucka, this is our bus. What you doin' on our bus, you white bitch?"

I hit the stop bell and looked to the driver's rearview mirror only to see the man staring straight ahead and not acknowledging me. He was as scared as I was. Now making their way to the front of the bus, my new pals continued with their greetings.

"What you gonna do, you white mothafucka?" they called, inching their way closer. "You got the balls to roll with us, bitch? Bring it on, mothafucka, bring it on!"

No, I did not possess the balls to roll with a gang of angry, bitter street toughs who were seconds away from ripping me limb from limb. Instead, I leaned forward and pleaded my case to the driver.

"Um, sir," I whispered into his ear. "Could you possibly pull over right now and drop me off before these boys kill me? Um, do you think we could do that…like…now?!"

Fortunately, the driver pulled over and, in silence, opened the door. I shot out of that bus quicker than you can say "Honkey Lips" as the gang of boys threw random items at me and laughed and howled like a pack of hungry wolves. Slipping into the shadows, I waited for the bus to pull away and resumed my walk home. I would never ride a Detroit city bus ever again.

This episode was just one example of the difficulties I faced on my nightly transit; those long, tortuous walks home became an ever-increasing challenge as Detroit slipped further into chaos. Relying upon my self-imposed military training as a child, I'd duck behind parked cars at the sight of trouble of any kind, or hide in the shadows as slow moving vehicles crept by, loaded with young men looking for fresh meat to pummel into submission. I'd run for long stretches at a time until seeing headlights in the distance, then I'd dip behind trashcans and wait until the car cruised by; only after they were out of sight would I resume my journey home. I soon became a master of stealthy travel by night, relying upon my wits, stamina, and vision to make it home safely every single time. And, as it would turn out, these experiences would become invaluable the further I grew into manhood.

Summer of 1981 was a blast, spending days with my Dark Haired Angel, going on day trips to local lakes and beaches, engaging in picnics and endless hours of youthful passion. At night, I worked as a pizza chef and rocked out with the crew at The Colonel's. On nights I didn't have to work, Andrea and I would go to concerts and restaurants, exploring her neighborhood—a neighborhood that was yet untouched by the mass exodus of Detroit's unemployed.

Drive-in movies were another favorite pastime, and I doubt that

Andrea ever saw a single film, as she was occupied with entertainment of a different sort. Those days and nights were filled to the brim with fun, passion and exploration of every kind; they gave me a true sense of comfort and acceptance that I had never experienced before. I would always be appreciative of my time with Andrea, my Baby, my Kitten, my Pumpkin, my Love Cub, during this period of my life, for it would prove to me that love and acceptance were real, and available to anyone with the constitution to bring them to fruition. Andrea showed me light in a bleak world, and I'm here to tell you that I held on to it as powerfully as I could for as long as I could, for the remainder of my days at Servite.

THE 1981 FOOTBALL SEASON

As the golden days of summer once again gave way to autumn—my favorite time of year—the mighty Panthers of Servite High began fall practices for the 1981 football campaign. Gathering at the school even before fall classes began, we got to work. As I've mentioned, the training rituals of Coach Hanson were extreme; the twenty or so kids who initially made up the team quickly dwindled in number to about fifteen within the first week, as some kids found the workouts too much to handle.

One of Coach Hanson's favorite tortures was an exercise known as "352s." In order to get our attention, praise us or berate us, Coach Hanson devised an activity that was nothing short of absurd. He mapped out a course on the park we practiced at, and we'd be forced to sprint (yes, I said *sprint*) for 352 yards at full speed with all our gear on, time and again. 352s became a staple of our practice routine and an activity we all grew to despise. Kids would vomit, cramp up, become woozy and fall over in pure exhaustion, as sometimes we'd be forced to endure five, eight, sometimes ten 352s in a row. For many, many years to come, and even to this day, I will see the number 352 everywhere I go — on clocks, billboards, books, license plates, advertisements, magazines, and in numerous other forms — and it's as if the ghost of Coach Hanson is still relentlessly hounding me.

Another favorite of the coach's practice regimen was taking us to Jefferson Avenue in St. Claire Shores, home of Detroit's rich and prosperous, where he'd run us for hours at a time in front of the local residents. As pampered young girls in their Mercedes-Benzes and Audis rolled by, we'd be sucking wind and gasping for air, our bodies whimpering under the endless torture. And of course, Coach Hanson let us know exactly what he thought of us, announcing to the world that he had a crew of pretty young girls as his football team, a crew that couldn't find a single pair of balls among them, and were as useless as his son's dirty diapers. The weakest of the team simply stopped showing up for practice and threw in the towel rather than be subjected to Coach Hanson's ways.

In fact, the starting quarterback quit the team and walked away after only three practices, leaving us in a precarious situation. Suddenly, we were without a leader. Looking at the group of guys left standing, Coach Hanson threw me the ball and said that I was now the starting quarterback for the Servite Panthers — a position I knew nothing about, and cared for even less.

Quarterbacks were pretty boys who didn't like to mix it up with the guys. They were glory-seeking prima donnas and crybabies who walked around with sunglasses clinging to their pretty faces and bubble-headed bleach-blondes under their arms. I was blue collar, lived in the trenches, and worked for a living. And perhaps more troubling, I had absolutely no experience playing the position of quarterback.

Expressing my concerns, I approached Coach Hanson shortly after hearing the news. "Coach," I began, "I think you have the wrong guy. I'm a defensive end and fullback. I can't be quarterback."

"Oh yes you can," Coach Hanson countered. "Besides, you're the only one left with half a brain. You're now the starting quarterback."

Suddenly, with only three weeks remaining until the first game, I was the number one guy for the job. In short order, I had to first learn how to properly throw a ball, and then attempt to master a position that some guys spend their entire lives perfecting. I needed time...but Coach Hanson was not what one would call a "patient man." I quickly learned an entirely new language I never knew existed, hearing cuss words and degradations of the most colorful kind, as Coach Hanson gave me all the encouragement I needed to forge ahead.

"God-dammit, Acquaviva, you're one of the most worthless, pussified, ball-less, shit-eatin' faggot rednecks I have ever known!" he'd cry in frustration while whipping a ball at my head.

As opening day approached, my anxiety levels reached new heights; I looked to my teammates and wondered if I'd even survive the season. Of the fifteen guys left on the squad, I was among the biggest. Most of the guys assigned to protect me were small in stature and appeared to be no bigger than most freshmen. To top it off, I had not even come close to mastering my position, and was as clueless as a landlocked sailor when it came to navigating my team through troubling waters. It was going to be one long, brutal season, but I was simply too proud to quit. So I strapped on my helmet, hoping for the best while preparing for the worst.

And the worst is what I got.

I will always remember opening day of the 1981 season for as long as I live, and in reality, I'd have a hard time shaking it from my memory even if I tried. We were playing Dearborn Divine Child, a school from Detroit's outer suburbs, on a classic fall afternoon with bright, sunny skies. As both teams lined up on their respective sidelines, I looked out across the gridiron to size up our opponent. Divine Child fielded a team of some sixty-plus guys who stretched across the full length of the sideline. The biggest guys were in the middle of a line that tapered off to the smallest at the ends. Their J. V. team could have beaten the shit out of us. The guys on the ends of that line were bigger than most of my teammates.

Looking to either side of me, I saw seven guys to the left and seven to the right, all looking scraggly, unkempt and painfully undersized. It wasn't that we lacked the heart or desire to be a good team—we were some of the toughest hombres you'd ever want to meet. It was simply the fact that we didn't possess the same talent, size, or mechanics that most teams had on their J. V. squads. To the one side of me were the likes of Tony Collins, a cat with a heart as big as Texas but who had about as much focus as a special ed kid at gym time. To the other side was Jimmy Black, a skinny little guy who loved to play, but appeared as a child lost in a man's game, with his jersey sticking halfway out of his pants and his helmet forever askew. I hung my head and let out a long, agonizing sigh as game time arrived. When the game finally began, so did the fiasco of the 1981 football campaign.

I fumbled the opening snap, only to have Coach Hanson unleash one long explosion of expletives, which rang in my ears for the entire game. When I finally did complete a pass, I was so excited that my teammates had to corral me—they needed to get me back into the huddle so that I could call the next play before being penalized for delay of game…which, of course, happened.

"God dammit, Acquaviva, get your fucking head out of your ass, son!" Coach Hanson cried, exposing me to a sentiment that I would hear all season long.

I believe we lost that opening game 56-7, our lone touchdown coming late in the game on a kick return against freshman replacements.

There was a night game played in some of the most brutal weather I have ever encountered: freezing, gusty winds that blew stinging snow in our faces as we negotiated a field and ball that were as hard as concrete. There was a fiasco at Orchard Lake St. Mary's, way out in the suburbs, and the only game my grandparents on my mother's side ever attended. We lost 70-6. Homecoming was an even bigger disappointment for Coach Hanson, losing in a monumental way and not even crossing the 50-yard line until late in the third quarter. Every outing was a mess as I fumbled, bungled, and stumbled my way through game after game, desperately attempting to become a quarterback in the line of fire. The whole thing was pathetic, if not absolutely hilarious. But the coupe-de-grace of the season, without a doubt, was the De Porres game of late September, 1981.

De Porres was an all-black school on Detroit's west side and smack-dab in the heart of some of the worst neighborhoods the city had to offer. Traveling to their field was bad enough, but once we got off the bus we were overcome with a feeling that we were now taking our lives into our own hands. De Porres' home field was some random park out in the middle of an even more random neighborhood, consisting of run-down houses and sketchy businesses that butted up against it. Upon our arrival, local residents emerged from their homes, with coolers and lawn chairs in hand, to root for the local team. There was an overpowering sensation that they knew something we didn't.

We wouldn't have to wait long to find out what that was.

As our team of stooges began its warm-up routine, Coach Bangor, who was now assistant coach for the varsity squad, encouraged us with strong words designed to inspire our courage.

"Ok, boys!" He cried while walking among us. "You've got this one! Let's take it to 'em and give 'em hell!!"

It was then that our opponent showed up for the big game. As they filed off the bus I couldn't believe what I was seeing, and when Coach Bangor lowered his head and mumbled something about playing "ringers," all I could do was lower my own head. These were not high school kids coming to play a simple game of football against the Servite Panthers. These were grown men recruited off the street to make our experience on the west side one we'd never forget. They walked right through our warm-up lines, laughing and snickering, as they looked down at us and let us know exactly what they were going to do once the game began. "We're gonna fuck you up, mothafuckas," and "You're in for a long day, bitches," were just some of the sentiments I heard as they walked through our shabby lines.

Some of these guys were so big that their uniforms didn't fit properly. Some had full beards and mustaches, and enormous frames that were layered with muscles. I guarantee you that their coach went out into the neighborhood and convinced a group of nineteen- and twenty-year-old gang bangers to fill out his team. I could even hear the recruiting speech he gave ringing in my head: "Hey, boys, want to have some fun this afternoon? I'll pay you each $50 to play for me and show these chumps from the east side how we do it on the west side! Come on, boys, let's have a gay old time and knock some heads into oblivion!"

It was that day which proved to me that the recruiting practices at the college level are as crooked as a politician in a New Orleans whorehouse. We lost the De Porres game the moment those ringers piled off the bus. When the game finally did start it was a descent into pain unlike any other I had experienced on a football field. It was a freaking joke from the opening kickoff.

Trying to stop those guys when they were on offense was futile as grown men slammed through our lines like Panzer tanks. They ran the ball to the left, threw to the right, and sent their 6'1", 200 pound tailback right up the middle for 30-yard gains every time he touched the ball. Their wide-outs were bigger than our interior line. Their quarterback was some goon who told *us* exactly where he was going once the ball was snapped, then ran right over us while following linemen who were big enough to start for the University of Michigan. When we finally did get to play offense, things only got worse. Leaning over my center, Jerry McAlister, I could clearly hear those De Porres boys...and they were having a ball.

"Gonna rip your fucking head off, number 20!" they'd call to me.

"Better say your prayers, bitch, 'cause you're about to meet your maker!"

They weren't exaggerating. On the snap of the ball, I'd drop back to pass, only to have four to six guys sandwich me in a group tackle that exposed me to an entirely new realm of pain. Getting to my feet, Coach Hanson let me know just how much of a little girl I was. And when I staggered back to the huddle, I would try to encourage my teammates.

"Come on, guys, I'm getting my fucking ass kicked back here, man! Slow the motherfuckers down before they kill me!!"

"Are you kidding, Larry? Did you get a good look at those guys? They're fucking huge, man!"

"I have been looking at them, man, every time they drive me into the ground like I'm a fucking stake and they're the hammer! Dammit, man, block the motherfuckers!"

And so it went...for four excruciatingly long quarters. Getting back into the huddle, I'd have to smack Jerry in the helmet to loosen the cobwebs from his head, and he'd have to do the same for me. Tony would be so out of whack that I'd have to call to him just to get him back to the huddle.

"Tony, the huddle's over here, man!"

Skinny little Jimmy Black would be so discombobulated that he'd keep asking, "Is the game over yet? Is the game over yet? I thought I heard the whistle..." as I pointed the way back to his team.

"The whistle is in your head, Jimmy. Don't worry, man, it's almost over," I'd lie.

One time, as soon as the ball was snapped, four guys leaped right over my offensive line to sack me, even before I took a single step. Another time, after getting the snap cleanly, I dropped back to pass only to have half the defense in my face. Without looking, and to save my own life, I simply threw the ball away, not caring where it landed, as I crumbled beneath the weight of the entire defensive line. Of course, the ball was intercepted and run back for a touchdown, something that did not get past my coaches. Coach Hanson let me know *exactly* how he felt about that play.

When the game finally came to an end, I had been sacked more than fifteen times, threw at least five interceptions, and fumbled three more. To this day, I have never known the final score and don't ever care to. Enough was enough.

Sometimes it's best just to let certain things slip into the dustbin of history.

The 1981 Servite High football campaign ended in a 2-8 record. How we managed to win those two games is a minor miracle and was, on some level, a victory in itself. The fact that we managed to keep our shit together long enough to win those two games is a testament to our sense of pride, forged far away from the degradation of the experience. As I would continue on with my relationship with Coach Hanson, I'd begin to sour on organized sports altogether, only continuing because I loved the camaraderie, the training, and the competition that the experiences brought. Nothing more.

In the summer of 1981, my mother finally remarried. After several years of playing the field and searching for a man she truly loved, she accepted the proposal of Mr. Rob Taylor. Rob — "Mr. Rob," as we affectionately referred to him — grew up outside of Philadelphia, was well educated, book smart, sweet, and incredibly gentle. He respected our mother, loved her dearly, and treated her well. In short, Mr. Rob was everything our mother needed.

Mr. Rob was trained as a journalist, and had spent several years in the Baltimore area writing for a living. Shortly after their marriage, I began hearing rumors that my mother and Mr. Rob were thinking of relocating to the vicinity of Baltimore to start anew. And in the winter of 1982, those rumors were now becoming a reality. Back in the spring, and utilizing the connections that Mr. Rob still had to the area, both he and my mother were going to move to Annapolis, Maryland and accept jobs as writers for The Washington Times newspaper in Washington, D. C. With this move, my life would change.

My mother strongly urged that I make the move, and looking at the state of affairs of not only the city but at Servite as well, I decided to accept the offer. I could have stayed had I really wanted, but I also knew that it was best to leave the city. It was one of the hardest decisions I ever had to make...but one I knew I had to accept.

And the reason the decision was so difficult was, of course, because of Andrea. I would have to leave my Dark Haired Angel behind. The pain I felt was untouchable, and would always linger in my heart as I forged ahead in time. It was a tough decision, but one I knew I had to endure if I was going to have any chance at becoming my own man.

Andrea and I loved each other so much that if I had stayed, our romance would have been doomed. In Detroit, my options would have been limited. Odds are, we would have fallen into the same pattern as my parents had: getting married following graduation, cranking out a litter of kids, and settling into a life of unfulfilled dreams and endless disappointments. I would have found a job in a factory or machine shop somewhere, hated what my life had become, and taken out my frustrations on Andrea and our children.

Even at age sixteen, I knew that my only shot at success was to leave the dying city behind and make the move to Annapolis. Even at that age, I knew that I had a restless soul, one that was destined to search for meaning in life, and that I would not have found the answers I needed in Detroit. To have stayed would have been unfair to not only Andrea but to me as well. As spring approached, I broke the news to my Dark Haired Angel and informed her of the move. It was a bad time for both of us.

The plan was to finish out the year at Servite, then help Mom, Mr. Rob, and Katherine move to Annapolis. I'd spend the summer with Michael and Paul in the old house on Goulburn Avenue, making the move myself in late August. That summer would be one of the most bittersweet periods of my life. I knew that I had been given a rare opportunity to better my life, but I also knew that I was leaving the girl of my dreams behind in the process. I felt as if my heart was being ripped in two; but I also knew that if Andrea and I were to have any chance of a lasting relationship, I would have to make the move—and make it now. Truth be told, as I write this, those same sickening feelings hounding my soul back then are crowding my heart now, forcing me to relive one of the most painful episodes of my life. I would not wish these feelings upon my worst enemy...they were, and still are, overwhelming and heartbreaking.

Despite this, the summer of 1982 was fun, living in the old house on Goulburn with Michael and Paul, where our life remained no different than when mom was still there. But now we had to pay all the bills while still fending for ourselves, taking responsibility for every aspect of our lives; the only difference now was that mom was more than 500 miles away. I remember even having to do my laundry with an old-timey washboard, since mom had taken the washer and dryer with her to Annapolis.

As those summer days crept on, the sorrow filling our hearts began to overwhelm Andrea and me. It made it difficult to be with one another; as much as I loved her, I knew that our time was limited, and those feelings of pending separation loomed over us like a dark cloud.

As August approached, I remember feeling that I just wanted the pain to simply go away; I was having difficulty dealing with the tears, the lingering self-doubt, and the fear of the unknown. I didn't want to hurt her anymore, and I certainly didn't want to feel the pain crowding my own heart.

I awaited the departure day like a condemned man would his execution date.

That fateful day finally did come, but to be completely honest here, I don't remember much about it. As I had done with so many other episodes in my life, I simply blocked it from my memory. I had spent my entire life at 17129 Goulburn Avenue on Detroit's east side. I had watched firsthand as not only my beloved neighborhood began its descent into chaos, but the entire city of Detroit — the city I loved — slip down the tubes as well. And now, the love of my life, my Dark Haired Angel, the girl I had been dreaming about since I was a small child, would no longer be by my side. The pain had become too much to process. Topping things off was the knowledge that I'd rarely even left the city — and now here I was, staring at a whole new life, knowing not a single soul in this new, alien land, fraught with who-knows-what. I believe that mentally, I simply shut down and refused to accept the pain.

I remember holding on to Andrea and never wanting to let go. I remember the crushing tears, promises of eternal love, and pain too powerful to comprehend. I remember the stinging self-doubt of leaving my Dark Haired Angel behind. It was a feeling of loss that ruptured my heart in ways I could not then fathom, and still cannot to this day. I remember walking away from everything I had ever known and feeling like I was dead inside.

And if I thought I knew what culture shock was at Bishop Gallagher, I was fooling myself in ways too broad to calculate. My new hometown — that of Annapolis, Maryland — would make Bishop Gallagher look like the slums of the west side of Detroit. Annapolis, Maryland, in short order, would show me just how different the world can be, and just how isolated a young man could feel. My life, for better or worse, was truly about to begin.

10. ANNAPOLIS, MARYLAND

MOLLY HAILEY WAS A TALL, BLUE-EYED, BLOND-HAIRED BEAUTY, CLASsically educated, and hailing from a tight-knit, well respected family. She was book smart, ambitious, and aspired to attend college since the day she could remember. She pined for a successful career at a very young age. Her father had graduated from Northwestern University, having met Molly's mother at that same school where she was studying to become a nurse. Molly was groomed for perfection, and given every opportunity needed to thrive.

And Molly Hailey, from the moment I met her, was way, way, way out of my league. She somehow characterized my entire experience in Annapolis: from the moment I arrived, I was in over my head.

If I thought the experience of leaving my Dark Haired Angel behind was difficult, I was fooling myself in ways that I couldn't fully grasp, because writing about my time in Annapolis is downright unsettling. From the moment I walked the streets of the city, I felt like a young man stumbling blindly through a fireworks factory with a blazing torch in his hand. I felt like I'd explode from the feelings of self-doubt bursting inside me. I felt ill-prepared, ignorant, backward, and unworthy. I felt stupid, uncouth, brain-dead and dumb.

I felt defeated.

Annapolis—Maryland's state capitol—sits midway between Washington, D. C and Baltimore, and is home to the United States Naval Academy. The town is filled to the brim with politicians, military brass, Midshipmen, executives, lawyers, and those who have inherited ungodly amounts of money for generations. Annapolis, and Anne Arundel County, is one of the richest regions in the nation, if not the world. And here I was—a simple, hard-working kid from the east side of Detroit—placed smack dab in the middle of one of the ritziest places known to man. I felt as if I had just landed somewhere between Rodeo Drive and Wall Street. I had never felt so out of place, and no matter what I would do, I would never fit in.

The first thing I realized about my new home was that I wanted out from the moment I arrived. Just like Bishop Gallagher, everything was clean, antiseptic, and devoid of diversity. Everyone was white, appeared affluent, and seemed absolutely money-driven. There seemed to be no struggle, no hunger, and not much drive for anything but more riches, more wealth, and higher status. From the moment I set foot in Annapolis, I knew that *this* was *not* what I was looking for in life.

Despite this, I just did as I had always done: threw myself into the situation with everything I had. Once settled, I immediately got to work in my new home.

Now, not only did I feel like an alien in a foreign land, but I suddenly felt that my life was moving at lightning speed. I felt as if I had no firm foundation to stand upon—out of control, lost and uncertain, attempting to absorb this new world while my mind and heart were still stuck on the east side of Detroit. But I also felt that I needed to shed my past and accept my newfound freedom. I knew that despite what I felt in my heart, I had to remove Andrea from my mind and get on with life. And walking through the doors of St. Martin's High School for the first time, that is exactly what I did.

St. Martin's High School, home of the Saints, was located in downtown Annapolis along the shores of Spa Creek, which feeds into the Chesapeake Bay. St. Martin's and Annapolis were in a beautiful area surrounded by enchanting harbors, vast waterways, quaint little shops, fancy boutiques, and ritzy restaurants. Downtown Annapolis had an historic feel to it, being founded as the state capital in 1649, an aspect that immediately appealed to me. There were cobblestone streets and rustic old buildings dating back to the 1600s, giving a visitor the sense that one had just stepped back in time.

Despite my trepidation at stepping through the doors of St. Martin's High School for the first time, I was somewhat put at ease before too long; the kids, regardless of station in life and background, immediately accepted me as one of their own. Looking back on it now, I believe that I was really nothing more than a novelty to these kids, but I accepted their efforts at friendship nonetheless.

St. Martin's, with no more than 500 kids in the entire institution, was a small school and news travelled fast. Shortly after my arrival, I learned that a rumor had been circulating that a kid from Detroit was going to be enrolling as a senior. As my sister Katherine and I walked through the gym on that first day—where the entire school had gathered for orientation—I felt all eyes fall upon us, as if we were the latest science project come to life.

The student body immediately became hushed; I could hear whispered conversation as we walked before the kids. In a strange turn of events, I suddenly felt that everything would be okay, and that my time at St. Martin's would be tolerable on some level, if not completely enjoyable. I realized that these kids were as nervous and excited as I was, another aspect that put me at ease. From that first day of school onward, I threw myself into the culture as deeply as I could.

Now, as I said, no matter what I would do, the harsh, stone-cold truth of the situation was that I would never feel like I truly fit in. I was not one of *them*. These kids were a part of the elite, and although I made quick friends and was accepted as their peer, I had no misconceptions about where my fellow students had come from — nor that it was definitely not the same place *I* had come from. And another truth was that these kids were wild, wide-open, privileged sons and daughters of Annapolis who'd had opportunity handed to them from the day they were born; it was a reality as foreign to me as a page-boy prostitution ring on Capitol Hill.

Unlike Servite, which had less than twenty percent of graduates moving on to college, St. Martin's boasted a ninety-five percent college attendance rate. The school was a college preparatory institution where kids jockeyed to enroll in the likes of Georgetown, Loyola, Johns Hopkins, and Harvard. Being the average student I was, I felt like I had just walked into an Ivy League school myself. Little did I know that things had only begun to get strange...and soon, they would get more than a little uncomfortable.

On one of my first days at St. Martin's, I was walking the halls when, in an eerily similar instance to my time meeting Coach Hanson at Servite, a man walked up to me and introduced himself.

"Hello, son, I'm Coach Moore," he said. "Tell me that you're a lacrosse player."

"No, sir," I replied while shaking his hand. "Football, basketball, and baseball are my sports."

"Well, come springtime you'll be playing lacrosse for me. We don't have a baseball team."

"Lacrosse? What the hell is lacrosse?"

"Come see me in my office after school and I'll show you."

And so began my tenure as a lacrosse player for the St. Martin's Saints of Annapolis, Maryland.

Another bizarre aspect of life in Annapolis was that my sister Katherine and I were now living in a suburban environment, alone with our mother and stepfather. There were no siblings, no thriving neighborhood, no city streets, and no urban chaos. It felt like we were living in a freaking resort. Although it was a modest suburban home, our new house certainly wasn't our little box-house in Detroit. And on top of it, the vast majority of the time mom and Mr. Rob were in Washington D.C., working for *The Washington Times*. It was like we had just stepped into the Twilight Zone. And one of the things I instantly noticed about the other kids at St. Martin's was that their parents were home even less than ours—a dicey proposition with obvious consequences. In short, these kids had money, opportunity, and very little supervision, and they partied like it was 1999 every single night.

Shortly after my arrival at St. Martin's, I spotted Molly Hailey—and she spotted me. Instantly we began to hang out. Molly introduced me to just about every kid she knew, and she'd known most of the kids at St. Martin's since she was a small child. St. Martin's had a grade school attached to it, and a lot of the kids had attended the institution for all twelve years. From day one, it was one party after the other, with an endless slew of kids hosting fiestas, which boasted no parental supervision.

Their parents were politicians who traveled to Europe, lawyers who traipsed around the country, naval officers who shipped out to ports all over the world, and people who had the means to do just about whatever they wanted whenever they pleased. In fact, besides Molly's parents (whom I got to know well during my time at St. Martin's), the number of parents I actually met could be counted on one hand.

Just about every day someone new had a party, and dozens of kids would crash these soirees. The houses these kids lived in were nothing short of absurd in opulence and design. Four-story houses in wooded communities were the norm: grand in-ground pools set in massive backyards; houses on waterfronts with ski boats and jet skis; Mercedes Benzes always at the ready. These kids had every cool gadget and knick-knack you could possibly think of. And these parties, I would soon come to see, were wild, mad, free-for-alls with drugs, booze, and sex raging throughout the night. My head was spinning from the decadence.

In fact, Maryland had just changed the drinking age to twenty-one, but anyone born before a certain date was grandfathered in and could buy alcohol legally. Most of the senior class could drink at age eighteen. And boy, did we take advantage of that law. To demonstrate how wide-open things were, the president of Students Against Drunk Driving (who shall remain nameless) was a junior at St. Martin's; he was once pulled over while driving with a pony keg placed in his back seat, sucking nonstop on the hose, as drunk as a sailor on midnight leave. It was a particularly egregious offense, but while I don't recall his particular punishment…I remember for certain that he was around for the next week's festivities.

Now, just to make this clear, Molly Hailey and her family were about as blue collar as St. Martin's got. They lived right down the street from us, had five kids, and were not at all rich or pretentious. Molly's dad worked his ass off as a consultant for an advertisement firm and made sure that his kids understood what work meant. Even though they had opportunity, the Hailey kids understood the effort involved in living as they did, and were very appreciative of their situation. Molly and her siblings were good people, as were her parents. Subconsciously, it was probably one of the reasons Molly and I gravitated towards one another; we both understood what work meant. And having my girlfriend living just down the street with ultra-cool parents made for fun times as well. I learned the ropes of the partying lifestyle in short order. In fact, I passed the class with flying colors.

Sports at St. Martin's were a trip. Lacrosse, I would come to see, was a sport these kids took seriously; the state of Maryland was ground zero for the game. But even those practices were nothing compared to my training in Detroit, including Assumption Grotto. Upon my arrival, I began practice for the 1982 football campaign, and came to see that the experience would be a walk in the park. It wasn't challenging in any way, and actually grew to frustrate me; I felt that none of my teammates were taking football seriously.

But before long...neither did I.

Hell, during games, and while in the huddle, my teammates were more concerned about where the party was that night, and who was fucking whom, rather than the play we were about to run. Fucking and partying were the main focus, and although we did have some success on the field, we were no better than an average team. Still, we had our moments — and the highlight of the 1982 football season was, without a doubt, the game against Gallaudet High in early October.

Gallaudet was a team from the Washington D. C. high school affiliated with the college of the same name. Gallaudet University, I would come to learn, was one of the leading institutions in the country dedicated to educating deaf and blind kids. Of course, being the sensitive kid I was, arriving at their campus, I immediately convinced myself that I needed to go easy on these deaf kids. But as life goes sometimes, my assessment of the situation quickly became a classic lesson of "never underestimate your opponent," and from the opening kickoff I realized why.

During warm-ups, and as we watched the kids of Gallaudet preparing for the game, we could hear them grunting and making sounds unlike any other we had heard before. In their pre-game drills, and upon contact with one another, it sounded as if they were being abused in ways that were not registering in our brains. These sounds were alien, unnerving, and completely unnatural. Being a team captain, I remember having conversations with my fellow teammates before the game, discussing the fact that we should go easy on Gallaudet and being afraid of hurting them once we began hitting. Every player embraced this sentiment, and as kickoff approached, we'd established our game plan: just go easy and cruise to a trouble-free win. We could not have been more off the mark if we ourselves were blind men throwing darts in the middle of a windstorm.

On the opening kickoff, I sauntered down the field only to have a kid from Gallaudet lay me out and then stand above me while grunting and howling like a lunatic. When I stumbled back to the huddle, I saw that my teammates had been greeted in the same fashion.

"Fuck this, boys!" I cried. "Deaf or not, let's take it to these fucks!"

My teammates agreed. Although a tight contest, we did win the game—just barely. We went home with the victory in hand, and with an entirely new respect for the boys of Gallaudet. One of the most unusual aspects of playing a deaf and mute football team was how they signaled the beginning of an offensive play: following them up and down the sideline was a massive bass drum on a dolly. To begin each play, and once they were set, a fellow teammate would strike the drum with a mallet, sending the vibrations through the field and to their feet. Once they felt the vibration, they began the play. Truly ingenious stuff. Beethoven would have loved Gallaudet High School.

By then, I'd grown to 6'1" and 205 pounds of solid muscle, and being a decent athlete, I had a relatively successful senior football campaign. I was made team captain, voted most valuable player, and earned honors in both First Team All-County and All-Tri-County. Nearing the end of the season, and realizing that I had one year of football eligibility remaining, the assistant coach approached me with a proposition.

"Larry," Coach began sternly, "if you were to stay one more year, use your last year of eligibility and train exclusively with me, I guarantee you that I could make you a Blue Chip prospect and get you a full scholarship to a Division I university. What would you say to that?"

"Um, Coach, you do know that I'm a senior, right?"

"Yes I do," he countered, "but you have one more year of eligibility remaining. Stay with me, get your grades up, and I'll make you one of the best college prospects in the state. You have all the tools necessary to be a great player. What do you say we give it a shot?"

I looked at him like he had just been released from the Anne Arundel County loony bin.

This guy wants me to stay another year in high school, I thought in disbelief, *and prolong my torture for another full school year? Is he out of his freaking mind? There is no way I would extend my stay and put myself through one more day of this bullshit—let alone an entire freaking year! This guy must be completely crackers if he thinks I would!*

Biting my tongue, I declined his offer and moved on with life. But I do believe that he thought *I* was the one who had lost his mind, turning down a chance for a free ride to any college in the state. Well, such was my life as a knucklehead on the banks of the Chesapeake Bay...

As I tooled through the fall, I began to realize that these kids at St. Martin's were years beyond me academically. In fact, I slowly realized that I'd begun several classes that I'd never be able to complete: calculus, chemistry, and advanced Spanish were all whizzing completely over my head. Pleading my case to one of my teachers, she came to agree with me (especially once she reviewed my progress). She then made the proper arrangements so that I could drop each.

Chemistry was gone for good, and I was shipped off to freshman level geometry and Spanish, actually sharing classes with my sister

Katherine and her freshman classmates. Those scenes were hilarious. Katherine and I would sit together in the rear of the room as the rest of the students snickered and cracked wise about the knucklehead senior who couldn't hang with the big boys. I would have Katherine tutor me, and whenever the teachers turned their heads, I'd cheat off her notes. In fact, our geometry teacher doubled as coach for the freshman girls' basketball team, of which Katherine was a member. This teacher/coach let me know in no uncertain terms that the only reason I was passing his class was because the football team needed me for the next game. (I guess it's beneficial to know people in high places from time to time.)

One day, nearing the end of the school year, a teacher told me to go see the guidance counselor in order to weigh my options after graduation. Having been clueless during my entire stay at St. Martin's, I remained true to form with a follow-up question: "What's a guidance counselor?" The teacher pointed the way and sent me to see the woman who was supposed to change my life. Upon entering her office, I took a seat as the counselor reviewed my records. Obviously not too impressed, she put the file on her desk and asked me what I wanted to do with my life once I graduated. I told her that I didn't have a clue. She nodded her head in understanding, closed my file and said, "Well, the military is always a good option for kids like you," and called for the next student. As I got to my feet and walked out of her office, I was even more confused than I was when I first walked in. Such was my academic experience at St. Martin's High School.

These kids were preparing to enter the next phase of their lives with college, careers, and everything else that went along with it, while I was still trying to get my bearings on where I even was. These kids were taking SAT's and College Board exams, writing college applications, and taking extra-credit courses to pad their resumes; I was wondering if I'd even make it through my senior year. If it weren't for Black Sabbath,

The Doors, and The Ramones, I would have lost my mind that year. Once again, music was the only thing keeping me sane.

My relationship with Molly began to strain as well, along with every other relationship I had with my fellow classmates. After the novelty of being the new kid wore off, reality began to set in. These kids were being groomed for success and working their way towards financial Nirvana while I was still lumbering through life like a street kid from Detroit. School was making no sense, and the world—far different from what I was accustomed to—was becoming more confusing by the day. I suddenly began to see Molly for what she was, and in turn, she began seeing me for who I truly was. I felt inept, powerless, and directionless. I no longer felt like one of the gang.

Chris Dodson was a kid I had met while playing football at St Martin's. Chris was a sophomore with the body, disposition, and intellect of a college freshman. He was street-smart, funny, and as wide-open as they come. Shortly after meeting Chris, I began to understand why he was such a loose cannon; his family life was a mess. Chris' relationship with his mother was nonexistent, as the woman simply removed herself from the family by drowning her sorrows in a bottle of booze. Chris' father was also a drunk who beat the shit out of Chris ever since he was a small child. By the time I met Chris in the fall of 1982, however, he'd had enough and learned to retaliate, involving himself in violent brawls with his father that left nothing to the imagination. For obvious reasons, Chris and I were like two peas in a pod.

Immediately, Chris and I began to run wild, partying, mixing it up, and getting crazy. We'd drive to Washington D. C. and hit the bars, getting as drunk as we could. Chris and I became fast friends, and we would spend my senior year getting into one ridiculous scenario after the other, all under the watchful eye of Molly.

Molly and her family had known the Dodson's their entire life, and Molly had a soft spot for Chris that was nothing short of matronly. Because of this, she never frowned upon our friendship, although it did test her from time to time. Getting to know Chris led to one of the few friendships I had at St. Martin's that seemed to matter, and despite its volatile nature, it was one that brought, on some level, a sense of security. And still…some of the situations Chris and I got ourselves involved in were nothing short of moronic.

Chris was the St. Martin's equivalent of Eddie Haskell: engaging, charismatic, and seemingly as sweet as they come. Get the guy on the street, however, and he became a maniac. Many, many times we'd be cruising down the road late at night, just listening to music. Suddenly, Chris would pop to life from the passenger's seat, crank the music, blast the heater, flip on the windshield wipers, hit the high beams, roll down the windows, honk the horn incessantly, push my seat back as far as it would go and turn off the ignition, all while howling like a lunatic. The guy was absolutely glorious. He was my senior year equivalent of Dean Moriarty.

We ate mushrooms together, dropped mescaline, and smoked PCP, knocking side view mirrors off parked cars as we tripped balls and ran down the street like psychotics. It was here where I began to come back into my own, feeling my roots while rebelling against everything safe, secure, and nauseatingly wholesome; I felt I was pushing the limits of sanity itself.

Chris and I would sit in the parking lot of the school before football games, smoking copious amounts of marijuana and listening to Black Sabbath and The Doors. We'd discuss just how fucked up the world was, and the fact that the planet was on a collision course with total self-destruction.

It was here, with Chris, where I resumed my search for meaning in life, and realized that I couldn't settle for the status quo—on any level. I started forging a plan to break free from the restraints of a normal life.

Chris and I would hang out with some of the brothers he knew. Sitting around and getting high with these cats was wonderful, discussing the absurdity of racism, and hate in general, while listening to Herbie Hancock, Prince and Parliament/Funkadelic—my first exposure to this great music. Partying with those guys was hilarious, and sometimes affirming; their girlfriends would tell Chris and me that we were some of the coolest white boys they had ever met. We'd return the favor by letting them know just how sweet they were.

Once, Chris and I bought three cases of cheap beer and took off for Ocean City, Maryland—a cheesy, tinker-toy excuse for a "resort" along the Atlantic Coast. Once we arrived, I could barely get out of the car I was so inebriated. Immediately jumping into the ocean, a mighty wave took my drunken ass under, disorienting me, and causing me to lose my sense of balance; I couldn't find the surface. While fighting for my life and quickly losing oxygen, I suddenly burst from beneath the waves, gasping for breath and wondering how I had just survived such a mess. We then cracked open another beer and resumed our search for more mayhem.

Another time, Chris and I decided to get wild with the boys from St. Martin's and push the limits once again. Piling into three cars (one of which was my mother's old-school, early-1980s Ford, which we called "The Brown Whale"), we tore down Bay Ridge Drive like mad NASCAR drivers on a mission, with Chris and I picking up the rear. Suddenly, the lead car slammed on its brakes in the middle of the two-lane thoroughfare to downtown. The car directly in front of us was a small Italian job with three of our classmates inside. We slammed into those guys with the Brown Whale like a torpedo hitting broadside, sandwiching them between two vehicles and nearly ending their lives. I saw the guy in the backseat bounce around like he was on a mini-trampoline. How they survived that wreck with barely a scratch is beyond me, for it was truly a scary scene.

Another night, Chris and I thought it would be a treat to drink absurd amounts of peppermint schnapps and smoke ridiculous amounts of hashish; the result was that I woke up the next morning out in a ditch somewhere, a mile or so from the house. (It took me more than fifteen years to be able to handle the scent of peppermint schnapps and another five just to be able to drink it again without gagging.)

For Mother's Day 1983, Chris and I — feeling enlightened from a load of mushrooms — stole exotic plants from the William Paca House and Garden on Main Street as presents for our mothers. My mother was very suspicious of those plants, but could never prove anything. To this day, she doesn't know the truth about where they came from. (At least until she reads this. Sorry, Mom.)

One sunny afternoon in the spring, Chris and I were in downtown Annapolis with a few friends from St. Martin's. Off in the distance we spotted a young, hippie-looking cat who stood out among the rich and coddled inhabitants of the lunchtime crowd like a sore thumb. Inquiring as to who he was, someone from our crew enlightened us.

"Oh, that's Lawrence," my friend Stella told us. "He graduated from St. Martin's a couple of years ago. People say that he ate too much acid, started hitchhiking across the country, and lost his mind. They say he went over the edge and has never come back."

Observing the kid, he looked absolutely normal to me.

"That sounds like an interesting life," I said, looking to Chris.

To this day, I still have that image of Lawrence preserved in my mind, and the feelings of freedom and rebellion his story instilled within me. Lawrence will never know the inspiration he gave me, or the notion he planted in my mind, because I never even met the cat.

New Years Eve, 1982. Mom and Mr. Rob were out of town for the holiday, so Chris, Molly, and I thought it would be a gas to invite a select few of our friends over for a small get-together. Katherine, was down the street babysitting. Even though the parental units forbade such shenanigans while they were gone, I broke the rules and told some kids to come over and hang out. As evening came, Chris, Molly, and I iced down some beers and broke open some bags of chips. But what we thought would be a nice, small gathering of close friends quickly turned into a fiasco. Within an hour or so of start time, we had a major problem on our hands.

Kids I didn't know began to show up. Kids from Katherine's freshman class walked through the door and asked where the booze was. Kids from down the street crashed the party, as well as kids from other schools, other neighborhoods, and other districts. In a matter of hours, we had kids partying on the street in front of the house, relieving themselves in the neighbor's yards, and passing out on the front porch. Kids were in every room of the house, dancing like freaks, fucking in the closets, and breaking things like it was a college frat house. Household items began to disappear, rooms were being trashed, and kids howled like banshees out in the backyard. There was a fight on the front lawn, a boyfriend/girlfriend drama in the kitchen, and some guy running down the street naked. Once again, I was in way, way, way over my head.

It was this night that I once again saw just how different I was from these kids. They simply didn't care about consequences. To them, it was just another party, just another place to drink and get high, and just another place to get wild, as they could have cared less about the outcome. And now, I was one of them. At one point, I simply had enough and threw everyone out. Left alone with Molly and Chris, it looked as if a bomb had exploded, not only in the house but outside as well. And to top it off, we had less than 24 hours to clean up the mess before mom and Mr. Rob returned home.

Immediately, we all got to work.

Cleaning, scrubbing, washing, and sweeping were followed by dishwashing, vacuuming, and laundry, then relieving the yard of debris and clearing the street of trash. Taking a break for sleep in the wee hours, Katherine and I resumed in the morning. We washed walls, mopped floors, wiped down windows, cabinets, chairs, tables, and doors. We moved things back into place, aired out the house, polished everything to a T, and reorganized as if our lives depended on it (which they may have). By the time Mom and Mr. Rob returned home, everything was in order and as tight as a drum. There was no sign of a misplaced coaster, let alone a major blowout. Everything was perfect…or so we thought.

When Mom and Mr. Rob walked through the door, Katherine and I acted like little angels, inquiring about their trip while telling them just how boring and uneventful our evening had been.

"Oh, you know, we watched T. V. and ordered a pizza," I lied. "Yeah, I was in bed by 11:00 P. M. I was really tired…"

"That's nice, honey," mom said, opening the cabinet door beneath the sink.

That's when the jig was up. Mom immediately popped up and said, "Goddammit Larry, you had a party didn't you?!?"

I was dumbfounded. Not being able to deal with the guilt, I broke down on the spot and confessed everything. It was the first and only time Mr. Rob ever raised his voice to me. I took full responsibility and accepted my punishment like a man, but what that punishment was is anyone's guess. I assure you that it was *not* severe. By then, Mom and Mr. Rob (a father of four children himself) had mellowed out considerably; they'd both had enough of discipline and anger.

In fact, years later, my mother told me that both she and Mr. Rob were not mad at all, and felt that they needed to act sternly simply because it was expected of them. She also told me that the only way she knew something was amiss was when she opened the cabinet beneath the sink where the cleaning supplies were stored. Inside, she saw that the Lysol can had been moved from the back of the cupboard to the front; on a hunch, she assumed that we'd had a party and cleaned up afterwards. She also said that if I hadn't confessed, they would never have been the wiser.

Oh, the bitter ways of a guilty conscience; it has hounded me my entire life.

The second half of the school year was equally brutal, dealing with feelings of inadequacy, disappointment, and insecurity. I felt like the quintessential fish out of water. Besides my friendship with Chris, the only other elements of school life that kept me focused in any way were the coming of lacrosse and the spring theater season, two events I had never been exposed to, but immersed myself into, nonetheless.

Lacrosse turned out to be a great game, and I made the varsity squad simply because of my athletic prowess and nothing more. I knew zilch about the game but had a great time; St. Martin's was one of the best teams in the city and had actually won the state championship the year before. It was a lot of fun watching those guys play. Practices were a blast as well, as I got to scrimmage against the starters on a daily basis. I'll forever be appreciative for the experience of playing high school lacrosse.

Recently, my sister Katherine reminded me that when picture day came for the 1983 Varsity Lacrosse team, I added my own flair to the experience. Sitting cross-legged in the front row, I placed my hands on my knees, smiled for the camera and stuck out both my middle fingers as the picture was snapped. This brilliant move caused quite a sensation, forcing the school to remove the picture from the yearbook and spend the extra cash to shoot another team photo while producing a supplement to be added later. Katherine also reminded me that Coach Moore was *not* happy with my decision to rebel at such an inopportune time.

The spring theater season was also a nice diversion, exposing me to the world of serious acting for the first time. The play selected for the year was Neil Simon's "Don't Drink the Water," a hilarious romp that was a stitch to perform. I had a minor part with few lines, but when opening night arrived, I would come to steal the show, despite my inexperience on the stage.

When it came time to deliver my lines, I got caught up in the absurdity of the moment and began to lose my composure, laughing hysterically. Molly, who played my lover, lost her poise as well. With the two of us attempting to hide our laughter, the guy standing next to Molly was soon affected. In a matter of seconds, the entire cast, some twenty people, began laughing, followed by the capacity crowd that filled the auditorium. For more than ten minutes everyone in that hall laughed uncontrollably, creating a scene of bedlam that was hard to top. It was an unforgettable moment and one that proved to me that acting was a part of my genetic makeup, putting me on a thespian path that I have followed to this day. Spring theater was an outright hoot.

As graduation day approached, Andrea—with whom I still stayed in contact—informed me that she, her little sister Maggie, and their mother were going to come to Annapolis to watch me accept my diploma. Feeling uncomfortable with the proposition but excited as well, I professed elation at their impending visit. This would be the second time Andrea would come for a visit, the first time being for Homecoming back in the fall.

Even as I write this, I feel uneasy—because, in the end, this is how my time in Annapolis affected me. And to have Andrea back in my world only added to those feelings of uncertainty. Back in the fall, when she came for Homecoming, she knew that I was seeing someone else but we both carried on as usual. By the time graduation rolled around my head was swooning with confusion for a number of reasons, and having Andrea there would only increase my anxiety ten-fold.

I felt torn between two worlds, locked in a confining space somewhere between the distant past and the unknown future. I simply didn't know how to act, how to feel, or what to say. In reality, I don't think I handled those visits very well and felt an entirely new level of confusion come crashing down on me. And my mother, I came to learn later, was *not* happy about how I handled the visits. When Andrea and I were alone, everything was fine and normal, but when we were in the world of St. Martin's, I felt lost, bewildered, and unsure of my intentions. I simply lost touch with reality.

And I'm certainly not happy or proud about how I acted during this time and have apologized profusely to my Dark Haired Angel for my actions time and again, but she swears I never did anything inappropriate and that I treated her well. To be honest, I really don't remember much about it. I felt like I was being ripped in two while not understanding which direction I should take. It was, without a doubt, a most confusing period in my life, like so many others I had lived through... and it didn't help with my outlook on life, or myself, in any way either.

LIFE AFTER HIGH SCHOOL

In early June of 1983, I graduated and prepared to move on. As my fellow classmates anticipated fruitful college careers, raging frat parties, vibrant campus life, and the beginnings of lucrative job offers, I still had no clue as to what I wanted to do. The debacle of St. Martin's was over, I had seen Andrea off, and was as lost as ever, so I decided what to do next: get a new job, and get straight to work.

The day after graduation, my brother Michael and I moved into an apartment together. Michael had recently relocated to Annapolis to get a fresh start; the situation in Detroit was getting progressively worse by the day. He felt that he'd have a better opportunity at chasing his dreams in Annapolis, and I could not have been happier that he made the move. Despite our volatile childhood, I always loved Michael, and looked forward to getting to know him as a young adult. And boy, would we have fun together, because shortly after moving into our apartment, the third member of our "Stooges Crew" came to town and joined in the mayhem. This third Stooge was our stepbrother Robby.

Robby—Mr. Rob's eldest son—was, and still is, a beautiful guy. Having spent a considerable amount of time with us during our final two years in Detroit, Robby was well known to my brother and me. Robby is intelligent, talented, compassionate, and one of the funniest cats I have ever known. And now he was in Annapolis, moving in with mom and Mr. Rob, even as Michael and I settled into our new apartment. The adventures Michael, Robby, and I would have would be nothing short of hysterical.

During that summer of 1983, the three of us would form a bond that was magical. Michael and I put our animosities aside, as if they never existed at all, and with Robby now in tow, our trio would run rampant: baseball games in Baltimore, bar hopping in D. C., late night partying in Annapolis, crabbing in the Chesapeake Bay…and endless days of getting to know one another. With those two boys by my side, and our sister Katherine yet to graduate from St. Martin's, the Acquaviva/Taylor clan became a force of nature that would tear through the streets of Annapolis like a fury. That summer would be a blast.

But first, I needed a new job.

Chris Keegan was an average, All-American kid who loved baseball, Black Sabbath, and chasing skirt. He was funny, intelligent, and had a positive outlook on life that was refreshing and pure. He came from a good family, loved swimming, and like us, wanted to spend the summer following his high school graduation having fun and partying. The only difference between Chris Keegan and the rest of our Annapolis crew was that he suffered from cerebral palsy, and was confined to a wheelchair every waking second of his young life.

Shortly after settling into the apartment with Michael, I answered a want ad in the newspaper that looked interesting. The position being offered was as a caretaker for a kid with cerebral palsy. Chris' father, a successful businessman who traveled much of the time, wanted to hire someone to watch out for Chris and show the kid a good time during the summer. And this was how I met Chris Keegan—I was the lucky guy who landed the job.

Upon that first day with Chris, I was shown the ropes of caring for a kid who suffered mightily from a disease that ravaged his body in ways that are hard to accept. Chris could do nothing for himself. When I arrived in the morning, I'd get Chris out of bed, bathe him, dress him, feed him, and exercise him. I'd brush his teeth, comb his hair, prep him for the day, and address every single issue he might encounter under my watch. And Chris' dad...well, he simply gave us a stack of cash and told us to have fun.

"Larry," Mr. Keegan said on my first day, "you're a good kid and I love Chris dearly. Because of his condition, we don't know how long he will live. I want him to have fun, but I'm going to be out of town a lot. Whatever he wants, you let him have it and don't worry about the expense. I'll take care of that. Now you kids have a great summer, and be careful."

"Yes, sir," I replied, "I think I can handle that."

And fun is exactly what Chris and I had. Every morning, after getting Chris ready for the day, I'd ask him what he wanted to do. And every day Chris would let me know. We'd head to Baltimore and catch baseball games at Memorial Stadium with the Orioles. We'd hit the aquarium, museums, restaurants, bars, and Inner Harbor of the city. We'd head to D. C. and traipse around Georgetown, The Smithsonian, the zoo, and high-end malls—where I'd often wheel Chris right into a gaggle of pretty young girls. Unfailingly, they'd gather around and shower him with affection.

"Oh, you're soooo cute," they would squeal as they kissed his cheek and held his hand. "You're just the sweetest little thing, darling," they'd coo, bending over and inadvertently hanging their breasts in his face.

Chris would giggle and bounce around in his chair as he attempted to reach around with flailing hands to squeeze some ass. Everywhere we'd go, pretty ladies would gravitate towards Chris and give them their attention. And Chris and I took advantage of this phenomenon every chance we got. The guy was a chick magnet. And grown men would walk right up to us, hand Chris a $20 bill, say "Have a good time kid," then just walk away as we attempted to absorb what had just taken place. These episodes gave me a modicum of hope about the human race; it proved to me that there was still a level of goodness in the world that had yet to be tapped, a truly refreshing reality in a realm teetering on the edge of darkness.

Chris' favorite activity was going to King's Dominion, north of Richmond. King's Dominion was a theme park boasting numerous roller coasters, some of the best the world had to offer at that time. And Chris would want to ride every single one of them, over, and over, and over...

"Rarry," Chris said to me upon our first visit, "anyone wiff a wheelchair gets to gow to the fwont of the wine ewewy time." Because of Chris' condition, he slurred his speech, but I mastered interpreting his lingo in short order.

"No shit," I replied. "Well damn son, we're going to have some fun now, aren't we?"

That summer we'd go to King's Dominion some half dozen times, always rolling right past the lines of people waiting to take a spin on the coasters—some of whom had waited two, three, sometimes four hours for a single ride. I'd wheel Chris straight to the front of the line where he'd tell the attendant, "I want thee fwont caw." The obliging fellow would seat Chris at the front of the ride, and I'd settle in beside him. Part of the protocol for wheelchair-bound customers was to allow them as many consecutive rides as they wanted; sometimes we'd sit in that car for six, seven, even ten times in a row or more. All the while, Chris would howl, laugh, scream, and cry out from the top of his lungs. I'd sit next to Chris, with my arm firmly around him, laughing and howling right along with him as we rode every single roller coaster in the park time and again. Those trips to King's Dominion were a scream, man, an absolute scream.

As I said, Chris loved to swim, and we had access to a pool whenever we wanted. One of his neighbors, who lived in a massive house next door, had a spacious indoor pool, some fifteen feet wide and more than thirty feet long. It dipped to more than twelve feet in the deep end, and was encased in a grand, weather-proof wooden structure. That pool house was beautiful. Chris and I would spend many an afternoon in the pool, and Chris absolutely loved the experience. I do believe that in the water, he felt somewhat normal.

Picking Chris up from his wheelchair, I'd hold his four-foot frame in my arms and jump right in. I'd then pull Chris around as he kicked and paddled with frail and uncontrollable limbs. When Chris would tire, I'd sit him up on the edge of the pool as I'd continue doing laps.

Often I sat Chris on the edge at one end as I swam to the opposite side and returned, making my way back to him in a matter of seconds. One particular day, however, I'd swum to the opposite end, then—as was my norm—turned to look at Chris before my return lap.

He was gone.

Stricken with panic, I pulled myself out, ran along the edge, and quickly spotted Chris: he was at the bottom of the pool, flailing about helplessly, struggling to survive. In the few seconds it had taken me to swim the length of the pool, he'd lost his balance and fallen into the water. Diving down, I scooped Chris up and raced for the surface. When I broke free with Chris in my arms, he cursed me relentlessly while pounding on my chest with limp, feeble hands.

"God dammit Rarry, you almost killed me, you bastawd!" Chris cried while gasping for air.

I apologized, sincerely and profusely; but suddenly, I was overcome with laughter. The release of panicked tension—the realization that my greatest fears had been averted—was just too much. Chris and I would howl about that incident for the rest of the summer, and relive the experience time and again, but we also knew that we had just dodged a major bullet.

I would never let Chris out of my sight again.

Chris had two older brothers who loved him dearly and were very appreciative of me spending time with him. One night, while we were all out having dinner and getting drunk, we began tossing around the idea of taking Chris to Baltimore and hooking him up with an escort. His brother Jim told us that he was good friends with a particular woman who could accommodate the request; after all, he reasoned, it was Chris' eighteenth year of life, and it was high-time to get laid.

We immediately put the plan into action. Over the next few days, Jim contacted the woman to make a date, then gave Chris and me the address where the rendezvous was to occur.

On the day of the big date I bathed Chris, then dressed him in a nice pair of pants and a slick, buttoned-down shirt. I brushed his hair neatly and made him look sharp. But as we prepared to leave the house and head to Baltimore for the liaison, I looked out the front window to see Jim pull up in his car, hastily get out, and run for the front door like a man on fire.

"Larry!" Jim cried as he entered. "Man, we can't do it! We can't do it! The date's off, man. The date's off! Shelly caught wind and she's pissed!"

Shelly was Chris' stepmom—a beautiful, blond-haired woman who, as a stewardess, traveled quite often. But now, she was back in town—and worse, she had somehow heard about our plan to take Chris to Baltimore for his romantic encounter. Shelly was on the way to lay down the law, and I was suddenly Public Enemy #1. For some unimaginable reason, she was not happy about me taking her baby boy to see a hooker in Baltimore and getting him "serviced. " Upon hearing this news, and fearing for our lives, we got Chris into Jim's car and hightailed it out of there, spending the evening at a local bar getting drunk.

Over time, Shelly eventually simmered down. But we never got Chris laid—a regret I still have.

As summer came to an end, so did my relationship with Chris. He was enrolled at the University of Maryland for the fall semester, and was preparing to move to campus. I was actually a member of the interviewing team responsible for finding Chris a full-time attendant, and once we settled on a suitable candidate—a sharp, twenty-year-old law student—I pulled the kid aside and told him to look out for my little buddy in every way possible.

"Don't ever leave him unattended in a pool," I joked. "And if you ever have an opportunity to get him laid, take it!"

My time with Chris Keegan was over, and I would move on to the next phase of my life, forever carrying the memory of Chris in my heart, and my time with a kid who was one of the toughest young men I have ever met. Chris Keegan was a great guy.

In the fall of 1983 I, too, enrolled in school—at Anne Arundel Community College just north of Annapolis. Studying who-knows-what, I spent the fall playing football and hangin' out with the girls. Both endeavors would prove to be interesting.

With Molly moving on to the University of Rochester in New York State, our relationship was effectively over, giving me the opportunity to spend time with whomever I pleased. I took advantage of the opportunity and began to play the field. And with Anne Arundel Community College boasting a football team, I decided to spend another year abusing myself on the gridiron. Now, if I thought Coach Hanson at Servite was a prick, I was fooling myself mightily, for my new coach was a man who would come to define the term "dickhead."

The coach of Anne Arundel, a man whose name I have blocked from my memory, was actually a former NFL quarterback for the Denver Broncos. Although his career was short, only a year or two, he did hold the dubious distinction of throwing five interceptions in one quarter—a feat which no doubt added to his abrasive personality.

This guy would do and say things that were simply wrong. He'd cut guys down verbally in ways that were way over the line. He challenged players to fights during games. He would throw things, like chairs and clipboards, and snap towels at the guys in the shower, like a freaking frat boy. The guy was a complete moron. He effectively hastened my decision to leave the team before the season even ended—and although the coach had a lot to do with ending my football career, it was actually a hit I took during a game that convinced me that I was, in the end, not really a football player in the first place.

Anne Arundel Community College, just like most junior colleges, was a place where players would go to sharpen their skills as they vied for scholarships to bigger schools; there were several guys on our team trying to get into the University of Maryland. Stepping into their world opened my eyes in a big way—I had never experienced hitters like that in all my years. These guys on the junior college level were straight-up headhunters who could hit like Mack trucks.

I was a second-string tight end who rarely saw action in games. In fact, I didn't play my first game until the seventh week of a ten-game schedule. And I was only put in then because the starting tight end got hurt. It was the fourth quarter, and we were losing big. We had the ball at our own thirty-five yard line following a penalty. We were looking at third down, with twenty-five yards to get the first down. Lining up in the huddle, the quarterback looked at me and said: "Acquaviva, I'm throwing to you over the middle." Once he called the play, we broke the huddle and I got in my stance. This was my big chance.

Upon the snap, the play worked like a dream. I held my block for two seconds, released my man and sprinted forward. Once behind the linebackers, I cut across the field and looked up to see a perfectly thrown ball fall right into my hands. As I grasped hold, I ran for the sideline, cut up-field, then sprinted with all my might. When I saw a defensive back heading my way, I told myself that I'd take the hit, step out of bounds, and celebrate a forty-yard gain.

What I wasn't expecting was to get my clock cleaned.

As the defensive back—a short, stocky guy with rabid eyes—approached, I lowered my shoulder to absorb the hit. But the guy came at me with the force of a runaway train, hitting me like a brick wall and laying me out as my right shoulder crumbled from the force of the collision. Ignominiously, this brutality had taken place right in front of the opposing team's bench; while lying on my back and writhing in pain, I was quickly surrounded by a pack of howling, cackling numbskulls who informed me just how much of a pussy I was. As I staggered to my feet, it took every ounce of energy I had just to walk across the field and get to my sideline. I had pinched a nerve; my shoulder was dead and my season suddenly over. I would never play organized football again, and in all honesty, would never want to. I could not have been happier.

Immediately following my position as a caretaker for Chris Keegan, and at the beginning of the fall semester, I had found a new job. Both my brothers Michael and Robby were salesmen at a Sears' store, and they found a position for me in the warehouse. Initially being offered a sales job myself, I quickly realized that I wasn't blessed with the same charm and charisma required to be an effective salesman, and decided to stick to my blue collar roots, becoming a warehouse employee. Michael, Robby, and I would spend our days working at Sears and our nights partying at the bars.

And partying is what we did best.

We'd hit every bar we could find in Annapolis, whooping it up with the locals, flirting with the ladies. Many years later, when reflecting on this period of my life, I remembered that there were several times when I had completely blacked out with no recollection as to how I got home. And the truly scary thing was, *I* was the one driving. Not good, my friend, not good. Despite these flirtations with disaster, Michael, Robby, and I sallied forth like the nimrods we were.

One of the greatest aspects about my brother Michael was that ninety-seven percent of the time, the guy didn't drink, giving Robby and me a ready-made designated driver forever at our disposal. Although sober, Michael would get as loopy as we would, laughing, joking, and cutting it up like he was three sheets to the wind himself. A truly amazing phenomenon, and one that Robby and I grew to love and appreciate.

Michael would drive when we went to D. C., where we'd hit the bars of Georgetown. One of the places we regularly frequented was called The Meat Market, and that was exactly what it was — a freaking open market for wholesale flesh trading. Now, truth be told, I've never enjoyed places like that, where wasted bimbos stumbled about so drunk that they didn't even know what planet they were on, let alone who you were. I've always enjoyed getting to know women, spending time with them and hearing their tales, dreams, and aspirations. I was never big on one-night stands. In light of this, The Meat Market was an eye-opener, a huge place where hundreds of kids would congregate and get so drunk that it came to resemble a degenerate Turkish whorehouse. Fights were a constant distraction, and talking to women an impossibility. It was like you were expected to knock a woman over the head and drag her to the alley to have your way with her. Not my style. The Meat Market was a scary place.

Michael, Robby, and I, and whomever else we recruited for these junkets, quickly formulated a rhythmic routine for our Georgetown excursions. We'd begin by trolling the ritziest neighborhoods of Georgetown, locating glitzy parties that we'd crash like we were long-lost pals returning from a summer abroad. And these were not just some random frat parties we'd crash either; these were elegant, highfalutin soirées in multi-million dollar homes, hosted by the cream of D. C. society. We're talking tricked-out nineteenth-century manors with pampered gardens, surrounded by wrought-iron fences and picturesque, tree-lined streets. We'd walk right into these places where lawyers, doctors, politicians, and hip young professionals hobnobbed—dressed to the nines, sipping on expensive French wines, nibbling imported cheese, and discussing the market and their inflated stock portfolios.

"Um, can I help you?" A pretty, young socialite would ask upon our arrival.

"Oh, hey!" we'd counter. "Don't you remember us? We met at Robert's lake house on the Chesapeake back in the spring. That Robert, man, I tell ya, he's a character, isn't he?"

"Um...sure..." She'd counter while looking as confused as a pauper on the French Riviera. "Oh yeah...um...Robert...sure."

"So, is the booze over here?" we'd continue. "We just got back from a day of sailing and we sure could use a snort!"

"Uh, yeah, right over there. The bar is right there. Um...good to see you..."

"Great seeing you too, sweetheart. We'll talk to you soon." And so it would go as we brushed shoulders with the elite of Washington D. C.

One time, however, we took the experiment too far. At one house—a beautiful home with gorgeous, hardwood floors, European furniture and the best accouterment money could buy—Robby and I found ourselves in the master bedroom, as drunk as two pea-brains could be, laughing at the absurdity of our masquerade. Suddenly, Michael burst into the room. The jig was up.

"Dudes," he called in a hushed and frantic tone, "we have to leave right now. These boys aren't happy."

As we stepped into the hallway, we were greeted by the linebacker corps of J. J. Crew: several tall, muscular, and chiseled boys straight out of G. Q. Magazine who were not pleased with our charade.

"We don't know what your game is, boys, but we don't like it," one of the gentlemen informed us. "We suggest that you leave now."

And leave is exactly what we did. We were escorted all the way to the street as the crew of Adonis's threatened to end our lives right there on the spot. Swift and crafty diplomacy was the only thing that allowed for us to survive the experience, and I'm here to tell you that we survived by the skin of our teeth.

Such was my life in the wilds of high society.

Baltimore was another place we traveled to frequently, and we spent a lot of time partying there. Baltimore was my kind of town: blue collar, seedy, and boatloads of fun. And Baltimore, to my delight, had "The Block," an old-school red-light district in the heart of downtown. Back then, The Block covered some four-to-six square blocks of the city's interior, and was home to dozens of the most wretched sex shops, strip joints, peep shows, adult movie theaters, and nightclubs you'd ever want to see. Those places were glorious, with cheesy, boisterous neon lighting, and frequented by drunks, drug addicts, dope peddlers, pimps, whores, perverts, street bums, nut-jobs, and misfits. I simply loved the place. Being eighteen and as dumb as they come, I fit right in.

One night, when so drunk I could barely stand, I wandered into an adult movie theater. This was one of those places with private booths where you'd feed quarters into a machine that showed snippets of X-rated movies for just minutes at a time. Stepping inside one of the booths so I could stop the world from spinning, I nestled in to take a breather from the nonstop debauchery on the street. Suddenly, I heard a lone, male voice calling to me from somewhere on the outer fringes of comprehension. Confused by this, I began searching for its source.

There in the corner, to the left of the door, was a hole in the wall a couple of feet above the floor. The man was calling through it. Getting to my knees and fighting through a wicked drunk, I politely asked the man what he was in need of.

"Your cock," he called through the hole. "Put your cock through the hole and I'll suck you off!"

Looking at the hole while sitting in a darkened, seedy movie booth stinking of stale beer, vomit, and dried jism, I weighed my options and determined that it would *not* be in my best interest to place my vulnerable penis through a random hole where an even more random wacko was awaiting a thrill. I then elected to gather my bearings and hightail it out of there to find my brothers. This was my first, and last, exposure to "Glory Holes."

Our stepbrother Robby was studying to be a psychologist, and I'm here to tell you that the guy was a born therapist. A young man with a kind, inquisitive, and compassionate heart, Robby had filled the role of family shrink from the time we met him. He was a natural. But sometimes, his compassion and curiosity concerning the human condition became a liability.

As we stumbled around The Block one night, drunk as sailors, I located Robby in a private-booth movie house. He was in the lobby where they sold VHS porno films, dildos, sex gadgets, and lingerie amid the bright, flashing neon lights. Robby had corralled a young couple, a man and a woman who were in the theater doing who-knows-what. The first thing I noticed about this unusual union was that the man—a rather large, strapping, and muscular fellow with glasses—was not pleased with the conversation Robby was having with him. I soon understood why.

"But I'm just trying to understand," Robby said, scratching his head. "Why would a woman like her be in a place like this?"

"I don't give a fuck what you don't understand, jack-off," the man growled while gazing hard at Robby.

"But she's so pretty and this place is so seedy…"

"Look motherfucker, we enjoy fucking, get over it," the man continued, now pushing Robby as the woman, obviously offended, shook her head in disbelief. "Who the fuck are you, motherfucker? Are you the fucking morality police? I could give a fuck less about your confusion and what you think about us. And I'll tell you something else, *bitch*…"

"Come on, bro," I interjected, pulling Robby out the door as this very large and now seriously pissed-off man continued to poke him and threaten bodily harm.

Robby was still confused about the situation even after I got him to the street. He was attempting to bring cohesion to a place that knew only decadence and nothing more. He's a good man, Robby.

One night, on the way home from The Block, we spotted a street bum asking for handouts, and in our loose state of mind, decided that it was our duty to take care of him. We loaded him into the car and decided to take him back to Annapolis.

"Oh man, you can sleep at our parent's house," we promised. "They won't care, they love bums!"

When mom woke the next morning, she went downstairs to do a load of laundry. There on the pull-out couch was Sam, the Bum from Baltimore, snoring away and stinking of cheap gin and stale Vienna sausages. I'm telling you now, our "enlighten the homeless" experiment did not go over well. The tale of Sam the Street Bum has only become more precious and unforgettable as time goes on.

During the spring of 1984, I decided that it would be a hoot to join the local rugby team, The Severn River Rugby Club. This would prove to be a wild romp through controlled mayhem unlike anything I had ever experienced. To put it mildly, rugby players are insane. It was here where I received my second concussion, and witnessed some of the most vicious hitting I had ever seen. Game after game I saw things I never thought possible as I attempted to hang with cats who embodied pain.

One game, I blocked an opposing player's kick and went on my way to rejoin the action. Suddenly, the man ran up from behind and blindsided me with a punch to the face that rocked my world. Having learned a thing or two by this point, I waited until the guy was looking the other way and threw my body into him with all my might. Laying him out, I stood over him as he writhed in pain. When he looked up, he smiled and extended his hand. And when I pulled him off the ground, he slapped me on my back and said, "Good hit kid, keep it up." Together, we rejoined the match.

At another game—this one in Washington D. C. — an opposing player split his head open upon making contact with someone's knee. I watched in awe as the man made his way to the sideline, sat on the bench and cracked open a beer. His girlfriend then pulled out a needle and thread from her purse and stitched up his wound as if she was mending a pair of jeans. Once the wound was sealed, the man polished off his beer and went back into the game.

I was a "left prop," one of the guys on the front line of the scrum. In one game, the man I was to oppose — the right prop directly across from me — was a lean, wiry man in his early 40s. I was certain that I'd have a field day with the guy. Again, never underestimate your opponent, man. This guy had my number from the opening kickoff.

Whenever we got into the scrum, this cat put a hold on me that had me incapacitated every single time. He would put the Spock death-grip on me that kept me off-balance and rendered my strength useless. I had no leverage, no power base, and no ability to utilize my advantage as he dictated everything I could do for the entire match. It was a great lesson, and one that proved to me that brains win over brawn every time.

If the games were wild, the after-parties following these matches were nothing short of absurd. Both teams would gather at a pub, drink ridiculous amounts of alcohol, sing songs while arm in arm, and get crazy. Fights would break out, chairs would be thrown, tables would get thrashed about, and grown men would go at it like wild dogs. When these altercations came to an end, both teams would again link arms and sing: traditional barroom ballads, expounding the glories of bedding down loose women, busting heads of ancient foes, drinking to excess and roaming the world in search of infamy.

Guys with missing teeth, cracked heads, blackened eyes, and swollen knees would get so drunk they could barely stand. Any women brave enough to hang out at these parties would eventually be overwhelmed and carried around the bar, slung over some random guy's shoulder like a cavewoman, as fellow teammates smacked her ass and grabbed some tit. Disputes on the field would be resolved in the bar, and lifelong friends would become bitter foes as team loyalty superseded school ties.

The world of rugby was an excursion into lunacy on a level never before imagined, and proved to me that I would never want to experience it again. Enough was enough. I'd had my fill of contact sports.

But back in the fall, while still playing football for Anne Arundel

Community College, we'd had a road game that took us to Western Maryland College, located in the plush, rolling foothills of Westminster. From the moment I arrived on the campus of the Green Terrors, I was enchanted; it seemed to me the quintessential collegiate setting. While walking across the quad, my feelings were only confirmed as I heard the sound of The Romantics blaring from a dorm room. Hearing one of my all-time favorite Detroit rock n' roll bands wafting across the quad was akin to seeing an oasis in the midst of a desert; it instantly hooked me where it counted — in my musical soul.

I knew right then and there that I needed to attend school at Western Maryland College.

When I returned home — following the debacle of junior college football — I dropped out of school and did whatever was necessary to enroll at Western Maryland for the fall semester. For the remainder of 1983 and throughout the summer of '84, I continued to work at the Sears warehouse, stockpiling cash, and preparing for college life.

Western Maryland College would become an experience that opened my mind to an entirely new world. It became an important stepping stone that convinced me that the pursuit of education — every day of your life — was as important as breathing in the morning air. It would also become an experience that would put me in a mountain of debt for many, many years to come, and exposed me to the true nature of higher education in America.

As my days at Western Maryland began to unfold, so would my mind, initiating a journey that I would ultimately never even come close to completing. Hold on to your hats, people, hold on to your hats — for this crazy motherfucker was just getting started.

And I would never look at the world in the same light, ever again.

11. WESTERN MARYLAND COLLEGE

IN MID-JULY OF 1984, I MADE MY WAY TO THE CAMPUS OF WESTERN Maryland College in Westminster, Maryland; my aspirations of becoming a "real" college student had suddenly come true. Upon my arrival, I was informed by school administrators that my high school resume needed some fleshing out, and that I'd have to take a couple of classes to be accepted as a fulltime student. Once informed, I got to work.

I settled in, familiarizing myself with my new surroundings as I began taking classes. Immediately, I met people and made friends. There were many other students already there taking summer courses—working, living nearby or on campus, and preparing for the school year in some way. One cat informed me that the grounds crew might be looking for some help, and that I should swing by the physical plant to inquire about a job.

Western Maryland College had a nine-hole golf course on its campus, and maintenance of the links and the school grounds required a small army of workers. I was hired on the spot. Another girl told me that the theater—always in need of crew members to help build sets and work as stagehands during performances—was hiring as well. Within my first two days at Western Maryland I was taking two courses, had two jobs, and a crew of people to hang with. It was a great start to a wonderful period of my life.

Western Maryland College was a small liberal arts school founded in 1867. Boasting a student body of less than 2,500 kids, it was a Division III school. The campus was beautiful, with uniform red brick buildings and a rolling landscape generously populated with mature maple, oak, and hickory trees. The school was small enough that you didn't feel overwhelmed by a sea of kids, but sprawling enough that you had room to breathe.

By the time I arrived on campus I had let my hair grow to below my shoulders, wore a leather headband, rock and roll t-shirts, and bleached-out jeans. In those first weeks, most of the other kids on campus were either football players preparing for the upcoming gridiron campaign, or theater majors getting ready for the fall theater season. I elected to hang with the actors — working in the theater, smoking massive amounts of dope, and getting wild with the thespians. Those early days were sublime, spending my evenings with a beautiful, dark-haired actress named Amelia, and partying at night with her troupe of actors for hours on end.

This was my introduction to theater life, something I'd be involved in throughout my time at Western Maryland.

A week or two after my arrival, I was called to the financial aid office, where I was informed that there was an issue with my tuition. I inquired about what options were available. A staff member, who had a series of documents already spread out across her desk, told me that if I signed these papers, I'd be allowed to continue on with the college experience. I readily agreed and signed everything that was put in front of me. When I asked her what I was signing, she was elusive, to say the least, with her answers.

"Oh, this will allow you to keep going to school," she said as she shuffled one document after the other in front of me. After I'd signed the final papers, she picked up the stack, smiled a warm smile and said, "There, you're all set for the year."

Feeling content, I stood, shook her hand and resumed my day. What I didn't realize was that I was signing my life away for a single year of schooling. Many months later, when I received a notice for the payment of a nearly $10,000 debt, I felt bamboozled. I had walked blindly into a situation I knew nothing about, had no guidance of any kind on how to navigate the academic process, and was—to put it sharply—given inaccurate information so that the school (and the bank that gave the loan) could ensure their high-dollar fees from a clueless kid who knew no better.

This, unfortunately, was the first of many episodes that proved to me that in the end, the system of higher education has one goal in mind and one goal only: to bilk desperate kids out of tens of thousands of dollars every year for their own gain. These institutions put kids into debt for many, many years to come, sometimes for the remainder of their lives, simply so professors can maintain tenure (something I think is absurd), football players can play homecoming games for alumni, and college presidents can maintain a certain lifestyle of caviar, champagne, and vacations to Paris and Milan. The university system, I came to see, was one of the most elitist programs in the world, and continues to maintain an exclusionary, if not criminal, element to it. Yet, if we don't properly educate and employ our people, how can we expect to have a thriving nation? It's a problem.

Late in August of 1984, kids began arriving on campus for the fall semester, and I moved into my dorm room. There I met the kid who would become my roommate, Dan Emory. A biology major, Dan was smart, funny, and had a great love for music. To top it off, Dan enjoyed smoking marijuana. Right off the bat I had found another kindred spirit.

A day or two after fall classes began, I met another kid while hanging out on the quad. Luca Rossi had dual citizenship in Italy and the U.

S., was well-traveled, intelligent, and possessed a fiery sense of humor, unlike any I had encountered. I liked him immediately. During that first conversation with Luca, I asked him what he was studying.

"Philosophy," Luca answered proudly.

Being the knucklehead I was, I snickered and asked him another question that proved my ignorance in a fresh and obvious manner.

"So, what do you guys do, sit around and talk about the meaning of life?"

Without blinking an eye, and with a curiously stern look on his face, Luca replied; "Yes, that is exactly what we do."

With that simple response, my life would change, and my view of the world — and of higher education in particular — would be altered in ways that would prove to be irreversible. Luca gave me a stack of books to read: Herodotus, Thucydides, Homer, Plato, and others...many others. In the traditional Greek manner, I became his pupil. And the things I would learn would become the foundation of my educational experience from that day forward.

On the day I received my first check for my job as a member of the school grounds crew, I asked a fellow employee what bank he used to cash and deposit his checks. The employee — a crusty old cat named One-Armed Bob — gave me a look that implied that I had simply lost my mind.

"What the fuck are you doin' messin' with banks for, boy?" Bob challenged as he continued to service a lawnmower.

Bob had lost his right arm as a child while working on his father's farm back in Illinois. His shirt had become entangled in a combine blade; the machine ate his arm up and spit it out. Bob, in his early 60s when I met him, had never let his disability slow him down. In fact, the man could outwork most students, and was a master mechanic who could fix just about anything.

"What do you mean, Bob?" I asked in confusion. "I need to open a bank account so I can cash my checks."

"Only fools use banks, boy," Bob continued while chewing on a wad of tobacco. "Didn't you ever hear of The Great Depression?"

"Of course, but what does that have to do with me cashing my check in 1984?"

"Everything, boy! I lived through The Depression and I watched as those fucking banks took everything from everyone in our town! *Only fools use banks, boy!*"

"I appreciate that, Bob, I really do. But banks can't do that kind of thing any more."

Again, Bob looked at me as if I had just fallen off the turnip truck.

"You keep telling yourself that, boy, just keep telling yourself that. I'm here to tell you son, banks — and *especially* the government — can do whatever they want whenever they please. And if you think you've got a say in the matter, boy, you're dumber than you look!"

"Well, what do you do with *your* money, Bob?"

"I bury it boy, in my backyard, in Mason jars!" He said sternly. "You think there's safety in this world, and there ain't. There's just power and greed. The sooner you accept that, the better off you'll be. Trust me boy, if I'm lying I'm dyin'."

I stood in silence as I watched Bob disappear into the shop and mulled over his words. By now, I had been studying the history of the world for more than fifteen years, and in an instant, it all came crashing down on me. The lies, the deceit, the corruption; the insidiousness, avarice, and malfeasance of mankind surged to the forefront of my mind.

I looked at the check in my hand, slipped it into my pocket and walked on.

I wouldn't deal with banks for many years to come following that conversation with Bob, and to this day do not trust them for as far as I can throw them. Cats like One-Armed Bob and Luca Rossi, when all was said and done, were all the education I needed, and fortunately for me, I was just getting started.

Besides meeting Luca Rossi and One-Armed Bob, I had also met Peter Cabell Banks, a perfect storm of personalities. Peter was a couple of years older than me, studying film. An intelligent guy with a great sense of humor, Peter was also the grandson of Cab Calloway, the legendary band leader and jazz innovator. The fact that Peter had such dynamic family ties was a real treat, but discussions about his grandfather were non-existent. What Peter loved, and what I loved about Peter, was film. In short, the cat turned me on to some of the greatest films the world has ever seen.

I'd make my way to Peter's dorm room—a rustic, loft-style apartment on the top floor of one of the dorms—and smoke ample amounts of marijuana to get my mind right. Peter would then greet me, show me to a comfortable chair, dim the lights, and prepare me for what was to come. Standing in the soft light of the room, Peter would offer subtle hints about what I was about to see. Then he'd pop in the film and step to the side. My eyes would become fused to the screen.

The Clowns, On The Waterfront, Fanny And Alexander, North By Northwest, La Strada, Days of Heaven, Apocalypse Now, Koyaanisqatsi, Amadeus and dozens of other films suddenly became a part of my educational odyssey, leaving an indelible and long-lasting impression on me. Peter would walk silently around the room, offering snippets of insight and background knowledge at appropriate times, while creating an experience that obliterated any I was having in the classroom.

When the films came to an end, Peter and I—sometimes with Luca and other friends—would sit for hours and discuss not only the films, but life as well. I began to see a connection, a melding of worlds; the real, the surreal, the infinite and the inner, coming together in a kaleidoscope of color, sound and texture that allowed my mind to expand and release. For the remainder of my time at Western Maryland College, Peter and his films would become a staple, a sanctuary, and a means to explore those mystical questions of life.

Luca and I would sit for hours ourselves, getting high and drinking beer as we discussed what I was reading, dissected what he was learning, and peppered each other with the great questions of life. These discussions delved deep into the human condition, and unleashed a segment of my mind that was just waiting to be set free. With Luca's guidance and friendship, I would come to see that what existed all around me was teeming with mystery and subtlety; to question reality was as essential as breathing.

I came to see that learning, university, and the true essence of those concepts did not restrain themselves to stagnant dogmas and antiseptic institutionalized settings. I came to see that when man first became conscious in the distant pages of history, the concept of university was unleashed upon him in its purest form: "I think, therefore I am." This is what philosophy did to me. I suddenly began to see the educational system as a constricting force, far removed from the truest form of education. I began to see that whenever two or more people are gathered in the name of higher thought, no matter where you are, that *this* is learning, that *this* is education, and this—in its most basic and righteous form—*is* university. Not only did I begin to question everything I saw, I began to question college life as a whole.

One day, while taking a lunch break with One-Armed Bob following a morning of cutting, trimming, raking and snipping, Bob and I began discussing the state of the world. This was the time preceding Iran-Contra, Sandinistas, American Death Squads, and Ollie North. This was a period when dimwitted Ronald Reagan, The Master Puppet, was the front man who was preparing for the mass murder of tens of thousands of indigenous peoples throughout El Salvador, Honduras, Guatemala, and Nicaragua, all for the sake of the almighty American dollar. Bob and I were discussing just how fucked up the world was.

"Well, you just better hope they don't draft you, boy, and send you somewhere to kill some folks," Bob said as we gnawed on our sandwiches.

"Draft me? There hasn't been a draft since '73. They won't do that shit again, man."

"Boy, you *are* dumber than you look. If you think they won't draft again, you're as foolish as I've always thought you were. The government man can do *whatever* he pleases *whenever* he pleases. Haven't I taught you anything, boy? You're the first generation who hasn't been drafted since I was born. If they want you, they'll take you, end of story."

Again, Bob had me dumbfounded. As I watched him finish his lunch, I knew deep down inside that he was right about everything he had told me, and immediately began to delve deeper into the history of mankind. There I began to unearth an infinite amount of information on just how corrupt and selfish man can be. One-Armed Bob was quickly becoming one of the smartest people I knew at Western Maryland College, and the things he would teach me would become invaluable as I grew older.

While I worked at the campus theater, I was also taking acting classes there; my experience at St. Martin's and performing in "Don't Drink the Water" had whet my appetite for the discipline. My time in the world of acting only enhanced my rebellious spirit, only fueled my passion to question everything I saw. And the man who would encourage my angst—pointing me in the direction I would follow for the remainder of my days—was named Max Nixon.

Max, a professor of theater, was tall and wonderfully poised, sporting wild, unkempt hair and a roundish face. A man in his late 40s, he had a regal air about him, and moved about the stage with the elegance and fluidity of a cat. The man embodied theater.

Theater, and acting, began to make more sense to me, as if a veil of illusion had been lifted, exposing me to the true essence of existence. One of the first things Max taught me was that in every aspect of life, we are merely acting and performing a part to fulfill certain tasks. When we go to the grocery store, we are performing the role of shoppers. When we go to the doctor's office, we are acting as the patient. To our parents, we execute the persona of children. To friends, we become confidants, and to romantic interests, lovers. In an instant, Max solidified Shakespeare's "All the world's a stage" in a manner that was logical and pure, destroying the myth that actors are a rare breed among us. He proved to me that we all act, all day long, everywhere we go, and with everything we do. The only difference between those who act for a living and the rest of us is, Max opined, is that actors understand this charade and are willing to exploit it for myriad of reasons…the least of which is to make money.

From the get-go, Max asked us to expand our horizons, look deeper into ourselves, and explore the inner reaches of comprehension. He taught us to look at an apple for what it was, and to dissect the act of eating it in a way that was natural and true. A painter paints; he does not throw a baseball. A painter holds his brush and creates streaks of color and texture upon a canvas. A baseball player throws a ball, and when he does, he lifts that ball over his head, reaches back and flings his arm forward, releasing the ball in the direction he wishes it to fly. Max had us focus on these movements, instead of taking them for granted—always comparing, contrasting, analyzing.

Some of those acting exercises were glorious, setting me down a path I am still on, and made me realize that I had actually been following them since the day I became conscious. One exercise Max gave us was to walk through the theater, every part of the theater, adopting the state of mind of a character of our choosing, while passing by fellow students and interacting with them. This exercise proved to me once again that we are all merely actors every second of every day and that to separate that reality from our conscious selves is tantamount to not living a life of clarity.

In another exercise, we were assigned a Shakespearean character and told to perform as that person exiting a certain scene in the corresponding play, essentially extending that character's involvement into a moment from everyday life. My character was Feste, the fool, from the play "Twelfth Night." Following Act I, Scene V, where my character has a conversation with Olivia, I exited the scene—a time when Feste is no longer vital to the story—and enacted a scenario where he went to the market, bought supplies for dinner, and played a game of hide-and-seek with a little girl he met on the street. What a joyous experience that was, and one I will always remember. A character does not stop living simply because he is no longer visible. A character is *alive*, has dreams and lives life just like everyone else. To act is the play, to live is the act.

Another exercise Max gave us was gathering at the front of the stage and having a fellow student impersonate you, essentially showing the world how you are perceived. This exercise altered my life in ways for which I was not quite prepared.

The girl who impersonated me was a seasoned actress from the school's acting troupe. She made her way to the back of the stage, paused to gather herself, then walked before us with her head held high and her shoulders firm and proud, sauntering in front of us as if she owned the place. The confidence she exuded was overwhelming, and her portrayal of my self-awareness astounding.

After the exercise was over, I asked the girl if that was how she truly saw me. Without hesitating, she said "yes," and went on to tell me that when I walked into a room, it was as if a man on a mission had just entered. She said I carried myself in a way that projected an air of certainty and subtle power. I was floored. With the endless confusion swirling in my head, I had never once considered how I was viewed by others, but once I saw it I would never forget it.

I recommend that exercise to every human being on the planet.

Now, the coupe de grace of the acting experience occurred late in the spring of 1985. As beautiful weather blossomed on the city and people flourished beneath the bright, blue skies of downtown Baltimore, I embarked on an experience that would simply blow my mind. Max paired us with a random partner, asked us to create a character of our own choosing, and assigned us to specific areas throughout Baltimore, Washington D.C., or Westminster, where we were to bring our characters to life. My partner and I were assigned to the Inner Harbor of downtown Baltimore, and the character I settled upon was a suspender-wearing, black-glasses-sporting, pencil-pushing nerd—but a nerd who stood 6'1" and sported 210 pounds of solid muscle. With my ponytail hidden in the top of my white, buttoned-down shirt, I looked like a cross between Christopher Reeves and Erkel.

When my partner and I arrived at the Inner Harbor—an area populated with numerous restaurants, bars, and gift shops, all attended by hordes of people—we were both bubbling with excitement. My partner—a beautiful, dark-skinned girl of Hispanic heritage named Elisa—was a tough, streetwise gal who dreamed of a career in the Army. She was dressed as a man, and with her firm and unyielding disposition, pulled it off well. The assignment called for us to separate and explore our environs while interacting with the people of the city, so we bid each other good luck and went our separate ways. Walking up to random people, I began to interact with them like the nerdy, book smart cat I was supposed to be.

"Um, excuse me, sir," I'd begin in a nasally voice while adjusting my glasses. "I'm searching for the Baltimore Aquarium and was wondering if you might direct me to its location. You see, I've recently submerged myself into the artistic endeavor of drawing with graphite pencils upon acid-free, manila paper and would love to use the aquarium as my subject, as the architecture reflects a certain combination of modern design and clean, linear forms not common to the area..."

Staring at me like I had just landed from Planet Cuckoo, these people would immediately play along, not certain if I was acting, performing, or just a crazy kid who was a little too loose in the mental department.

"Uh, sure, son," they'd respond while looking me up and down. "It's right over there, on the opposite side of the harbor."

"Well, thank you kind sir, and perhaps you might be knowledgeable enough about the area to recommend an appropriate restaurant, as I am currently feeling the distant pangs of hunger nipping at my insides. I have been informed that Maryland blue crabs are a succulent dish and have been curious to expand my culinary horizons." And so it would go, as I walked around the Inner Harbor looking for "straights" to ply my talents upon.

An hour or so into the experiment, I was feeling confident—so confident that I decided to push the limits of reason.

In the distance, occupying a wide concrete stairwell that lead to a strip of restaurants and bars running alongside the harbor, was a group of bikers. They were hanging out, drinking, and smoking cigarettes.

These cats were rugged looking, with long, greasy hair, leather pants, and shit-kicking boots. Each wore leather vests displaying their biker affiliation. Spotting several women in the group, all donned in biker regalia, I felt certain that my masquerade would be a big hit with this crew. Walking right up to them, I began my spiel.

"Um, hello good people," I said while extending my hand in a friendly gesture, "my name is Bartholomew T. Rothschild III, the 'T' standing for Thaddeus, my great uncle's name on my mother's side, who was an engineer for the Baltimore and Ohio Railroad back in the 1920s, the period known as 'The Roaring 20s'. But I personally prefer the more mellifluent description of the era; 'The Jazz Age', a term which combines the dawning of a new musical epoch and the, well, how shall we say, the old-world continuum so prevalent in the country during that period..."

"Hey, partner," the woman closest to me suddenly interrupted. "Shut up."

By now, some ten to twelve bikers closed in on me, including a few women, and I could tell that they were not enjoying the performance as much as I was. In fact, I suddenly felt that I was a breath away from having the entire membership pounding me into a tiny speck of dismembered pocket protectors and Buster Brown shoes. As I internally debated what to do, I felt a sudden tug on my shoulder. I turned to see Elisa as she forcefully pulled me down the stairs and away from the agitated group of bikers — all of whom were cursing, spitting, and letting me know just how much they'd love to turn my cock-sucking face into a punching bag.

"Are you crazy, Larry?" Elisa chided as she continued to pull me down the stairs. "Those guys are an actual biker gang. You're lucky you're not dead."

When I looked over my shoulder and back at the gang, I was greeted with an explosion of inappropriate hand gestures and threats of subjugation in a manner that had me suddenly concerned for my safety. Hightailing it out of there, we made it safely to Elisa's car and headed back to campus. The experiment had suddenly come to an end.

Despite that unfortunate incident, the experience at the Inner Harbor was eye-opening in many ways, and gave me an insight into acting that I would not have found in any other way. Many years later, while running with Widespread Panic, I'd take my street theater antics to the people of Athens, Georgia, and show them the ancient art of improvisation (with similar reactions being the obvious end result). Although it would be a somewhat more successful experiment, it did evoke similar responses that once again put my safety into question.

What can I say? I've always been a man of adventure.

For the one year I was at Western Maryland College, I simply threw myself into every aspect of college life that was available. Dorm life was a riot as Dan and I ran wild with the geeks, freaks, dweebs, and nerds of the fourth floor. Crazy, free-for-all parties would erupt throughout the week, exposing me to the world of boozing and other collegiate festivities.

One of our favorite pastimes was filling a 25-gallon garbage can with grain alcohol and fruit punch. Utilizing a six foot-long lacrosse stick, we'd stand on a chair, place one end of the stick in the can and suck on the other end until filled with the tasty beverage. Having someone cover the opposite end of the stick with their hand, you'd then tip the stick up and drink the alcohol. This was known as "Lax Bongs," Lax being a reference to lacrosse, and this would ensure that you not only ended the night in a drunken stupor, but that you'd be left with a wicked hangover that would linger for days.

Many afternoons would be spent playing golf on the school's course with a group of friends. Carrying coolers of beer as well as our golf clubs, we'd enhance the experience with a round of bong hits upon completing each hole, and invariably wind up stumbling off the golf course after completing the final hole. Dan and I even played several rounds of night golf, and on one such outing, Dan hit a hole-in-one on a par 3 hole one night. We were both so astonished upon finding his ball in the hole that we jumped around like kids on Christmas.

There were Saturday afternoons watching football games in the fall and Tuesday evenings watching basketball games in the winter, all the while cheering on The Green Terror at the top of our lungs. There were celebrations every weekend—throughout the week, in fact—and intramural basketball and volleyball games just about every time you turned around. There were endless nights at the pub, bong sessions in between classes, long philosophical debates with friends on lazy afternoons, and studious discussions about everything under the sun until the wee hours of morning.

Being a healthy, vibrant nineteen-year-old kid, I explored the world of college coeds as well. I elected not to have a permanent girlfriend during my tenure so I courted as many girls as I could. One night, while hanging with the freaks of the fourth floor, we all proceeded to get as drunk as hobos at a track-side hoedown. There was a beautiful brunette named Jennifer among us, and when it came time to end the festivities, it was apparent that Jennifer needed assistance to make it back to her room. I volunteered for the task simply because I was the only one remaining who could still walk. Wrapping my arm firmly around her, I all but carried Jennifer to her room as she let me know just how much she would enjoy spending the night with me.

Once inside her room, Jennifer proceeded to strip her clothes off, lay naked upon her bed and exposed her full, feminine form to me in wondrous fashion. I gazed at her glorious frame and was transfixed by what I saw; I was only moments away from ravaging her. As I contemplated the possibilities, however, something inside spoke to me, telling me that to take advantage of a vulnerable female in such a condition was terribly wrong. Is that how I wanted to get intimate with her? Instead, I elected to stay beside her as she continued to tempt me, waiting until she drifted off to sleep before I headed back to my room.

When I met the boys in the dining hall the next morning, they prodded me for steamy details about my evening with Jennifer. Even before I had the opportunity to tell them the disappointing news, Jennifer walked up to the table, leaned over, and whispered into my ear.

"Did we do anything last night, Larry?" she asked.

"No sweetheart," I replied. "I waited until you fell asleep and went back to my room."

Jennifer threw her arms firmly around my neck and kissed my cheek repeatedly while thanking me for being such a gentleman. Her reaction was incredible, a lesson I never forgot, and one I have carried in my heart all these years.

My brother Michael, who was studying at Fairview State University in Fairview, West Virginia, came to visit me numerous times at Western Maryland. Those weekends were a riot, getting to hang with Michael while introducing him to the freaks and partying until the early morning hours. Michael—still limiting his drinking to special occasions—would get as crazy as my friends and me, cutting it up and raging like a madman, despite being sober.

One night, after a long evening of merrymaking, Michael and I found ourselves in my dorm listening to music. In the soft light of the room, Michael was sitting on the bed opposite me when he began to apologize for how he treated me when we were kids, becoming overwhelmed with guilt for something none of us had control over in the first place. Touched by his gesture, I tried my best to put Michael's heart at ease.

"Man, I really appreciate that, Michael, I really do," I said as my mind basked in the beauty of the moment, "and I accept your apology. But bro, we were kids, in a tough and violent situation we couldn't escape. There really is no need to apologize; we were all guilty of something back then. No one escaped it."

"I know, Larry," Michael countered. I could see his eyes shimmering in the dim light of the room. "But that does little to ease the guilt."

"I know how you feel, bro...I know how you feel," I replied, drifting off. "I love you, bro, and no need to apologize ever again, you dig?"

After a short pause, Michael finally said, "Yeah, you're right, Larry. I love you too, man." And off to sleep we went.

To this day, the subject has never again been brought up.

When winter began, Dan decided that he wanted to cultivate several marijuana plants in our room, utilizing his expertise in biology and the botanical arts. I was not only happy to accommodate this new endeavor, but assisted Dan in every way possible. When Christmas break came, we did everything necessary to ensure the healthy maturation of the cannabis while we were gone.

What we didn't anticipate was maintenance men entering our room to replace our windows. When we returned, not only were the plants gone, but a summons for a court date had been left in their place.

The court date was no big deal; we accepted the fine and community service without a fight. But this is not the point of the story. As Dan and I entered the courtroom and took a seat, a man in a black t-shirt and camouflage pants was standing before the judge with his back to us. He had long, scraggly hair and a big rebel flag on the back of his shirt. The judge was reading off a long list of charges that included assault and battery on a woman, illegal possession of a firearm, and violation of parole.

When the judge finished with his chastisement and gave the man a seemingly harsh sentence (five years without parole), Dan and I were struck dumb when the man turned to face the gallery. There, on the front of his shirt for all to see, were the words "Kill 'Em All And Let God Sort 'Em Out" in big, white letters. Dan and I looked to each other and shook our heads in astonishment. The cat might as well have been flipping the judge off while telling him to burn in hell. Maybe someone should have told him to change his shirt before entering the courtroom. I don't know, just a thought.

Now, in the midst of this mayhem, you may be asking yourself, "When did this guy have time to go to class?" Well, the reality was that I did have time, but the further the school year went on, the less I attended. And the reasons for this were simple; I didn't feel like I was learning anything from most of the professors I had. Some looked as bored as I felt while listening to their uninspired lectures. This was another glaring issue I had with formal education from the time I could remember: if a teacher isn't passionate about sharing their knowledge, how could the students be in accepting it?

Outside of Max Nixon, I had only one other teacher in my time at Western Maryland who made me excited about learning, and I'm emphasizing the word "excited" in this statement. This teacher was a subtly beautiful, bookish-looking woman with short, dark hair and glasses. She reminded me of the quintessential sexy librarian who hid behind a "Plain Jane" façade. But when she began discussing the ancient Romans, the class she was teaching, she would suddenly become overwhelmed with passion.

As she spoke of Caesar, or Pompey, or Cicero, or her favorite, Mark Antony, she would become flush with amorous delight. As she recited verse from memory, her small, perky breasts would rise and fall beneath her sweater as she gazed into the past and brought to life all the passion, all the sensuality, and all the glory of those great men—and she, in turn, would have every guy in her class hanging on her every word. As if suddenly becoming self-conscious about the effect she was having on her male students, she would immediately snap out of her trance, change her demeanor to the bookish professor of Ancient Roman Civilization she was, and carry on...until she once again became lost in her historical fantasies. That woman was a wonderful teacher. I'll never forget the affect she had on me (or the rest of the boys in her class) for as long as I live.

The rest of the teachers I had were dull, boring, passionless automatons who trudged through every day like they were on the Bataan Death March. Speaking in even, monotone voices and appearing as if the classroom was the last place they wanted to be, I had to fight through the nausea of disaffected rhetoric to find purpose for being there myself. As the year went on, I simply lost interest, and realized that I was learning more from open discussions with my peers than I was from these listless, aloof professors. This reality only added to my disenchantment with college life, creating a deeper wedge between myself and the absurdity of university policy, while sending me down a path I found increasingly more appealing: that of open rebellion towards the university system.

It was during this time that I would blow off class and head to the library, reading books, essays, and magazines pertaining to every facet of history—essentially becoming my own teacher. I would spend entire days and nights in the library, reading one volume after the other; my mind absorbed these tales like a sponge. Following these sessions, I'd head to a friend's room and continue discussions about anything that came to our minds.

One of my friends had a video documentary on World War II. For an entire week I sat in his room and watched twenty-two hours of that documentary over and over, smoking one bong hit after the other, becoming so absorbed in the content that I'd lose track of time, forgetting meals, oblivious to where I even was. This is where my college experience was heading, and this is where I felt I needed to be. It was a manifestation of attempting to deal with confusion: internally, where my emotions still quivered with echoes of the past, but also externally—towards an educational system I could no longer respect.

Instinctively—perhaps defensively—I rebelled.

This disenfranchisement only became stronger and more apparent as time went on, causing me to seriously rethink my time in college.

And when I first began to receive bank notices for a ridiculous school bill later in the year, I felt cheated, taken advantage of, and used. This feeling would become so powerful that I'd eventually be unable to break free of its allure, and actually grew to embrace it, putting me at serious odds with the entire higher educational system. (Another conversation with One-Armed Bob near the end of the school year only added to my disillusionment, fueling the fires of discontentment until I couldn't stand the heat any longer...but that tale will come later.)

But there was one more crucial element of my college life that needs to be examined—one that literally came knocking on my dorm room door one night, and one I thought I'd never be a part of in a million years: that of The Preachers, a group of guys who, over time, would prove to be as crazy and reckless as me.

Funny how things work out.

THE PREACHERS

From the moment I walked onto the campus of Western Maryland College in the fall of 1984, I began hearing crazy rumors and wild stories about a mysterious group of guys known as The Preachers. Their legend was striking, intimidating, designed to put the fear of God into everyone who came into contact with them...and it worked like a charm. It was a mythical reputation, larger than life, and one that preceded them like a fierce and dominant army from the pages of ancient history. The Preachers had people cowering in fear before they'd even met them. They were, without a doubt, the bad boys of the campus. Further explorations into who these secretive and menacing cats were revealed their true identity: the fraternity of Delta Pi Alpha. And even further research unmasked their troubling past.

The year before I arrived on campus, the Delta Pi Alpha fraternity had lost its charter and been forced to disband. Kicked off school grounds, the frat had been obliged to close its doors and move their operations underground, even though they were the oldest, longest-lasting fraternity in school history. The reasons for the ostracization were plentiful: inappropriate hazing rituals; excessive underage drinking; wild, out-of-control parties; disregard for school policies; fighting; intimidation; and general rabble-rousing. The school had been forced to take a stand. And the fact that one of their hazing rituals had made national news months earlier did not help The Preachers' cause in any way either.

The previous spring, a new recruit was force-fed excessive amounts of alcohol, taken to a field in the farmlands of Western Maryland, stripped to his underwear and tied to a tree. The following morning, a farmer making his rounds found the kid unconscious, near freezing, and close to death. The farmer saved the student's life, but with this final incident, the school had had enough. The Preachers were no more, and became a skeleton crew of their former selves.

By the time I had arrived on campus, the reputation of The Preachers was nothing short of terrifying. Fellow students told me to go nowhere near them, to avoid them at all cost, and that to enter their world meant trouble on a grand scale. The more I heard about them, the more appealing their rebellious reputation became.

Although no more than fifteen members remained by the time I arrived, The Preachers still maintained their status as a fraternity — illegally, mind you — and upheld their reputations as rebels and outcasts with a continued reign of terror. On occasion, I would see one of these guys, and exchange respectful greetings, but felt that it was best to keep my distance. By this time, I'd had enough of confrontation and unrestrained machismo, deciding that it would be in my best interest to stay away from a group of guys who relished in such insanity. But as winter recruiting season hit full stride, it was rumored that The Preachers were once again looking for fresh meat.

And, it was also rumored, they didn't recruit just anyone.

The Preachers wanted the toughest, coolest, baddest cats available to them, and doggedly pursued those they considered worthy. So why they began hounding me so relentlessly was anyone's guess. I was a pot-smoking, poetry-reading, philosophy-preaching, music-loving actor who would much rather court the ladies and make art than swill bad liquor and kick ass. But the one aspect about me that might shed light on the situation was that I was a big, strong, rugged-looking cat with long hair hanging down to the small of my back. If I didn't act the part of a Preacher, I certainly looked it—and to fraternities, well... appearance is everything. So I was on their radar.

Being a kid who has always taken pride in walking through life as his own man, observing the fraternity life was an eye opening experience. To witness their rituals and secret handshakes always confused me: why, I thought, would anyone ever want to be a part of a group that relished in such normalcy and all-out conformity? The fraternity mentality went against the grain of every fiber of my being. Fraternities, I thought convincingly, were not for me. But the one thing I didn't realize at the time was that The Preachers were not your average fraternity. They were rebels, they were outcasts, they were pariahs—and they did not care an iota about rules and regulations. They, I would come to see, flew in the face of convention, breaking the mold of your average fraternity in a monumental way. These boys put Animal House to shame. And no matter what I would do, The Preachers would continue to hound me; they were dead-set on making me one of their own. It now became a test of will.

It all started so innocently: just a knock on my dorm room door one evening, as I sat studying for an upcoming test. I opened the door and was shocked to see two members of Delta Pi Alpha, smiling and greeting me like I was a long-lost friend. I had heard rumors that they were going to pursue me, and now here it was; the time had come. Immediately, they forced their way through the door while complimenting me on my choice of music, the posters on my walls, books on the tables, and the hipster knickknacks strewn throughout the room. I could tell that they were trying to sell me something from the moment I met them, and now began the chess match. Both of these guys were big, strong, muscular football players who had tough reputations and intimidating dispositions; I knew instantly that they were making nice with the compliments just to soften me up.

"Look, guys," I began, "I appreciate you taking an interest in me, but fraternities aren't for me. I just don't think it would work out. Thanks again, but I need to get back to the books."

Showing them gently to the door, one of the guys continued with his recruiting spiel.

"Hey, man," he countered while grasping my shoulder, "we're having a party Friday night off campus, why don't you swing by and meet the boys?" He handed me a slip of paper with an address on it.

"Sure," I replied. "I'll see what I can do," and I closed the door behind them.

Although flattered that they thought I was Preacher material, I wanted nothing to do with the lifestyle. But I must tell you, the stories I had heard about their initiation week *did* perk my ears. I heard that it was tough, brutal, and unforgiving. I heard that most people caved in and succumbed to the abuse in short order. I had lived through Detroit; I had lived through my time with Coach Hanson; I had lived through my own home life and a real-life version of "The Lord of the Flies."

So now, naturally, I wondered: *could I handle The Preachers?*

Putting these thoughts to the side, I resumed studying and carried on with life as if it were just another day. But if I thought I was getting off easy, I was underestimating the tenacity of The Preachers.

The truth is they were just getting started.

Over the next several weeks, and as winter gave way to springtime, the recruiting process reached a fevered pitch. The man The Preachers faithfully sent my way was Norm Dennison, one of the brothers I had initially met at my dorm room when the recruitment began. Norm was a great guy with whom I shared a lot of similar interests. Despite his "jock" façade, Norm was intelligent, curious, funny, and loyal—and above all, he loved The Preachers. He was determined to make me a member of his fraternity simply because he believed that my unorthodox lifestyle, mixed with my strong physical attributes, would only enhance the mystique of The Preachers.

Another aspect of my life that you may need to understand to fully appreciate my state of mind at the time was that by the time recruiting season came, I was a balls-to-the-wall, angry, confused, and bitter young man. Again, there was a perfect storm brewing that came to a head at the most inopportune time.

I was angry about my childhood; I was angry at the state of the world; I was angry about the confusion swirling in my head and I was angry at who I was. I could see the possibilities in life, but felt that I didn't know how to pursue them. I felt as if I was put directly behind the eight ball and without the proper tools to pursue my dreams. I felt disenfranchised, unworthy, and perpetually ignorant about everything other than what I held in my heart. And I believe that Norm and The Preachers understood this, and appealed to those shortcomings while pointing the way to open rebellion. I've always worn my emotions on my sleeves and could not hide them if I tried. I was a walking time bomb, moments away from igniting.

In short, I felt lost. And that's when I was found—by a gang of Preachers.

Norm continued to appear at my dorm room, at the library, at the theater, outside my classes, and at parties, ceaselessly expounding the positive virtues of his brotherhood. The test of will had hit full stride. Norm and I began having debates and in-depth conversations, not just about The Preachers, but life in general. Norm was a smart guy, and these conversations became hilarious, if not completely addictive on an intellectual level, as he would make a move and I would counter. Norm would digest my words and throw something back in my face that I'd have to think about long and hard. Then I'd counter again. And so it went, back and forth, move after move, and over time I began to respect Norm as an intellectual peer, someone with whom I could discuss just about anything. In turn, Norm began to respect me as something more than an average recruit. He began to see me as not only worthy, but someone who could potentially obliterate the stereotype of the meathead Preacher in one fell swoop.

Slowly but surely, Norm began to make headway. And slowly but surely, Norm and I became friends. One night, as recruiting week loomed, Norm showed up at a study hall as I prepared for an upcoming exam. It was then that Norm broke through my resistant veneer.

"I don't know, Norm," I reiterated, "a fraternity? It's just not me, man."

"Look at it this way, Larry," Norm expanded, "I know that you're a man who loves adventure. So view this experience as just that: a new experience that you can add to your life story. Imagine," he said with a convincing flair, "you — a hipster, rock and roller, philosopher-artist guy — joining the bad boys of campus and running with the outcasts of the school. It's a perfect match, man, and I guarantee that you'll never have an experience like this ever again. And the fact is, Larry, we don't want someone who thinks like everyone else. That's what we're all about: independence, man. Fuck this school and their policies, bro. What good is living life if you don't try to buck the system that breeds conformity? This school doesn't want us, and we don't want them."

Suddenly, Norm began to make sense. Yeah, I thought, all I'm doing is committing to the experience. Nothing more. And it was an experience that might assist in fighting through my perpetual confusion. After all, in my state of mind, I knew that I was in the midst of a fight — a fight to, in the end, preserve my sanity. Suddenly, I viewed The Preachers as an adventure, a chance at a unique experience, one that (as I gleaned through the endless stories I'd heard about The Preachers) not everyone could handle. All of a sudden it became a challenge, a moment in time that could come around only once in a lifetime. I now began to see The Preachers as an entity that fought against conformity while maintaining a façade of normalcy. They were, in essence, rebelling against rebellion. It was an appealing reality, and one I had never encountered before. Suddenly, I found myself nodding my head, extending my hand, and smiling like the Cheshire Cat.

"Okay, man, I'm in, I'm ready to do it. Fuck it; it'll be an adventure."

Norm and I hugged, laughed, and slapped hands like lifelong pals. I was now a potential new brother for the Delta Pi Alpha Fraternity of Western Maryland College in Westminster, Maryland. And as Norm had promised, it would be an experience I would never forget.

The initiation rituals of a fraternity, and especially The Preachers, are, to put it mildly, interesting. Although sworn to secrecy, something I have always held firm to, what I *can* tell you may be enlightening on some level. The Preachers' reputation as fierce and intimidating hombres held true. Once I was within the fold, the initiation period — known as "Hell Week" — was brutal and humbling. These guys didn't give a fuck about rules and regulations; hell, they weren't just a fraternity, they were an *illegal* fraternity. They simply did whatever they pleased. After all, who was going to stop them?

The whole point of the experience was designed to put you in your place and keep you down. The brothers of Delta Pi Alpha were adept at establishing a pecking order, assuring that potential new members understood who was in charge. The experience was pure mayhem and one that, in my rabid state of mind, I relished as I pushed the limits of endurance.

In fact, of the ten new recruits in my class, four dropped out in the first two days, succumbing to the physical and mental abuse immediately. The six of us who remained were forced to endure the wrath of the brothers on a daily, and nightly, basis. They'd show up at my classes, at my dorm room, in the library, at the theater, in the dining hall, or wherever else I'd be, and drag me away to continue the experiment of debauchery and torment on a scale I never knew existed. As angry and confused as I was, I grew to absolutely love the experience, rebelling and fighting against everything I viewed as normal and safe. I wanted the pain, I wanted the humility, I wanted the chaos and embraced the bedlam.

For the entirety of that week, my fellow new recruits and I were subjected to whatever the brothers desired. We were completely at their mercy as one painful and humbling experiment after the other rained down on us in wicked fashion. Hell, there were several times that *I* almost dropped out due to the abuse, but as Mama always told me, "Once you start something you finish it, for that is the true test of one's character." There was no way I was going to walk away from what I started.

The one thing I understood from the beginning of that week was that The Preachers absolutely loved breaking the rules. Standards that all other fraternities held firmly to were thrown out the window with The Preachers. There were no rules, no mercy, and certainly no room for weak constitutions. In fact, once I began hearing stories about how other fraternities approached their Hell Week at Western Maryland, and elsewhere, I was infused with a sense of pride; those other recruiting practices couldn't hold a candle to ours. I soon came to see just how unique The Preachers were.

All other fraternities were merely playing pattycake with their new members while The Preachers beat the ever-living shit out of theirs. They made us work for our place in the group, a badge of courage and pride I would wear proudly. After a week of some of the most bizarre and demanding experiences I had ever encountered, the light was now at the end of the tunnel, and I — a wild rock-and-roller from the east side of Detroit, Michigan — was one step closer to becoming a Preacher.

With the experience finally coming to an end, the culmination of Hell Week was highlighted by two distinct features once the brutality of the initiation was completed: the scavenger hunt and The Midnight Basketball Game, two more undertakings that would prove to be unlike any other. In order to become full-fledged members, it was imperative that we carry out these assignments — or the entire exhaustive, humiliating week would be all for naught. As it would turn out, the scavenger hunt was a blast, consisting of a weekend run to New York City with two other new brothers. Once in The Big Apple, we had to perform certain tasks, then provide proof of our prowess through photographs documenting our exploits.

Another recruit and I had to jump into the seal pool at The Bronx Zoo. As the seals howled and the straights looked at us like we were insane, we jumped around in that pool, swimming with the pudgy inhabitants, until informed by the brother taking the pictures that it was time to move on.

Our next stop was the Empire State Building. We rode the elevator to the top floor, mixing with the throngs of tourists, then moved out to the viewing area. Casually pulling a bong from a backpack, we sat in a circle and passed it around, puffing and taking pictures of one another as people milled around like it was just another day in the Big Apple.

We then had to steal a menu from Sardi's on 44th Street. The scenario involved pretending to take a seat at a table, just like regular patrons settling in for a fine meal; but once the menu was in our possession, we ran out of that place like we were on fire, snagging whatever else we could carry as we made a beeline for the door. The straights had no idea what was going on, recoiling in fear as we zoomed past, looking like lunatics. It was freaking hilarious, man.

Our final mission was to get an autograph from a celebrity, which, to our dismay, never materialized. There was a rumor that Bill Murray was in the vicinity, but our search for him ended in a wild goose chase. This part of the odyssey has always been a thorn in my side, and the perceived failure on our behalf remains tough to swallow. Upon our return to campus, however, the older brothers welcomed us with open arms, assuring us that we had not only survived Hell Week, but were now full-fledged members of Delta Pi Alpha.

Full-fledged, that is, barring one last assignment: The Midnight Basketball Game.

Western Maryland College was a small school, where secrets were hard to keep and relatively easy to dissect. The one rumor I had heard about (but never fully understood) was The Midnight Basketball Game. This was a mystery shrouded in secrecy and innuendo. I never could grasp what it was about, or who participated in it, for a variety of reasons—the main one being that the event had been outlawed by the school authorities. But the day after the six new members of Delta Pi Alpha returned from our scavenger hunt following Hell Week, we were informed what The Midnight Basketball Game was all about.

One night, we—the newly-ordained Preachers—gathered in one of the older brother's dorm rooms and were told to take a seat. We were then notified that at midnight, we were to dress in our new Delta Pi Alpha long-sleeve shirts and make our way to the gymnasium. There, we were to play a basketball game against the brothers of our rival fraternity: Gamma Beta Chi. Sounded simple enough, I thought. But then the older brothers added a twist: this game, they assured, would not be your typical roundball contest of putting a ball through a hoop in a gentlemanly fashion. This game — for all intents and purposes — had no rules. It would literally be a fight to the finish, the Last Man Standing, a test of brutality and endurance on a ridiculous scale, with not a single one of us escaping the punishment of what was to be essentially a rugby match performed on the unforgiving hardwood floor of the gymnasium. And since the game had been banned by the school, we were again about to buck the system and fly in the face of convention. The older brothers also informed us that most of the school would be there, drunk and wild, awaiting the return of a ritual that was so brutal, so crazy and out-of-control, that we were taking our physical and academic lives into our hands just to be a part of it.

As I sat in silence listening to the older brothers describing the final rite of passage in our journey to become members of this near-mythic fraternity, I again contemplated walking away and simply throwing the experience of the past week to the wind. *A brawl on a basketball court?* I thought in anguish. *Are these guys insane?*

But deep down, I knew I couldn't walk away now. I was in way too deep. And I also believed that, on some level, this ordeal would address the overwhelming angst ravaging my soul: I began to feel that it was something I *needed* to experience. As game time approached, I hit the booze and the bong to deaden my senses; instinctively, I knew I was entering a new strata of absurdity.

Along with my fellow new brothers, I gave into my fate and seized the moment; we were now gladiators going into the fight of our lives. There was no turning back now. When Zero Hour arrived, the boys and I gave our battle cry and emptied out into the quad, where — calling to us from just about every surrounding window — we encountered our peers, howling and encouraging us as we made our way to the gymnasium in a neat row.

As we approached the gym, we came upon even more students crowding the entrance; they parted like the Red Sea to allow our passage. We walked through the front doors, headed straight to the gymnasium and, upon entering, were astounded at the sight before us.

There, filling the stands to capacity, were hundreds of onlookers: students, faculty, townies, school employees, professors, cleaning personnel, local drunks, and even several children, all whooping it up, screaming wildly and crying out for blood. I couldn't believe my eyes. I felt like a lamb being led to slaughter, a convict being sent to the gallows, a Christian being fed to the lions. All the while, more and more people filed in, anticipating the spectacle of a group of knuckleheads beating the ever-living shit out of one another, all for the glory of blood sport. We had just entered the Coliseum and were about to unleash pure hell on one another for the enjoyment of the crazed, inebriated masses who cried out for carnage. They would not be disappointed.

While gathering on the bench and receiving the final motivational speech, we put our game faces on and listened intently to Norm.

"Now, boys!" He cried above the ceaseless chaos of the crowd. "Remember, there are no rules, no fouls, and no referees. The object of the game is to score as much as we can within the time allotted: four eight-minute quarters. Let's keep our shit together, let's help each other out, and DO NOT LOSE the game! Now, let's give 'em hell, boys!"

As in a normal game of basketball, there were to be only five players per side allowed on the court at the same time. The difference was that this game resembled basketball in only two ways: we were on a basketball court, and there was a basketball involved. Beyond that, everything was pure madness. Unlike a normal game where the contest begins with a gentle jump ball at center court, we were placed in a line opposite our opponents near mid-court, with a ball resting between us. A whistle was blown; both sides charged the ball, and each other, for possession of an object that was to become the focal point of so much pain. The game had begun.

I really don't remember much of the actual game. Perhaps it was one of those situations where, to preserve my sanity, I blocked it from my memory. But the things I do remember are disturbing enough and make me shudder whenever I think of them.

I remember running blindly down the court, with ball in hand, stiff-arming my opponents as they attempted to rip my head off. I remember having my legs knocked out from under me as I went up for a shot, only to slam painfully into the floor below. I remember elbows being thrown, fists flying, heads crashing into one another and even a blurred recollection of being thrashed into a wall as I went up for yet another shot.

I recall the endless roar of the crowd, the continuous instructions coming from the older brothers, the cries of anger, pain, and triumph resonating from both teams as young men attempted to prove themselves as worthy. I recollect being abused, slammed, punched, and kicked. I remember being spit at, laughed at, and blindsided. And I remember holding my own, retaliating wildly, and defending myself as madness swirled all around me.

I remember running headlong into an opponent—even though the ball was nowhere near him—and striking him with all my might, forcing him to crash violently into the floor. I recall taking out the man's legs who had initially taken me out, and watching in astonishment as he flipped in mid-air and plunged to the hardwood. I remember throwing elbows, body-slamming opponents, tackling my foes, and crying out in ravenous delight as another enemy player went down in dramatic form. And I remember, somehow, someway, scoring a basket as the game continued on in a violent, unforgiving pageant of pain and abuse.

I also remember wanting the experience to come to an end as soon as humanly possible.

That quartet of eight-minute periods felt like an eternity. I was forced to use every one of my senses, and every physical attribute I possessed, just to survive. *This scene is crazy, man!* I remember thinking. *These guys are trying to kill me!* Unflinchingly, I fought on. Relentlessly, I surged forth. Menacingly, I entered the realm of a madman. There was a moment of insanity, a flinch of lunacy, and a hair's breadth of dementia. I began swinging, throwing, kicking, and thrashing about at anything that moved. My mind went blank, my heart stopped feeling, and my soul became devoid of consciousness. This was survival, man, pure and simple, and I had to either fight my way through or wind up in the annals of those who didn't make it.

And yet, just beneath the protective veneer of mania, a less-deranged voice was asking: *When will this madness end? When will it end?*

Eventually, thankfully, the game did come to an end. And despite a plethora of bloody noses, black eyes, fat lips, cuts, bruises, and scrapes, every one of us walked away in one piece. Who won the game is anyone's guess, and has been forever lost to the dusty pages of history. And did it really matter who triumphed at such a ridiculous event as this? I do retain a distant memory of the score being 3-2, a testament to the brutality of the experience. The only thing that did matter was that all of us—Preachers and Betas alike—lived to see another day, and add our own chapter to the Tale of The Midnight Basketball Game.

Following the game, both fraternities gathered together to drink into the wee hours of the night, reliving the insanity of the farce, as one absurd story after the other made us laugh hysterically. Friendships were born, relationships forged, and memories solidified as we continued on with the college experience full-throttle. But none of us — and I mean *none* of us — would ever forget the gauntlet that we had just survived.

And that night, I became a full-fledged member of the Delta Pi Alpha Fraternity of Western Maryland College.

I was now a Preacher.

As spring crept on — and Hell Week, the scavenger hunt and The Midnight Basketball Game passed into history — I knew in my heart that my time at Western Maryland College was coming to an end. Once again, I felt that I truly didn't belong; despite the friendships made, the experiences I'd had, all that I had learned, and all that I had seen, college life was just not for me. I felt dissatisfied, disillusioned, and alienated. Looking at my fellow classmates — most of whom had strong family ties, guidance, direction, and support of every kind — I once again felt like I was as alone as I could possibly be. These kids were going home to internships and lucrative summer jobs; vacations to the Caribbean, or Europe, and other exotic locales; parental homes in Baltimore, D. C., New York, and Philly.

I didn't even know where I was going to live for the summer.

I felt lost, tapped out, disoriented, and angry. There was something burning inside me — something that I couldn't pinpoint, something that wasn't making any sense. I felt as if I needed more out of life... but just what that "more" was, I couldn't decipher. I felt I had to move on, take my chances, and search for something else, even though I knew it seemed unrealistic and far beyond my reach. I felt like I was splitting in two. I knew that, despite the potential for failure, I had to make a move.

One day, nearing the end of the school year, I was helping One-Armed Bob load some tables into a truck following a school function. It was the waning days of classes; graduation was approaching, and once again, I had found myself at a crossroads. Having just received my first notice for the overwhelming $10,000 debt to the bank just days ago, I became stricken with anger, and had no clue as to what I wanted to do with my life. As if Bob could peer deep into my soul, he told me to lower the table we were carrying and looked directly at me. Gazing hard into my eyes, he spit out a stream of tobacco juice, readjusted the John Deere cap and smiled.

"Boy," he began in his familiar, farmer's drawl, "why do you want to go to school for, anyhow? You know they let anyone through those doors who has the money, right?"

"What do you mean, Bob?" I replied in a self-conscious tone. "I want to learn."

"Boy, I've been working here a long time, and I see them givin' out those diplomas to kids dumber than you and me combined. Just because you can read the right books, answer the proper questions, and kiss the right amount of ass don't make you smart. There's a lot more ways to get smart, and fallin' into the right lines at the right time don't make it so. This 'ol place is a bigger racket than those casinos in Las Vegas."

I stood before Bob and continued to hold his gaze. His words hung before me like lingering cigar smoke. I took a deep breath; while he made perfect sense, his message only deepened my confusion. I looked up at the sky; it was a startling azure that day. Somehow, it was like seeing the firmament for the first time.

"Boy," Bob went on, "God don't care how many certificates you have sayin' how smart you are, all he cares about is that you do something good with your life and make the people you love happy and proud. Don't ever do things 'cause your *'sposed* to, do them because you *want* to. These places crank out diplomas like McDonald's cranks out hamburgers, and to me they're just the same: shit disguised as gold. Live your life, boy...live your life. Time on this planet is far too short."

In all my time at Western Maryland College, the best teacher I had turned out to be a one-armed farmer's son who most people wouldn't have given the time of day. I have carried Bob's words of wisdom in my heart, and have reflected upon them often in my life. I have met few who could hold a candle to his insight and strength; the world would be a much happier place with more men like him in it.

The semester finally came to an end. I bade farewell to Western Maryland College, packed up my bags, and reluctantly headed to West Virginia, the home of my mother and Mr. Rob. In one year of schooling, I had pushed the limits of exploration to the furthest degree possible; I'd experienced things I would remember forever, and met people who would never fade from my heart. My future was wide open, just waiting to be discovered, and the only thing I knew was that I could not settle for an ordinary life — on any level — for as long as I lived.

I also knew that in a very real way, despite the confusion hounding my soul, I was just getting started. I also knew that the journey would only get more interesting as time moved on, but what awaited me would even surprise this crazy motherfucker from the wild, untamed streets of the east side of Detroit.

Giddy up there, little pardner, giddy up! This wild man was just about to blaze new trails that he didn't even know existed, not even in the furthest reaches of his imagination. And he would come to see just how wild the world could be — just how crazy *he* could be — as he sallied forth through the great experiment called life.

12. TUCSON, ARIZONA

I ARRIVED AT MY PARENTS' NEW HOME IN CHARLES TOWN, WEST VIRginia, feeling restless and uncertain. Looking at a future that suddenly appeared vague and devoid of direction, I knew that life in a small West Virginia town was not for me. The only thing I was certain about during this period was that I didn't want safety, comfort, or security — I wanted the exact opposite. And I also knew that I didn't want university, religion, government, or even a career. All I wanted was experience, and cared little about how I got it.

A day or two after being with my parents, I took a drive to Leesburg, Virginia, where Mom and Mr. Rob worked for a small newspaper. My mother told me that there was a Greenpeace office in town, and I — being the young, adventurous kid I was — thought that this may be a good experience for me. Given my state of mind at the time, I felt that working for Greenpeace would be a perfect environment to explore the world while diffusing my angst.

I made my way to the offices, told them who I was, and offered my services.

"Well, what would you like to do with Greenpeace, Larry?" A female employee asked.

"Anything," I replied. "I'm ready for anything. Send me halfway around the world to save whales if you need to. I'm up for anything. "

"Well, do you have a college degree?"

"No, I don't,"

"Oh," she countered in a lofty tone. "Well, you can help stuff envelopes if you'd like."

I looked at that woman like the pretentious, self-serving dolt she was. Here was a strong, healthy, ambitious young man who was ready to lay his life on the line for seals, dolphins, turtles—hell, for humanity itself—and all she could do was offer me a volunteer job licking envelopes. I stood from my chair, shook my head in contempt, and walked out of there while cursing her arrogance. I would never again consider working for the likes of Greenpeace. Talk about elitism—Greenpeace wrote the book on it.

A day or two following this incident I received a call from my sister Maria. She was living in Tucson, Arizona, where she'd attended the University of Arizona, and subsequently met the man who would become her husband. Now married and expecting a child, Maria and her husband Don were operating an apartment complex, and had called to ask if I wanted to come out and work for them. I immediately accepted the offer. A couple of days later I was on a plane out of Washington, D.C., bound for the Grand Canyon State quicker than you can say "howdy pad'na", and preparing to start the next chapter of my life.

Though I'd never been west of the Mississippi River at that point in my life, I was nevertheless ready for the adventure, and embraced the opportunity with everything I had. Once again, I would not be disappointed, nor could I have ever prepared myself for what I was about to get into. My time in Tucson would truly be a Western Adventure.

The plan, after touching down in "The Old Pueblo" of Tucson, was to learn the ropes of managing the apartment complex. I was to take over the managerial duties after a couple of months training, which would allow

Maria and Don the opportunity to move on to greener pastures. Seemed simple enough to me...but once settled into my new environs, I quickly realized that my daily managerial operations would be anything but routine.

I soon discovered that this apartment complex—dubbed "La Fiesta Apartments"—was not populated with hipsters and swingin' singles, hepcats and kool kids, Johnnies-On-The-Spot and rock-and-rollers too cool for school. Rather, it became quickly apparent that this apartment complex, located off Speedway Boulevard in Central Tucson, was smack-dab in the heart of the Red Light District: it was chock-full of freaks, psychotics, outcasts, drug addicts, prostitutes, alcoholics, fairies, degenerates, wife abusers, knuckleheads, geeks, and all around down-and-out nut jobs. I immediately felt at home. These were the kind of people I had become comfortable with—no pretentions, no arrogance, no games. People like this were real.

The complex sat on Mabel St., two blocks north of West Speedway Boulevard. It was conveniently located across the street from a fleabag motel populated with streetwalkers and their pimps, and right next door to a homosexual nightclub. The rest of the neighborhood was equally stimulating, consisting mainly of liquor stores, pawnshops, nightclubs, greasy-spoon diners, and an assortment of destitute motels, apartment complexes, and low-rent housing.

In fact, on my first day there, while walking down Speedway on my way to a convenience store for some snacks, I saw approaching me a couple of young kids who appeared rather intoxicated, even though it was only shortly after noon. One of the kids, who seemed especially lit, carried a double-barreled shotgun that he slung over his shoulder like an old time desperado. As I passed by, I doubled up on the respectful gestures and appropriate salutations. Luckily for me, I don't think they even realized I was there; they walked right past me, laughing, joking, and stumbling like a couple of drunks at a Friday night soiree. Such was the flavor of my new home.

Despite the condition of the neighborhood and the apartment complex itself, Maria and Don welcomed me with open arms and made me feel right at home. They lived in the manager's apartment above the office, and furnished me with my own living space; I would take over their apartment once they had trained me and moved on.

With the manager's apartment being the exception, every other living space in the two-building, two-story complex was an efficiency unit — a one-room box with a small kitchenette and even smaller bathroom. Being twenty years old and single, I needed nothing more, and quickly decked out apartment 106 of Building One with all the hipster accouterment at my disposal. I was ready for the adventure to begin.

Those first few weeks with Don and Maria were hysterical as we explored Tucson and all it had to offer. There were excursions to border towns and trips to other tourist traps in the area. One of these was to The O. K. Corral in Tombstone, southeast of the city. There we enjoyed a cheesy tram ride that was suddenly ambushed by a gang of bandits; they jumped on the cars and demanded money and valuables from the tourists. I became so engrossed in the experience, and cowered in fear so convincingly, that the man portraying the bandit closest to us broke from his character and complimented me on my acting skills. My thespian chops had followed me to Tucson. I was now a nationwide sensation, man...

Don was a Mormon, and Maria had converted to the religion shortly before their wedding. This only added to the hilarity, as the two of them tried to convert me in playful (and sometimes not-so-playful) ways. What ensued were long discussions about religion, God, and all that other stuff, as Don and I would go round and round attempting to influence the other, all to no avail. Before long, we both realized that the other wouldn't crack, and simply put such shenanigans to the side out of respect for one another. Although the threat of conversion was always there, I never allowed it to get out of control. By now, I knew too much, and would never submit to the tainted allure of religion.

Immediately following my arrival, Don took me under his wing and showed me the ins-and-outs of running "the asylum"—a moniker that sounds harsh, but was, in truth, frighteningly fitting.

"Larry," Don cautioned one day as the training began, "these people can be...well...eccentric. One thing we do here is offer cheap housing to recently released patients from the Palo Verde Psychiatric Hospital. They can be...um...different."

Shortly after settling in, I began to understand just how different the clientele was.

There was Josie, a longtime resident who was as old as the hills and as disoriented as a wingless bird. Her special talent was walking the halls butt-naked while searching for someone, anyone, to dance a jig with.

"Come on, sweetheart, the party hasn't started yet," I would say when I saw her roaming the halls in her birthday suit. "Let's get you home in case your date shows up early."

"Oh, Larry," she would reply while stroking my cheek tenderly, "you're such a sweet boy."

There was Enrique, an incredibly charming and engaging transvestite who took a liking to me from the moment we met. I returned the favor, spending time with the flamboyant Puerto Rican while watching movies, drinking beer, and listening to music in his apartment as we discussed the gossip of the day. Enrique was one of my closest friends at the apartments, and accepted my friendship unconditionally. He was a great guy.

There were Millie and Ron, a sweet old couple from Wisconsin who chose the La Fiesta Apartments as their retirement spot, and apparently elected to spend their golden years hanging out at the pool, drinking beer day-in and day-out, from sunup to sundown. I spent a lot of time with Millie and Ron at that pool, listening intently to their stories and sharing my own. They were really good people.

There was Allison, a beautiful, vivacious, blond-haired young woman with striking green eyes and a personality that was equally enticing. Allison was a perfect example of the people who populated the La Fiesta Apartments. Though she was one of the most beautiful girls I had ever met, Allison was also remarkably sweet and unpretentious, grounded in a way that seems to elude most beautiful people. She had a two-year-old son named Michael and was working two jobs to support him—but I never once heard her complain about her situation. Despite her tough lot in life, she was as bright and warm as the Arizona sun. Allison and I would become close friends and spent a lot of time hanging out together, talking and drinking beer. Perhaps the most comforting aspect about our relationship was that I never once felt compelled to engage in sexual relations with her; despite her irrefutable beauty, I couldn't help but view her as a sister. We remained solid friends throughout my stay at La Fiesta.

Then there was Joe the Plumber, a soft-spoken, lonely retiree who was once a master plumber and now called a one-room box his home. I spent many, many days with Joe, inquiring about his life and offering friendship to a man who was obviously struggling from loneliness and depression.

One Monday morning, as I began my day, I noticed that the door to Joe's apartment was ajar. It then occurred to me that I hadn't seen old Joe all weekend long; I became concerned. Knocking and getting no response, I gingerly opened the door—and there, slumped over a card table that he used for dining, was Joe, still as the Painted Desert. I knew instantly that he was dead, and I also knew that he had taken his own life; beside him was an empty bottle of pills and a one-page note that he had left behind to no one in particular. According to the note, Joe was tired of being alone and felt no reason to go on living any longer. It was truly a sad moment. Joe was a kind, compassionate and sensitive man whom I liked a lot. To this day, I have a picture of Joe, one I found on his bed when I discovered his lifeless body. I slipped it in my back pocket before I called the police and have held onto it for all these years. I was determined to never forget Joe, and never have.

These were the kind of people who resided at the La Fiesta Apartment complex, the folks I would grow to love and respect as my Arizona adventure progressed. The La Fiesta Apartments were the perfect place for me, and the perfect environment for my state of mind. I could relate to these people, confide in them, and, most importantly, understand them; for when all is said and done, we are all just one step away from being destitute and alone. Life at La Fiesta proved this. But another lesson my time at "the asylum" taught me was that no matter how hard we may try, no matter how hard we may wish, and no matter how hard we may fight, some souls are just too far gone to ever bounce back from mental illness. And despite our best intentions, some people may never escape the demons that torture their souls and deceive their minds.

It's a truly sad reality, one that I recognize...but still have difficulty accepting.

Once Maria and Don had moved on and left the complex in my charge, I began to master the intricacies of my position. By far the most appealing aspect of my duties was spending time with the asylum's inmates, perhaps because I counted myself among them. I basked in the general wackiness of the day-to-day goings-on, and although most people were harmless, there were others who were downright scary.

There was one mysterious cat—a pimp—who lurked in the shadows and was rarely seen by anyone. On the rare occasions where I'd catch a glimpse of this resident wraith, I quickly found out that looking him in the eye was a dicey proposition; those dark pools were devoid of life and screamed of foul intention. In truth, the guy scared the ever-living shit out of me.

There was another kid, younger than me, who beat the crap out of his pretty, dark-haired wife on a daily basis. Every time I saw her, she had shiny new bruises, which she futilely tried to conceal behind sunglasses and long sleeved shirts. She reminded me of the young girl who lived next door to us on Goulburn Avenue in Detroit when I was a kid. Several times, I contemplated intervening; I pulled her to the side on occasion to see if she was alright. Within seconds, the kid would show up, grab her forcefully by the arm and whisk her away, no doubt to unleash a new round of abuse on her for even talking to me. It was a sad situation.

And there were some residents who were just too far gone for their own good, wallowing in demons that brought them to the edge time and again. One day, one of those people appeared at the door of the La Fiesta Apartments, and in one of the most disturbing episodes I had ever encountered, showed me the true nature of severe mental illness.

The La Fiesta Apartments' arrangement with the Palo Verde Psychiatric Hospital was a beneficial union, allowing recently discharged patients to become re-acclimated with the world while learning how to live on their own. One day, as I sat in the office doing paperwork, a caseworker by the name of Stephen Townes came knocking on the door. With him was a dark-haired, scraggly-looking kid who appeared to be no older than me. It was obvious, right from the get-go, that this kid had lived a rough life. He was quiet, shifty, calculating, and tense, and had an air about him that screamed of instability.

"Larry," Stephen began as the two nestled in the office chairs beside me, "this is Dusty. He's going to be your new resident."

"Hey Dusty, how are you today?" I extended my hand.

Dusty, never looking to me, barely lifted his hand as he sat cross-legged and stared at the floor in uncomfortable silence. I knew instantly that this kid was going to be an issue.

Following the usual paperwork, Dusty stepped outside for a smoke. Stephen took advantage of his absence to corral me and impart some much-needed insight into my new resident.

"Larry," Stephen said while looking at me with cautious eyes, "this kid has some issues but we're confident he can assimilate. Just in case there are any problems, here's my personal number. Don't hesitate to use it."

I gazed at the number, knowing instinctively that it wouldn't be too long before I used it...but committed myself to offering Dusty a fair shake nonetheless. Getting him situated in apartment 206 of Building One, directly above my old apartment, I hoped for the best and carried on with my normal routine.

But with the dawning of the new day, the severity of Dusty's issues would become evident.

Painfully, dramatically evident.

La Fiesta's efficiency apartments were small and poorly constructed. It was impossible to avoid hearing your neighbors watching T. V., listening to music, cooking dinner, making coffee—even snoring. Privacy at the La Fiesta Apartments was nonexistent, and one either learned to deal with those circumstances, or moved on to other accommodations as soon as practical.

Allison—who lived in Building One—owned a parrot she named Pedro, a gorgeous bird who thoroughly enjoyed speaking his mind. Pedro The Parrot was so vociferous that you could hear him talking to Allison from just about anywhere in the environs of Building One, and even into the wee hours of night. But rather than being annoyed, the neighbors embraced and enjoyed Pedro's chatter; Allison entertained a continuous stream of people who would stop by to engage the chatty bird and offer him treats.

Every tenant in the building was cool with Pedro...except one.

The morning after Dusty moved in, I was tending to my duties in the office when I heard an angry, boisterous male voice discharging expletives and unsavory expressions that blanketed the halls. Stepping outside the office, I followed the sound of the voice up the stairs, down the hall...and directly to room 206. There, through the cracked door, I could see Dusty; he was pacing, cursing, and pulling his hair as Pedro The Parrot, in the room directly across from his, engaged his new neighbor in unwelcome conversation.

"Goddamn stupid fucking cocksucking, piece of shit fucking bird!!! Shut the fuck up!!! Shut the fuck up!!!" Dusty cried.

As I gently knocked on the door, Dusty immediately fell silent. He stopped pacing and stood as motionless as a statue with his back to the door.

"Hey, buddy," I called out as I pushed the door open, "are you ok?"

Remaining silent, Dusty nodded with excruciating slowness. He didn't turn around.

"Yeah, old Pedro, he can do some talking, can't he? You know, maybe closing your door and turning on the radio might drown out the sound of his voice."

Again, Dusty stood in silence and slowly nodded his head. I gazed at him for several seconds and spoke up one more time.

"Okay, Dusty, I'm going to close your door, man. If you have any problems, let me know, ok?"

When I shut the door, I turned to see Allison at the entrance of her room with little Michael in her arms. Her striking green eyes were swimming with worry.

"That guy scares me, Larry," she confided as she soothed her little boy with caressing hands.

"He scares me, too, sweetheart. Close and lock your door and call me any time. Maybe he'll learn to relax."

Unfortunately for the residents of Building One, and Allison in particular, Dusty did not learn to relax. In fact, his behavior became even more erratic and unpredictable as that first day slipped into the next. I found myself going to his room just about every hour or so, and even during the night, as he continued to scream, curse, and explode with rage. Dusty, it became apparent, was a ticking time bomb.

On the afternoon of just the second full day of Dusty's stay at the La Fiesta Apartments, things came to a head.

Once again tending to my office duties, I heard Dusty screaming at the top of his lungs while pounding violently on a door that I assumed to be Allison's. By the time I ascended the stairs and turned down the hall, however, Dusty had disappeared into his apartment. When I reached his door, I peered through, as it again was slightly ajar, and there was Dusty, standing at the counter of his kitchenette, making a sandwich. I turned to Allison's door and knocked.

"Allison, it's me, Larry," I called out.

Allison cracked the door, just barely, only opening it when she saw that it was indeed me. I could see that she had been crying.

"I can't take this anymore," she whimpered. "He's scaring the shit out of us, Larry."

I nodded my head in understanding, told her to close and lock her door, and turned to Dusty's apartment once again. Quietly knocking, I pushed the door open and slipped inside. There at the kitchenette was Dusty, spreading mustard on a piece of bread with the largest, sharpest kitchen knife I had ever seen in my life. The fucking thing looked like a small machete, gleaming in the dim light of the room, and here was this nut-job spreading a condiment on a piece of bread half the size of the knife he was using. Keeping my eye on the knife at all times, I stepped in front of Dusty. Although seriously concerned, I had seen plenty of crazy episodes in my life; this one was no different than the rest. It was just another day in paradise for me.

"Look, man," I said in a stern yet compassionate tone, "we can't have you freaking out like this, Dusty, you're scaring the other residents. You've got to learn to relax, man, these are tight quarters and everyone needs to learn how to live with one another, do you understand?"

Dusty, never looking up at me, continued with the same motion of sliding that enormous knife across that same piece of bread. Without a word, he nodded.

"Now, Dusty," I continued while keeping my eyes firmly on the blade, "if we have any more problems, I'm going to be forced to call Stephen."

I was lying. I had already made up my mind that I'd had enough of his frightening, erratic behavior, and simply placated Dusty to ensure I'd leave his apartment in one piece. I had no intention of dealing with this kid ever again.

Dusty, making certain that the piece of bread was thoroughly covered with mustard, never looked up or disrupted his rhythm with that incredibly large and intimidating knife. I slowly slipped around him and backed out of the room, my eyes never losing sight of the weapon.

"Okay, Dusty, you take it easy and I'll talk to you soon," I mumbled, closing the door behind me.

I ran down the hall as fast as I could, bounded down the stairs two at a time, burst into the office, and grabbed Stephen's number from the corkboard on the wall. Dialing his number, I waited in silence as the phone rang.

"Stephen Townes here. How may I help you?"

"Stephen, Dusty's out of control, man. I think you need to come get him."

After an excruciatingly long pause, I heard Stephen sigh and answer in a tone that sounded defeated.

"We were afraid of that," he confessed. "Do you know if he has a gun?"

I thought to myself: *Did this guy just ask me what I think he asked me?*

"A gun? Why would he have a gun?"

"We just got a call from his brother," Stephen went on. "He may be missing a gun from his house. Dusty may have taken it."

"*Excuse me?* When were you going to tell me this, man?"

"We just found out. Now look, Larry, keep everyone in their rooms and lock yourself in the office. Police are on the way now."

Those ten minutes of waiting for the police to arrive were unbearable. Of course, I immediately thought of Allison and called her, assuring her that everything would be okay while urging her to barricade her door (which she did with a chair and bureau). I told her to hang tight until Dusty was taken away by the authorities.

When they did arrive, the police stormed through the front doors, up the stairs, and directly to Dusty's room. That's when I entered the hall as other residents emerged from their rooms. Milling around, we could hear the police enter Dusty's apartment and begin the process of taking the deranged young man into custody. Thankfully for everyone involved, Dusty went quietly and was never heard from again by the residents of the La Fiesta Apartment complex in Tucson, Arizona. To this day, I never got a clear answer as to whether or not Dusty had a gun, and truth be told, I prefer to keep it that way. Sometimes, not knowing is the best answer to the most troubling questions we are faced with.

With Dusty now gone for good, the wackos of the La Fiesta Apartments and I were free to carry on with life as normal. But fortunately for me, not only would that normalcy prove to be more interesting by the day, but it would also be kicked into high gear from that point forward. You see, shortly after Dusty was taken away, I met a new resident who would become my partner in chaos, and a guy I would run wild with for the remainder of my days in Tucson. The guy, Dave Lang, would prove to be one of the most interesting characters I had ever met, and the adventures we would have would be nothing short of moronic.

One day I was in the office doing some reading when in walked a man of average height, sandy-blond hair, and a refreshingly cheerful disposition. His right arm was in a sling and the right side of his face sagged, as though it were melting.

"Hello. My name is Dave Lang and I need an apartment," he said, extending his left hand.

"Hey, Dave, I'm Larry," I replied, returning the gesture. "Sure, man, take a seat and we'll set you up."

As David and I continued our conversation, I learned that Dave was in Tucson attempting to get his academic career back on track after a long hiatus. I told him that I was pretending to go to school myself, having recently enrolled at the Pima Community College.

"I don't know why I even try with college, man," I confessed. "I think I'm doing it just to appease my sister."

"Yeah, I'm having a hard time getting back into it myself," Dave added.

"Man, what happened to your arm and face?" I asked, leaning in to get a better view.

"Pretty fucked up, right?" Dave said while smiling. "I was in an accident down in Bermuda. It's why I dropped out of school."

Dave then went on to tell me his story. He was a Midshipman at the U. S. Naval Academy studying engineering. In the summer of 1984, while a junior at the academy, he was a member of a submarine crew who were on leave in Bermuda. One night, he and a group of friends rented some mopeds and cruised around the island, hitting the bars as they went. When closing time came, Dave suggested to his friends that they should wait a while—sober up before jumping back on their scooters. When the dawn finally began to break, Dave and his crew—feeling confident that they were no longer intoxicated—climbed aboard their mopeds and headed back to the base.

While traveling along a winding, two-lane highway, a car (ironically driven by a man who was stinking drunk) swerved across the median and ran Dave and his friends off the road. Losing control of his scooter, Dave teetered along the shoulder before careening to his right…where he hit a telephone pole at 40 miles per hour.

He woke from a coma two months later. His right arm was permanently paralyzed, the right side of his face forever damaged, and his dream of becoming a United States Naval Officer gone forever.

Now, after many months of therapy and psychiatric treatment for his depression, Dave was ready to try school again. But he admitted that he was still grappling with the fact that his lifelong dream was dead; he really didn't care about school—or anything else for that matter. He was from Tulsa, Oklahoma, and Dave's mother felt it would be best for him to move to a new city, start fresh, and enroll in school.

"But Larry," Dave went on, "I've got to tell you, man, I feel like I'm just going through the motions. I'm having a hard time concentrating on school. I just really don't give a shit right now."

I sat in silence and shook my head in understanding. Again, I felt a true connection with another resident of the La Fiesta Apartments, and realized once more that in an instant we could all be gone, all our dreams wiped from the face of the earth and our lives swept clean in the blink of an eye. As I looked at Dave, I smiled and offered my sage advice.

"What do you say we get you squared away, man? I'll help you move your things in, then we'll crack open a beer and shoot the shit."

"That sounds great, Larry. I could use some suds." He smiled a beautiful smile and shook my hand. Once again, I had found a kindred spirit.

From the moment Dave was settled, we began hanging out together. Dave and I had similar tastes in music and similar beliefs, as his world was shattered and now he had to rely on whatever he carried in his heart just to get through the day. There were no more illusions, no more privileges, and no more separation of class or economics. He was now just another guy trying to get along in life. Dave began to see the world for what it was, and I began to see just how quickly life can change. We were both reckless, disenchanted, and angry. And we were both fed up with the status quo, abhorring the idea of a stereotypically "nice, simple life": marriage, kids, and a dead-end, nine-to-five job. We both just wanted to get wild...and that is exactly what we did.

Two weeks into his stay at the La Fiesta Apartments, Dave moved into the manager's apartment with me, since the place boasted three bedrooms, a full kitchen and a large living room. I introduced him to the freaks of the complex, and we began hanging out with Enrique, Allison, Millie, Ron, and others. Every day we blew off classes while Dave helped me with my duties; we'd then proceeded to rage all day, and late into the night. We'd hit random campus parties at the University of Arizona and every college bar we could find around town. There we met kids who invited us to frat parties, sorority parties, and house parties.

We took trips to Mt. Lemon, spending entire weekends tripping on acid while camping under the stars. We'd take day trips to the desert, smoke insane amounts of marijuana, and goof on the sights. We'd spend hours listening to music, hours walking the streets of Tucson, and hours discussing whatever came into our minds. Dave's perspective on life, warped by his circumstance, was refreshing. The guy didn't mince words, nor did he hide his feelings, and he had a sense of humor that was biting and sharp. Dave simply didn't give a fuck about anything. It was a stimulating perspective, one I was all but too happy to embrace.

One night, Dave and I took another LSD journey and made our rounds about town, ending the evening at a Denny's restaurant on Speedway. We sat at our table, as loopy as two cartoon characters, when a pretty Hispanic waitress came and asked us what we would like. I placed my order and Dave placed his. The waitress then asked Dave how he would like his eggs cooked.

"How you lay your eggs?" She inquired in her thick, Latino accent, butchering the English language while holding pen to pad.

Dave and I laughed for an hour as we attempted to digest her words. Eventually the woman just walked off and left us alone. "If we could lay our own eggs honey, we wouldn't need you," we joked incessantly. "How you lay your eggs" would become a defining statement, the theme of our time together, as we continued our experimentation with fringe society. And things would only get wackier from there.

Margaret Sampson was a Pima Indian from the San Xavier Reservation south of Tucson. She was a heavyset girl with long, dark hair that she pulled into loose ponytails on either side of her head. She had a fresh, pretty face, big brown eyes, and a sweet personality that was engaging and innocent. I liked Margaret from the moment I met her.

Margaret was on a full scholarship to the University of Arizona and was studying to become a nurse. Margaret also sold marijuana that her cousins cultivated on the reservation; she became the main supplier of the herb at the complex.

Dave and I got to know her well.

The three of us would spend many nights in her room, drinking beer, smoking dope, listening to music, and trading stories. Margaret was a really cool girl, and fun to be around. But sometimes, people can hide behind cheery facades that mask what is truly in their hearts. And before too long, Dave and I would discover just how unhappy and confused Margaret really was.

One glorious fall afternoon, Dave and I were sitting around the apartment watching T. V. when we received a call from a friend. This kid — a student at the University of Arizona — had just received a shipment of liquid LSD, and wondered if we were interested in sampling his new product. We readily agreed. And so the next night, a perfect Friday evening, Dave and I would shoot for the moon and explore the outer reaches of hallucinatory recklessness.

When the new day dawned, Dave and I took care of our duties for the day and went out to purchase everything we needed for our experiment: beer, snacks, anything we thought necessary. Electing to stay at the apartment so we could control our environment, we settled in for an evening of regulated mayhem.

The apartment complex and the surrounding neighborhood were alive that night; there was energy, electricity — the perfect atmosphere for our odyssey. People were partying at every turn, and a feeling of brotherhood hung in the air. Ingesting a freakish amount of liquid LSD, Dave and I basked in the warmth of friendship.

We set up different colored light bulbs in the lamps and light fixtures, put on music conducive to our state of mind, and began searching deep and wide within ourselves as the experiment got underway. Tripping with Dave always ensured a good time; the guy relished delving far into his own psyche, diffusing the demons that hounded him, that relentlessly reminded him of shattered dreams and unrealized hopes. And Dave, with the right side of his face already appearing as if it were melting, only enhanced my altered perception of reality as the drug worked its magic. Looking at his face while in that state of mind never ceased to amaze me: his face would flinch, contort and change in form, as if it had a life of its own, sometimes becoming somewhat normal as time went on.

At one point, the experiment had reached a crescendo; Dave was spinning records on the turntable, and I found myself staring at the T. V. screen, listening intently to Hendrix's *Are You Experienced* as it blared from the speakers. MTV flickered silently in the psychedelic light of the room.

"Fuck, man," I said with my face only inches from the tube, "these fucking videos are insane, man. The fucking Pet Shop Boys, are you kidding me? They might as well be fucking each other up the ass, as gay as these videos are."

"Man, do people actually like this shit?" Dave asked.

"I mean, look at their hair, man. What the fuck are they, Barbie dolls?" I rubbed my fingers to the screen in an attempt to wipe it clean of the images.

"How did music become so bad so quickly?" Dave wondered. "If things keep going like this, music will just become a series of electronic beeps and pulses, man. Give me Hendrix any day, man. This shit sucks ass."

And so it went, the further the night crept on. Outside our door, we could hear the residents of the asylum getting crazy and running wild. On occasion, I'd walk the halls to check on the inmates. All was well... but getting crazier by the minute.

Now, at some point in the night, the absurd amount of LSD I had taken began to overwhelm me, and I was forced to lie down on the floor in front of the T. V. Where I traveled to next is anyone's guess, but I do know that I had reached the point of losing touch with my physical form. Able to hear the activity in the apartment and the music wafting through the air, I drifted outward to the distant reaches of the cosmos, and enjoyed the sights at the edge of consciousness. I have no recollection of how long I stayed in the stratosphere...but I must have been there for some time. Suddenly, I heard a commotion somewhere in the apartment and began to drift back into my body.

"Larry!" I heard David call in a manic tone. "Get up, man; the police are at the door. Get up, man!"

I opened my eyes to see Dave hovering above me with a concerned look on his distorted face. I shook myself from my stupor and pulled myself up on my elbows. There on the T. V. screen were Chrissie Hynde and The Pretenders, a beautiful sight to see. I always loved Chrissie.

And then—reality. *Cops?*

"What?" I said, getting to my feet. "The cops are here? Where?"

"They're at the door, man. They're asking for the manager."

"Holy shit," I replied as I shook the fog from my head. "Man, I better get my shit together."

I struggled to gather my senses as I made my way to the door. Taking a deep breath, I opened it. Sure enough, two of Tucson's finest were standing at the entrance, now looking at me with firm, stoic faces.

"Are you the manager?" One of them asked, staring me dead in the eye.

"Yes, sir," I answered as I tried to focus on him.

"There's been a report of a suicide attempt in room 106. We need you to open the door for us."

106? I fought through my confusion. *106? That's my old apartment... and Margaret...Margaret lives there now.*

Holy shit.

Margaret tried to kill herself?

"Uh, yeah," I said, attempting to comprehend the moment. "I'll meet you downstairs at the office—that's where the keys are."

I shut the door, raced through the living room (passing a stunned

Dave, still in lysergic shock and standing statue-still), went down the stairs, through the kitchen, and straight to the office door. Entering, I turned on the lights and grabbed the keys to room 106. I stepped through the office door, greeted the two cops, and immediately headed down the hall to apartment 106. My mind was racing in a hundred different directions, and as I slipped the key into the lock, I attempted to prepare myself for what was to come. But no matter what I would have done, it would not have prepared me for what I was about to see. At this point, I was a little *too* flavored.

When I opened the door, I was greeted by the sight of Margaret on her bed; she turned to face me. She had a look of pure horror on her face. In her right hand was a bloody kitchen knife and she had slit the wrist of her left arm. Her arm was covered in blood; it streamed into a pool on the floor below. I took several steps inside and heard Margaret cry out in a tone that was freakish and unnatural as she flailed around on her bed like a frightened little girl. It was all I could take. When I turned to face the cops, the expression on my face must have said it all. I felt all the color rush out of my body and I became stricken with debilitating weakness.

"Don't worry, son," one cop said as he placed a hand on my shoulder, having mercy on my soul. "We've got it from here. We'll let you know if we need anything else."

I turned and hightailed it out of there, quicker than you can say, "Oops, must be in the wrong place." Severely shaken, I headed back to the apartment. My night, in a harsh and sobering manner, had suddenly come to an end.

Despite Margaret's suicide attempt, Dave and I continued on with our wild ways. Looking back on it now, Margaret's brush with death should have been a sign that things were changing and getting out of hand. But Dave and I continued to mingle with the freaks of the apartment, and pushed the limits of logic to the extreme. We had both completely dropped out of school and become totally submerged in the partying lifestyle. Incrementally—inexorably—we began to lose touch with reality.

It was at this point where something came over me; something that began to gnaw at my insides like termites on fresh wood. Once again I was feeling unfulfilled, as if I needed more out of life. The restlessness I had felt for most of my life was starting to become overwhelming, and was pushing me towards uncharted waters.

Though confused as ever, I did understand one thing: whatever it was that I was searching for could not be found at the La Fiesta Apartments in Central Tucson.

It was time to move on.

Sitting in the apartment with Dave one day following a weekend of stupidity, I expressed my concerns to my roommate.

"Dave, I can't do this anymore, man. I can't live in this crazy place any longer. This environment is starting to wear on me. I need more, man, and this isn't cutting it. I think I'm going to head back east."

After a short pause, Dave agreed.

"Yeah, man, I've been thinking the same thing. I really need to get back to school and I can't do it here. I'm going to take my dead-ass back to Tulsa."

Two days later Dave packed up his car and began his journey home. Over the next week or so, I tied up my loose ends, said goodbye to the freaks of the asylum, and handed over the keys of the La Fiesta Apartments to my successor. Boarding a plane back to D. C., I would touch down in my old stomping grounds and resume my journey to find meaning in life.

My time in Tucson had left me yearning for something more—and I was determined to find it, even if it meant the end of my own life in the process. In retrospect, my time at the La Fiesta Apartments was an eye-opening experience on many levels. It gave me a clear understanding of not only the true state of mental illness in this country, but it also proved to me that all was not well in the world of psychological rehabilitation. Not only are our designated institutions for the care of the mentally ill overpopulated and under-equipped, they are grossly underfunded to the point of destitution—a truly scary thought. And it also showed me an aspect of my own personality that I desperately needed to get a grip on. Life at La Fiesta proved to me that everyone, and I mean *everyone*, can cross a line and find themselves in a state of dementia if they push the limits of logic too far. It would be a lesson I would never forget...but one, due to my personality and background, I would continually explore the older I became. What can I say? I've never looked for the easy route in life, and as the man said, if you're gonna be dumb, you better be tough.

Now, if I thought things had been crazy in my life up to this point... well, what would unfold over the next few years would prove to me, once and for all, that I was not destined for an average life. In fact, I would do everything I could, and with every fiber of my being, to ensure a life of adventure.

This wildcat from the streets of Detroit, Michigan was about to discover just how wild this world can be. And through these experiences, I would also come to find out who I was and what I needed out of life. In the end, that's not a bad place to be my friends, not a bad place to be at all...

EPILOGUE — BOOK I

THE QUEST, THE SEARCH, THAT'S WHAT WE'RE ALL ON. THAT SEARCH never ends, and it never goes away. And whatever that search is, is determined by each and every one of us. From the time I can remember, I always understood that I was on that quest. And I always understood that I needed to take it as far as it would go until I found that thing, that muse, which I needed to put my heart at ease. But in 1986, I didn't even know what I was looking for.

As I prepared for the next phase of my life, I felt as lost and uncertain as I ever had. But there was a rumbling in my heart, a calling that tempted me to hit the open road and take that quest to the next level. Subconsciously, I knew that music was so important to me that I needed to have her with me wherever I went. And over the next few years, I would come to understand that it was music that would keep me sane as I did search. Getting there, however, would be another issue. In the next chapter of my life, I would come face-to-face with that quest, and I would also challenge myself in ways I could never have imagined. It's amazing what we will do to find happiness.

Up until this point, I had tried everything I could find, from school to work to family, women, drugs, sports, isolation, history, religion, reading, philosophy, acting, and on and on. None of it brought me the satisfaction I was looking for. I felt frustrated, handcuffed, and stifled, but one thing was for certain, I also felt free. I felt free enough to do as I pleased, to get to that next level, and I felt free enough to take things to the extreme, and the extreme is what I got.

When you're backed into a corner, when you feel that you have no other options available but to break free of all that you've ever known, that's when you can begin to create a meaningful life. Fortunately for me, I had the opportunity to do as much, and, listening to my heart, that is exactly what I did. Although there was an element of fear hounding me, I had also seen enough to not allow that fear to dictate who I would become. And it would be that fear that kept me moving, kept me searching for what I truly needed.

Fear is a powerful thing. It is something that can cripple us but it is also something that can motivate us. I chose to let it motivate me. Now, I'm no badass. I've had my ass kicked enough, even by age twenty, to realize that *I wasn't* a badass. And growing up in Detroit I had known too many guys, and men, who could have eaten me for lunch. Detroit is a tough town. Always has been, and always will be. One of the many things I've always appreciated and respected about that city is that it will put you in your place time and again. Hell, the old neighborhood alone was enough to make me realize that I was just an average Joe looking to get by. But the other thing life in Detroit gave me was the ability to recognize trouble—to recognize who, and who not, to deal with. It was a powerful lesson and one that I've never forgotten.

Growing up in Detroit was a great way to prepare for life. It taught me so much—on a subconscious level—that it took me years, decades, to understand just what it had given me. As I embarked on the next phase of my life, I would come to rely upon that upbringing in ways that even now I have never fully comprehended. But I can tell you this much; if I didn't have that foundation, that experience of growing up in the Motor City, I would not have survived what I was about to get myself in to.

In the next few years I would embark on an adventure that sent me up to Canada, all over the United States, down into Mexico, across the open roads, into major cities, and along lonely highways. I would meet people who would inspire me, take advantage of me, help me, nurture me, beat me, scare me, teach me, and tempt me. I would search on my own, with others, take journeys of the mind, body and soul, and go places deep within myself that I never knew existed. I would encounter fear, beauty, longing, joy, and loneliness. I would understand madness, happiness, confusion, recklessness, desperation, and acceptance. I would survive by the skin of my teeth. But you know what; I would have it no other way. Because in the end, that search would bring me right back to where it all began; to my own heart, my own mind, my own soul, and my own life. It brought me right back to who I was destined to be. And through it, I would finally meet some very powerful, inspiring, intelligent, creative, and spiritual cats in a band called Widespread Panic. Those boys not only nurtured me once I found them, but they gave me all the tools I needed—the ones for which I was craving—to live a life of meaning, a life of substance. And after all is said and done, that's not a bad trade off. In fact, it's the best trade off I could have possibly hoped for. I'll take that any day of the week, my friends; any freaking day.

—Larry Acquaviva, July 2016.

THE STORY ISN'T OVER!

BOOK TWO OF
NOBODY CARES WHO YOU ARE
WILL BE AVAILABLE SPRING 2017

WWW.DEEDSPUBLISHING.COM

www.ingramcontent.com/pod-product-compliance
Lightning Source LLC
Chambersburg PA
CBHW021429080526
44588CB00009B/476